Internationalizing Higher Ed

Internationalizing Higher Education

Critical Collaborations across the Curriculum

Edited by

Rhiannon D. Williams and Amy Lee
University of Minnesota, USA

SENSE PUBLISHERS
ROTTERDAM/BOSTON/TAIPEI

A C.I.P. record for this book is available from the Library of Congress.

ISBN: 978-94-6209-978-4 (paperback)
ISBN: 978-94-6209-979-1 (hardback)
ISBN: 978-94-6209-980-7 (e-book)

Published by: Sense Publishers,
P.O. Box 21858,
3001 AW Rotterdam,
The Netherlands
https://www.sensepublishers.com/

Printed on acid-free paper

All Rights Reserved © 2015 Sense Publishers

No part of this work may be reproduced, stored in a retrieval system, or transmitted in any form or by any means, electronic, mechanical, photocopying, microfilming, recording or otherwise, without written permission from the Publisher, with the exception of any material supplied specifically for the purpose of being entered and executed on a computer system, for exclusive use by the purchaser of the work.

We would like to dedicate this book to Bruce and Felicity Williams, and to Timothy Robert Brandon Lee who have dedicated their lives to being present and engaged in a more wholehearted world.

TABLE OF CONTENTS

Acknowledgments		ix
Internationalizing Higher Education: Critical Collaborations across the Curriculum *Rhiannon D. Williams and Amy Lee*		xi

Section 1: Mindful Global Citizenship: Critical Concepts and Current Contexts

1. On the Hologram of International Education:
   With Raya Hegeman-Davis, Amy Lee, Nue Lor, & Rhiannon Williams   3
   Josef A. Mestenhauser

2. Promoting Holistic Global Citizenship in College:
   Implications for Education Practitioners   17
   Elena Galinova

3. The Challenges and Implications of Globalization for
   Undergraduate Pedagogy   35
   Marta A. Shaw

4. Institutional and Instructional Techniques to Promote
   Undergraduates' Intercultural Development: Evidence from
   a Multi-Institutional Student Survey   47
   Krista M. Soria

Section 2: Developing Intercultural Programs and Practitioners

5. Internationalizing Teaching and Learning: Transforming
   Teachers, Transforming Students   63
   Gayle Woodruff, Kate Martin and Mary Katherine O'Brien

6. Strategies for the Development of an Intercultural Environment   87
   Jill E. Blondin

7. Global Citizenship: Surfacing the Gap between Rhetoric
   and Reality in Internationalization of Management Curricula   101
   Diana Rajendran, Janet Bryant, Patricia Buckley and Ryan Jopp

8. Social Competencies in the European and Polish Qualifications
   Framework: A Tool for Designing Intercultural Environments   117
   Ewa Chmielecka and Izabela Buchowicz

TABLE OF CONTENTS

Section 3: Critical Reflections from across the Curriculum

9. Internationalizing Teaching and Learning in a Graduate Doctor of Nursing Program Curriculum — 131
   Mary Benbenek

10. Internationalizing College Algebra — 151
    Susan Staats

11. Illuminating a Course Transformation Journey — 171
    Catherine Solheim, Mary Katherine O'Brien and Scott Spicer

12. Social Media & Intercultural Competence: Using Each to Explore the Other — 187
    Barbara Gibson, Meredith Hyde and Troy Gordon

13. Developing Diversity-Related Competences in Creativity Workshop for Teachers — 201
    Adam Jagiello-Rusilowski

14. On Becoming a Global Citizen: Critical Pedagogy and Crossing Borders in and out of the University Classroom — 213
    Sahtiya Hosoda Hammell, Rose Cole, Lauren Stark, Chrissie Monaghan and Carol Anne Spreen

15. "Unpacking" International Experience through Blended Intercultural Praxis — 231
    Jane Jackson

Notes on Contributors — 253

ACKNOWLEDGMENTS

We would like to acknowledge our colleagues and students whose fiery passion for diversity, equity and the learning of teaching inspires us every day. We particularly thank Gayle Woodruff for her leadership and daily work in international education; Raya Hegeman-Davis for her editing and input; and John Magers for his overall and constant support.

RHIANNON D. WILLIAMS AND AMY LEE

INTERNATIONALIZING HIGHER EDUCATION: CRITICAL COLLABORATIONS ACROSS THE CURRICULUM

…the development of our students as individuals, as moral agents, as responsible members of their community, and even as global citizens, hinges on their ability to have meaningful encounters with issues of diversity rendered in terms of the global realities of our lives. (Charles, Longerbeam, & Miller, 2013, p. 49)

There is little doubt that higher education is facing unprecedented change—from evolving expectations for student outcomes, rapidly developing technologies, changing student demographics, to pressures and shifts in funding. Today's graduates need particular skills, awareness, and knowledge to successfully navigate a complex and interconnected world. Higher education institutions and practitioners are under pressure to be more attentive to internationalization initiatives that support increasingly mobile and globalized student populations and that foster the development of global citizenship competencies which include, "problem-defining and solving perspectives that cross disciplinary and cultural boundaries" (Hudzik, 2004, p.1 as cited in Leask & Bridge, 2013).

While there is growing awareness of the changing realities and expectations for graduates, that awareness is not yet systemically realized in undergraduate education. Historically, institutions and graduate programs have done very little to support faculty development related to teaching that supports intercultural development. Internationalization of the curriculum initiatives are growing more common and take an increasingly diverse range of forms, from service learning to study abroad. However, global citizenship competencies, the skills and awareness necessary for effective communication and participation in contemporary life, need to be developed and supported across the undergraduate experience if they are to reach a stage where they can be effectively implemented and expanded upon graduation. This is not unlike the normative understanding that disciplinary knowledge, and the ability to apply it skillfully and in unique contexts, accrues and develops longitudinally and as a result of multiple opportunities to practice, test, refine, and hone (knowledge and skills). This developmental process requires long-term and intentional support that is effectively embedded across the undergraduate experience. However, support is often focused on individual faculty or classrooms and initiatives are often ad hoc rather than systemic and comprehensive.

Scholars in the field contend that in order for effective internationalization to happen, internationalization efforts across disciplines and within majors require support in the form of both resources and infrastructure, from the institutional and college level (Clifford, 2009; Leask & Carroll, 2011; Mestenhauser, 2011). Furthermore, intercultural undergraduate classrooms should be informed by advances in our understanding of undergraduate learning, as well as by current technologies that provide powerful opportunities to support learning activities and that facilitate the development of mindful global citizens (Guth, 2013). Childress (2010) argued that, "the development of a critical mass of faculty supporters is key to integrating international perspectives into an institution's (work)" (p. 27). This requires building the knowledge and capacity to support intercultural pedagogy among faculty whose research or teaching specialization is not internationalization.

Faculty who want to support students' development as mindful global citizens do not simply need theoretical knowledge or current research, they need ideas and models for the practical application or use of that research and tips for continuing to develop within their own dynamic and shifting teaching contexts. In Lee, Poch, Shaw and Williams's (2012) *Engaging Diversity in Undergraduate Classrooms*, the authors argued that effective, substantive internationalization of the curriculum initiatives require *intentional pedagogy and informed practitioners*. Undergraduate faculty across disciplines benefit from practitioner-oriented scholarship on intercultural pedagogy that fully acknowledges and explores the experiences of various stakeholder-participants in authentic sites of practice. By their nature, authentic sites of practice are unpredictable and dynamic. They provide a context for critical reflection on obstacles, challenges, and the dissonance that occur between theoretical models and the practices for implementation in sites of practice.

While there is no one-size-fits-all or magical formula to this work, there are pedagogical principles and approaches, technological tools, and frameworks for assessment that scholar-practitioners have found to be useful in the development of mindful global citizens and the support of intercultural learning. This edited volume focuses primarily on supporting the design, pedagogy, and implementation of intercultural pedagogy in contemporary higher education contexts. The authors represent the range of institutional vantage points that participate in the work of internationalization and student development. Scholar-practitioners featured here include: institutional researchers, directors and key implementers of the EU/Bologna process in Poland (one of the newest members and one that is facing unprecedented change in the diversity of its students due to mobility), international partners in learning abroad programs, theorists and classroom instructors across a range of humanities, STEM, and social sciences. Their shared aim in these chapters is to investigate, to better understand, and to inform intercultural pedagogy that supports the development of mindful global citizenship. In selecting chapters to include, our goal was to feature the dynamic and evolving nature of this work, from its historical roots to its current implementation in both traditional classrooms and innovative, cutting-edge programs. We also sought to represent the spectrum of practitioners that are required to support the goal of intercultural development: advisers, teachers, scholars, and administrators.

In working with the contributors for this volume, we emphasized the importance of reflective practice and of grounding or contextualizing the scholarship within its specific site (whether that was a moment in time, an institutional location, etc). The chapters represent the range of contexts in which intercultural learning happens and is facilitated in institutions: from theory and institutional research that drives development of models, to implementation of broad institutional initiatives to build faculty capacity, to individual practitioners' efforts to incorporate, refine, and engage global citizenship and intercultural pedagogy within a particular course. We noted with interest, though not surprise, a common thread across these domains: authors consistently identified flexibility and adaptation as a critical component. That is, success in the dynamic site of practice didn't flow from adherence to a plan or model but rather it resulted from participants (faculty, students, program administrators) being willing to practice an ongoing process of assessment and reflection, navigating unpredictable relationships, and engaging dissonance and uncertainty. Just as intercultural effectiveness and mindful global citizenship require reflection, tolerance of ambiguity, listening, and collaboration so does the practice and refinement of intercultural pedagogy. Of course, the volume also features the tensions and complexities of varying viewpoints and experiences with internationalization work.

We have organized the chapters into three sections as follows:

Section 1: Mindful Global Citizenship: Critical Concepts and Current Contexts

The concept of mindful global citizenship relies on scholarship from several historically distinct fields of research, including intercultural competence, internationalization, and multicultural education (Arkoudis, 2010; Charles, Longerbeam, & Miller, 2013; Green, 2012; Otten, 2003). Given that those of us aiming to support this developmental process are also likely to come from a range of disciplinary backgrounds, the volume begins by providing a solid conceptual framework for mindful global citizenship. In addition, many of us who teach and support current undergraduates did not come of age in a globally interconnected, tech-rich environment, therefore, gaining more nuanced understandings of today's students seems core to effectively supporting intercultural learning and development. This section thus provides institutional research and current theory to help provide a dimensional and empirically-informed understanding of contemporary postsecondary learners, primarily in Western contexts.

Section 2: Developing Intercultural Programs and Practitioners

As Dr. Mestenhauser points out in the introductory chapter, given the relatively recent emergence of intercultural learning as an institutional priority, systems must learn how to create spaces for engagement and capacity development. The initiatives and programs described in this section seek to inspire intercultural learning in various sectors of the institution as well as promote ongoing discussions and collaborations. These chapters highlight the unique complexities of each system and how these initiatives have sought to navigate and work within these complex systems of practice.

Section 3: Critical Reflections from across the curriculum

In this section, contributors will present and reflect on program or classroom-based efforts to support, develop, and implement intercultural pedagogy. This section features diverse disciplines and undergraduate contexts and presents models for, and reflections on, supporting students' development in areas of global competency, such as the capacity to communicate with diverse others, seek out multiple perspectives, or share information/ products with diverse others.

Our goal is to stimulate critical action and reflection at the individual, classroom, and institutional levels and across different stakeholder groups. As Dr. Mestenhauser articulates in his interview with Nue Lor, it is critical to acknowledge and to actively promote the interdependence of the historically differentiated (and often competing) domains in which the work of "internationalization" has been done. His interview opens the volume and sets the tone and stage for the chapters to come. His capacity to look both back at 60 years of leadership in this field and to forecast ahead to what is necessary to sustain and strengthen our work has served as a point of reference for us in developing this book and we are grateful to him for his leadership, critique, vision, and tenacious insistence on mindfulness and interdependence, both of which can fly in the face of received and normative ways of doing things in the academy. Our hope is that as scholar-practitioners, the diverse chapters presented in this edited volume on internationalization within institutional sites of practice provide ideas, material for discussion with colleagues, and potentially guidance in each of your teaching and learning journeys.

REFERENCES

Arkoudis, S., Yu, X., Baik, C., Borland, H., Chang, S., Lang, I., . . . Watty, K. (2010). *Finding common ground: Enhancing interaction between domestic and international students.* Melbourne: Australian Learning and Teaching Council.

Charles, H., Longerbeam, S., & Miller, A. (2013). Putting old tensions to rest: Integrating multicultural education and global learning to advance student development. *Journal of College & Character, 14*(1), 47–58. doi: 10.1515/jcc-2013-0007

Childress, L. (2010). *The twenty-first century university: Developing faculty engagement in internationalization.* New York, NY: Peter Lang.

Clifford, V. A. (2009). Engaging the disciplines in internationalizing the curriculum. *International Journal for Academic Development, 14*(2), 133–143.

Green, M. F. (2012). Global citizenship: What are we talking about and why does it matter? *Trends and Insights for International Education Leaders,* 1–4.

Guth, S. (Ed.). (2013). *COIL Institute for globally networked learning in the humanities: Case studies.* SUNY, NY: National endowment of the humanities.

Hudzik, J. (2004). *Why internationalize NASULGC institutions? Challenge and opportunity.* Retrieved April 20, 2013 from http://www.aplu.org/NetCommunity/Document.Doc?id=38

Lee, A., Poch, B., Shaw, M., & Williams, R. D. (2012). *Engaging diversity in undergraduate classrooms: A pedagogy for developing intercultural competence* (ASHE Monograph Series). San Francisco, CA: Jossey-Bass.

Leask, B., & Bridge, C. (2013). Comparing internationalization of the curriculum in action across discipline: Theoretical and practical perspectives. *Compare: A Journal of Comparative and International Education, 43*(1), 79–101.

Leask, B., & Carroll, J. (2011). Moving beyond 'wishing and hoping': Internationalisation and student experiences of inclusion and engagement. *Higher Education Research and Development, 30*(5), 647–659.

Mestenhauser, J. (2011). *Reflections on the past, present, and future of internationalizing higher education: Discovering opportunities to meet challenges.* Minneapolis, MN: Global Programs and Strategy Alliance, University of Minnesota.

Otten, M. (2003). Intercultural learning and diversity in higher education. *Journal of Studies in International Education, 7*(1), 12–26.

SECTION 1

MINDFUL GLOBAL CITIZENSHIP:
CRITICAL CONCEPTS AND CURRENT CONTEXTS

JOSEF A. MESTENHAUSER

1. ON THE HOLOGRAM OF INTERNATIONAL EDUCATION

With Raya Hegeman-Davis, Amy Lee, Nue Lor, & Rhiannon Williams

INTRODUCTION

We are delighted to present a conversation with Dr. Josef A. Mestenhauser, Distinguished International Emeritus Professor in the Department of Organizational Leadership, Policy and Development at the University of Minnesota. The chapter resulted from a series of in person and written conversations that we were privileged to have with Dr. Mestenhauser. Dr. Mestenhauser was an early advocate of international education and has contributed six decades of pioneering research and practice, helping to define and legitimize this work as a field of expertise. He has published more than 120 books, monographs, articles and book and a recipient of Fulbright grants in the Philippines, Japan and Czechoslovakia. He served as President of NAFSA: Association of International Educators, ISECSI (International Society for Educational, Cultural and Scientific Interchanges).

Let's start with the basics. Why is international education important? What is the purpose?

American students are very lucky to have one of the most advanced educational systems, modern building facilities, parks and physical education programs, and libraries full of up-to-date books and magazines. They have many more advantages offered to them by their educational system than my generation or culture could even dream about. The best and greatest opportunities are, however, still awaiting, if the students and their teachers can see them. The opportunities do not come cheap – they must be earned. The "business as usual" of our educational system is not sufficient to gain the advantages.

So we need the key to the gate that opens these opportunities. The key is this relatively new field of international education (International Education) which has been here for more than half a century and is visible in virtually every university and college, but to many is still invisible.

The purpose of the field is to explain when, why, and how people in various cultures do and think differently from the way we do. This field of international education is complex and challenges both students and their teachers. But this is a positive thing because cognitive complexity is one of the most important competencies. Cognitively complex people accomplish more, recognize more problems, solve them more easily and effectively, and explain them to others.

One of the roles of international education is to ensure access to the largest knowledge base possible and to focus on the utilization of that knowledge in practical situations. If the cognitive map of our faculty and students is ethnocentric, then people think that the knowledge they do not know, in fact, does not exist. There is sufficient evidence that our students, both undergraduate and post graduate, are not being educated well enough to produce knowledge through research and that they receive only the minimum exposure to international subjects

What exactly is international education?

International Education combines two exceptionally complex domains, *"international"* and *"education."* *"International"* means the entire world, composed of hundreds of individual nations, thousands of cultures and languages, religions and sub-cultures, and the relationships among them. *"Education"* is not only the pedagogy used in teaching about such a world -that includes ourselves-, but the many theories of cognition, learning, motivation, transfer of knowledge, and thinking. Thus, in the arena of higher education, we distinguish international education as the field of knowledge and internationalization of higher education as a program of educational change to implement the concept into practice.

The vast literature about this field keeps growing exponentially but is scattered in virtually all academic disciplines and their sub-specialties in many countries. A cynic might say that we have more studies than knowledge about International Education. Nonetheless, as is customary in the social sciences, there is a large range of views about International Education. This complexity allows several interpretations and approaches to the field. Many individuals, including international educators and students, seek to simplify both the meaning and practice of international education in order to reduce this complexity.

For example, most researchers use a standard definition of international education provided and amended several times by Knight (2004), "internationalization of higher education is the process of integrating an international/intercultural dimension into the teaching, research, and service elements of an institution" (p. X), but this definition has many shortcomings. First, it is circular: international education is international perspectives. Secondly, international education is impossible to attain if it must be mainstreamed into every function of a higher education institution. I cannot even imagine how some 7,000 faculty and staff of my university might accomplish such a feat and educate some 50,000 students – especially in our culture that does not favor an omnibus approach to policy. Suffice it to recall two ill-fated omnibus bills, the international education act of 1966 and the present Obama care. Thirdly, to get out of the "omnibus – universality" dilemma, Knight employs an escape clause that individual institutions decide how to accomplish the "process" – in other words, everything goes. Fourth, by defining internationalization as a process, she ignores the product that results from the process and vice versa. Fifth, the definition makes no reference to knowledge, yet education is the name of the field that is all about knowledge.

So what definition would you offer? Can you provide a better definition of International Education, based on your years of experience?

Internationalization of higher education is a program of major educational reform designed to ensure that higher education produces globally thinking and knowing students able to work anywhere on short notice without prior preparation. As such, International Education consists of both formal and informal knowledge, cognitive, experiential, and implicit domains of learning, and it originates across multiple academic disciplines. My definition challenges some established wisdom and practices because the recent dramatically growing literature and research prefers the opposite approach; it tends to divide the field into smaller units of analysis and smaller size topics that tend to fragment International Education the same way that higher education is fragmented.

How then is International Education different from the traditional curriculum students pursue?

The curriculum students pursue is based on an established body of knowledge which is grounded in research and experiences that conveys to them the frontiers of their field, how much they already know in relationship to how much more there is to know. International knowledge does not have the same frontiers. It is "all over." Furthermore, typical curriculum is organized hierarchically from introductory to advanced, based on perceived complexity. International education hits us unexpectedly, at any time, and without regard to being introductory or advanced. It also challenges the typical production of knowledge based on our much cherished analytical thinking that reduces complexity to the smallest units of analysis. International Education does the opposite, it does not reduce the units of analysis but expands on them and brings several more to bear. Research evidence shows that only a small number of courses include the "international dimension" of any kind, that references to other countries are presented from a US perspective, and that the "infusion" is usually a limited amount of knowledge "injected" only at one time. How the international content is integrated with predominantly "domestic" emphasis remains a major issue that international educators seek to resolve. When

I worked in Indonesia, I found thirteen possible patterns that emerged when people attempted to insert and integrate foreign concepts (e.g. quality circles) that were being introduced into the native culture.

Furthermore, international education supports the idea of cultural heterogeneity and diversity as a great strength of the society of the future. Culture is not only the source of peoples' identities but also a screen that inhibits learning about others. Change is the most permanent aspect of modern living and if understood may bring about new opportunities perhaps never before available. The most common methods of changing peoples' minds are new mental representations (difference between "emic" and "etic") and multiple perspectives on issues.

You have argued that the concept and the field of international education needs reframing. Why is it necessary to reframe international education?

The most common method of our analytical tradition is to break down the field by different functions (study abroad, foreign students, agreements, etc) with which the field is associated historically and treat each separately. This conceptualization makes International Education into a "holding corporation" that has specialists in many aspects of the field. This format is consistent with a familiar pattern of analytical thinking. However, it allows some part to think of itself as the whole.

Ever since Bolman and Deal published their seminal work about reframing organizations, I started thinking how this theory might help reframe international education. The field has grown and expanded but at the cost of coherence and is thus a candidate for reframing. I am motivated to find a different way of thinking about the field than the current paradigm of instrumentalism, competitiveness, and pragmatism. In various publications, I have attempted to formulate such a new way of thinking about the field by doing precisely that – by re-framing it (Mestenhauser, 2011).

You are known for applying a systems approach to higher education. From a systems perspective, how is an institution better able to achieve its goals when all parts are working in unison?

In short, systems thinking and systems perspectives helps identify knowledge that is missing, streamlines administration, provides research materials, shows trends, and sees the whole and all the parts. All systems are interrelated and interdependent. Changes in one system or sub-system influence changes in others; change is a constant which explains the dynamics and movements we see every day. This is why we need to understand the historiography of the field, to see what parts changed over a long period of time and how they influenced other parts. Several scholars and practitioners of the field have recently paid attention to trends, but treat them very superficially. A trend is not something that happens over a short time, from one conference to the next, or is triggered by recently released statistical studies about student enrollments. Trends are changes that happen over a long period of time and are caused by both internal and external sources. That is another reason why understanding the history of the field is important to the systems theory, but it has been neglected by many practitioners and faculty.

You have proposed the idea of conceptualizing the work of international education as a hologram. Can you explain and elaborate on this idea?

I want to offer a new and different way of thinking about this large field. I look at International Education as a system of knowledge that is so complex that it cannot be understood through the established way of analytical and critical thinking. It can only be explained through several frames of reference, each part of a system, all seen simultaneously, as in a hologram. *The metaphor I use is a hologram – something physicists do to capture a picture of a subject that also contains all its parts.* Again, following Senge and Bolman and Deal, I present seven of these frames of reference that together form the system. The multiple "frame" method is most useful in social sciences whenever we need to explain complex phenomena, when variables are interdependent, and where the causes of problems lie in the system rather than in individual parts. Accordingly, taking such an approach, I suggest that international education can be understood by the following seven frames of reference:

1. Ideas, philosophy, peaceful relations, and cultural diplomacy;
2. Body of knowledge and corresponding intellectual competencies;
3. Form of inquiry;
4. Giant laboratory of international and intercultural relations;
5. Program of educational reform of higher education;
6. Business, economics, and employment;
7. Leadership as integrative force.

Many people see international education as structures, projects, or programs from which to pick and choose at random, as small pieces like dressing on a cake. The field is too complex to be divided by these projects and may discourage some from pursuing it. They miss knowledge of cognitive complexity that has become a requirement of many professions and is needed for promotions and professional advancement. As I explained above, but it stands repeating, cognitively complex people accomplish more, solve more problems, do so more effectively, and explain problems to others. In addition, research shows that complex explanations gain more credibility. Systems thinking is a multiplier of learning because it re-arranges the clutter in the brain by arranging masses of information into higher level categories, thus creating more space for new ideas (Mapes, 2003).

This is a lot to unpack. So let's begin with you elaborating on why the concept of cultural diplomacy is important to international education?

Modern international education started as an ideal of a peaceful world without wars. This frame will restore this dimension of the field because like it or not, everybody is a cultural diplomat of sorts. How we behave, what we say, what we do, and what we write about others and about ourselves is transmitted instantly, locally, and around the world, where it reinforces pre-existing positive or negative biases. Arndt (2005) traced the history of official US policy for international education in his encyclopedic work, which should be required reading for international educators, because it documents that universities are not the only places where international education is done. Governments play a very important role by both promoting and creating barriers for the field. The term "international education" was, in fact, coined for one of the US Government programs in Latin America.

Cultural diplomacy should not be treated as an isolated goal that is often labeled pejoratively as "ideology." It should be an ongoing process of learning. It provides a counterpoint to the self-centered paradigm of competitiveness and may be the only way to keep mankind from killing itself out, if we can figure out how to make this idea the property of a critical mass.

So then what are the practical implications associating cultural diplomacy with international education?

First, students should know enough about their own country so that they can explain it to others. Similarly, they need to know the mindsets of most their countrymen in order to explain to them people of other countries.

Second, students need to fully understand the cognitive consequences of ethnocentrism that Thomas (2002) defines as "an attitude that one's own cultural group is the center of everything and all other groups are evaluated with reference to it" (p. 44). Ethnocentrism, not globalization, is the antecedent of International Education. It causes misunderstandings, miscalculations, and as significant social science research shows, prejudice, contempt, stereotypes, and conflict. Ethnocentrism is difficult to change because it is both conceptual and perceptual: we do not know and do not want to know.

Third, explicitly identifying cultural diplomacy as a facet of international education calls attention to the vast growing and most sophisticated sub-field of International Education, intercultural communication, which is needed by individuals to interact with people of other cultures. There are ample academic literature, handbooks, and training programs available to hone one's intercultural communication skills (Deardorf, 2009; 2012). Not to be neglected are equally ample resources that address the important issues of cooperation and of peace and war.

What are the sources of knowledge that International Education comes from?

Most formal knowledge about international education originates in some fifteen social sciences and humanities, while much of international relations is conducted by technical, information, and scientific fields such as agriculture, public health, medicine, engineering, military, economics, business, and finance. This discrepancy allows many specialists to ignore cross-cultural knowledge and think that all they need is their excellence in their specialty. Groennings and Wiley (1999) attempted to identify the international dimension of key disciplines, but did not succeed. Several of these "hard core" social sciences are culture-bound in a way that was described by Ross (2004).

What is the significance of Ross' insights?

Ross' work confronts the need to think of International Education as an interdisciplinary field. Interdisciplinarity has become a very popular concept that is used commonly by higher education institutions to publicize themselves as being "world class" institutions. Unfortunately, the record of most institutions does not conform to these images. By far the greatest number of teaching faculty have been socialized exclusively within their own discipline and do not have the incentive or the foundation to conceptualize the theoretical framework for interdisciplinary cooperation. Each discipline has its own paradigmatic foundation into which it has a tendency to absorb the international dimensions of that discipline (Sperber, 2008). As a result, these faculty members simply juxtapose their discipline with others, without conceptual sharing, something that Klein (1990) has termed as multi-disciplinarity, not interdisciplinarity. Research has indicated that it takes about three months for graduate students to understand the logic of another discipline. Once mastered, however, additional disciplines may require as little time as one week to fully understand (Mapes, 2003).

One of the frames of reference in your hologram concept is, "a giant laboratory of international and intercultural relations." Can you talk more about this frame of reference so as to make it more concrete for me?

While this frame is the most visible part of international education, it is also the most neglected and misunderstood. Universities have become trans-national institutions and join other public and private agencies in hosting a number of other categories of people ranging from students, to research scholars, teachers, trainees, administrative and legislative leaders, journalists, parliamentarians, school teachers, and military personnel. In addition they institute joint academic programs, often joint degrees, and open branch campuses. Every human variable is involved in this massive movement of people and ideas. The scope of the exchanges is impressive; some estimate that as many as five million students study in countries other than their own. Their presence is an enormous source of research material for virtually any field of study. Unfortunately, this important sub-field has been perverted by a paradigm of competitiveness and reduced to recruiting foreign students to bring valuable funds into our countries. The US Department of Commerce reported that in 2012 international student contributed to the US 18.2 billion dollars. It is not just the US that is counting the presence of foreign students as business. Spain has announced that US students on study abroad in that country bring into it more than 200 billion Euros.

Due to the ethnocentrism mentioned earlier, foreign students are considered as outsiders so that knowledge and interpersonal relations can hardly be regarded as mutual and reciprocal – to the detriment of domestic students and the classroom instructors who lose a great deal of insights and new perspectives that these foreign students bring with them (Mestenhauser, 2002). Furthermore, the social psychology of ethnocentrism suggests that we teach them, not the other way around. One seldom seen loss is the potential to teach our students meta-learning and emic thinking. Foreign students have to overcome and adjust to the differences in educational systems which gives them an advantage in developing a coping strategy through acquisition of meta-learning (learning about learning). The skills and perspectives that foreign students come with and acquire here are needed by domestic students who also need the same unique learning that is not available in a typical lecture-based classroom or in study abroad.

You propose that international education is a learning multiplier.
How can that be when there may be issues of cultural gaps between
international and domestic students?

Integration of international students in the lives and cultures of our institutions and their mutual relationships with domestic students remains a major issue for international education. Intercultural communication skills are needed by both domestic and international students to bridge the cultural gaps. Undergraduate students have a unique opportunity to participate in the multi-cultural world that our universities are becoming.

Mutual and reciprocal relationships have more than social benefits. Students acquire new knowledge and perspectives that help them enlarge the opening to the brain (to allow more new information to pass through) and expand the long term memory through creation of new "bins" for new knowledge. To use an economics metaphor, the cognitively rich get richer. This is the basis for the claim that International Education is a learning multiplier. Some research suggests that the multiplier effect is a result of learning one thing in relationship to another. In other words, as the students study their specialty, and add, let's say intensive study abroad, that creates the multiplier.

What is the basis of international education as educational reform?

Unlike traditional educational reform, internationalizing universities is not a matter of a single step that can be legislated by government or institutions, but a continuous change that occurs on several levels and has multiple goals, such as from single to multiple perspectives, from simple to complex concepts and theories, and from ethnocentric to global consciousness. The reform should have two major objectives, first, to correct ethnocentrism, and second to provide students with frameworks for living and working in the future.

I like to recall what President Wilson was attributed as saying, "it is easier to move the cemetery than to change the curriculum." It appears easier to create a new course than to change the existing ones. The pattern that seems to dominate is that academic departments hire at least one "cross-cultural scholar" while the rest of the department does "business as usual."

Recent years have witnessed an exceptionally rapid and exponentially expanding production of knowledge in the form of concept papers, articles, journals, books, handbooks, and conferences in all fields that crowd the already busy curriculum beyond its ability to provide students with the breadth and depth of knowledge required for life and work in a complex society. Educators have a difficult task to handle this explosion of both domestic and international knowledge at a time when the curricular system is static and while students should learn more than the system offers. The only answer is that students must motivate themselves to learn more than the present credit system allows.

There is an increasing pressure on undergraduate students to conduct research. They should know that knowledge produced by research is almost always "etic" – from the perspective of an outsider (observer) looking in (Headland, at al. 1990); questions are formulated in the US by disciplinary frames. This is legitimate knowledge as long as the methodology is transparent because the "etic" method is probably the only one available to do cross-cultural studies involving more than one culture. When the "etic" approach does not consider its "emic" dimension, (the looking out from the inside), the research may produce misleading information and conclusions. The emic concept is difficult to teach because most faculty see it as a form of relativism.

Why is it important to view international education as an agent of change?

These are major changes that may challenge many peoples' firmly established views. Histories of educational reforms in democratic societies suggest that they are successful when there is perceptive leadership, simultaneous training (Fullan, 1991), and knowledge about how people think. Change is difficult, but people and institutions do change their minds (Gardner, 2004) and education and knowledge is the best method to produce change. Undergraduate students need to be globally educated if they wish to influence the change needed.

Can you see the risks of comparing higher education to business?

Comparing higher education to business is faulty comparative thinking. The same functions of business are present in government, in non-profit organizations, in private clubs, athletics, foundations, in families, and everywhere else that depends on income, expenses, and accountability. What is then missing? Ethics, context, and – of course – culture. Sedlacek (2011) is clear that economics neglects or ignores all three.

Many believe that International Education is a response to the negative aspects of globalization whose forces appear at a time when the institutions also face great need to respond to domestic issues and problems of funding, inappropriate forms of governance, massification (changes from elitist to mass education (Trow, 1961)), differentiation (new levels of educational achievement for diverse populations), and relevance to changing employment market. This formulation is an oversimplification.

Universities no longer have a monopoly on higher education. They face severe competition from private, for-profit organizations and consulting firms that offer and aggressively market courses and programs of education and training that siphon financial resources from established educational systems.

Recently in the news, several higher education institutions have received generous funding from the US federal government to further fund the study of international education, including the University of Washington, which received $16 million and Michigan State University, who was awarded $7 million. Why this interest now?

When the American Council on Education International Education identified the field as being "leadership driven" it had in mind its primary membership, the college Presidents. This might be misleading, because Presidents get selected for other reasons and priorities than international education and because most organizations have some seven layers of leaders who perform some – even if limited – leadership functions in various departments and colleges (Thomas, 2002). Furthermore there is a disconnect between "leadership" and "institutionalization (Scott & Davis, 2003). Arrows (1974) calls it an "impossibility theorem" that states we should "study people in organizations but do not draw conclusions about organizations, and vice versa" (page #). International education needs both leaders and structural abilities to institutionalize an institutional objective.

The early history of international education in the US faced colleges and universities with difficult questions about how to administer various aspects of the field. International Relations, Area Studies, and foreign languages became the monopoly of the academic colleges and departments, some of which had to be established first, while international students were traditionally assigned to Student Affairs. These assignments created a strict dual system of "academics" and "the rest" – a division that still persists in many instances. When the "field" grew to the point of expecting all functions to have some international and intercultural dimensions, international education became the most unique and different function of higher education. Virtually every unit established its own international "division."

What makes up the actual study of international education and what are the implications for International Education as an educational leader?

Higher education is full of examples of academic disciplines that study and monitor practice of a profession. For example, business schools study business; colleges of education study the teaching profession, schools of nursing study the nursing profession, policy sciences study public services, etc. However, there is no similar feature in international education. Gunnel (1989), coming from the field of philosophy of social sciences, suggested that the relationships between meta-practice and its academic counterpart, is one level of discourse. Such a relationship does not exist in international education where the meta-practice – international education profession – has acquired multiple levels of discourse. First level is the actual performance of the functions associated with the field. Second level of discourse is the rapidly growing opportunities for academic study and research of the field that informs the meta-practice. Finally, the third level of discourse is the effort to help internationalize most of the second level of discourse units. My own experience in the field persuades me that international educators possess the most comprehensive and data based knowledge that has no counterpart among the vast majority of the teaching faculty. Teaching faculty to become cross-culturally and internationally competent has thus become a function of international education professionals, as Woodruff et al. (this volume) indicates.

What should International Education mean to me as a student?

The imminent changes that should occur are changes in the minds of students and those who teach them. Many students live under the misguided notion that they will only work "at home" not realizing that the skills and knowledge they need in "domestic" employment ***are the same as those required*** of working globally because "local" has become "global."

What are the next steps needed to re-conceptualize International Education in using this hologram?

International Education must also integrate newly acquired global perspectives with "domestic" knowledge. As Wittgenstein asserted, "A proposition must use old expressions to communicate a new sense" (As cited in Sedlacek, 2011, p. 304). This adds another intellectual competence to others; integrative thinking.

Other countries are not standing still. International Education is being promoted, organized, and funded in the Russian Federation, in the European Union, China, in East Asian countries, in Singapore and Latin America. In the European Union students have in each country a National Union of Students that have together formed a European Association with headquarters in Brussels. This office is routinely consulted on legislative and administrative processes and is organized to produce valuable concept papers and consultations. It would be nice if we had something like this in the US and if our students stopped being just passive recipients of learning.

REFERENCES

Adler, N. J. (2003). *International dimension of organizational behavior* (4th ed.). Cincinnati, OH: South-Western Publishers.

Altbach, P. G., & Paterson, P. M. (1998). Internationalize American higher education? *Change, 30*(4), 36–39.

American Council on Education. (2008). *Mapping of internationalization*. Washington, DC: Author.

Arndt, R. (2005). *The first resort of kings. American cultural diplomacy in the twentieth century*. Washington, D C: Potomac Books, Inc.

Arrows, J. K. (1974). *The limits of organizations*. New York, NY: W.W. Norton.

Asia Society. (1976). *Asia in American textbooks*. New York, NY: Author.

Barrows, T. S. (1981). *College students' knowledge and beliefs: A survey of global understanding*. LaRochelle, NY: Change Magazine Press.

Bennett, M. J. (1986). Toward ethnorelativism: A development model of intercultural sensitivity. In R. M. Paige (Ed.), *Cross-cultural orientation: New conceptualization and application* (pp. 109–139). Lanham, MD: University Press of America.

Blanding, M. (2010, Winter). The brain in the world. *Tufts Magazine*. Retrieved September 21, 2010 from http://www.tyfts/alumni/magazine/winter2010/featurews/the-brain.html

Bloom, B. S. (1956). *Taxonomy of educational objectives: The classification of educational goals*. New York, NY: David McKay.

Bolman, L., & Deal, T. (1997). *Reframing organizations: Artistry, choice, and leadership* (2nd ed.). San Francisco, CA: Jossey Bass.

Bond, S., & Lemasson, J. P. (Eds.). (1999). *A new world of knowledge*. Ottawa, Canada: International Development Research Centre.

Brandenburg, U., & De Wit, H. (2011, Winter). The end of internationalization. *International Higher Education, 62*, 15–17.

Chandler, A. (2000). *Paying the bill for international education: Programs, partners and possibilities at the millennium*. Washington, DC: NAFSA, Association of International Education.

Coombs, P. H. (1985). *The world crisis in education: The view from the eighties*. New York, NY: Oxford University Press.

De Wit, H. (2013). *Trends, issues and challenges in internationalization of higher education*. Amsterdam, The Netherlands: Hogeschool van Amsterdam.

Fullan, M., & Stiegelbauer, S. (1991). *The meaning of educational change*. New York, NY: Teachers College of Columbia University.

Gardner, H. (2004). *Changing minds*. Boston, MA: Harvard Business School Press.

Gibbons, M., Nowotny, C., Schwartzman, S., Scott, P., & Trow, M. (1994). *The new production of knowledge: The dynamics of science and research in contemporary societies*. London: Sage.

Groennings, S., & Wiley, D. (Eds.). (1995). *Group portrait: Internationalizing the disciplines*. New York, NY: The American Forum.

Harari, M. (1992). Internationalizing the curriculum. In C. B. Klasek (Ed.). *Bridges to the future: Strategies for internationalizing higher education* (pp. 52–80). Carbondale, IL: Association of International Education Administrators.

Hayward. F. M. (2000). *Internationalization of higher education: A preliminary status report 2000.* Washington, DC: The American Council on Education.

Headland, T. N., Pike, K., & Harris, M. (1990). *Emics and etics: The insider/outsider debate. Frontiers of Anthropology,* (Vol 7). Newbury Park, CA: Sage.

Hofstede, G. (1984). *Cultures' consequences.* Beverley Hills, CA: Sage.

Hunt, J. G. (1991). *Leadership: A new synthesis.* Newbury Park, CA: Sage.

Kahneman, D. (2011). *Thinking, fast and slow.* New York, NY: Farrar, Strauss and Giroux.

Kahneman D., Slovic, P., & Tversky, A. (1982). *Judgment under uncertainty. Heuristics and biases.* Cambridge, England: Cambridge University Press.

Kegan, R., & Laskow Lahey, L. (2009). *Immunity to change. How to overcome it and unlock the potential in yourself and your organization.* Boston, MA: Harvard Business Press.

Klein, J. T. (1990). *Interdisciplinarity: History, theory and practice.* Detroit, MI: Wayne State University Press.

Klein, J. T. (2010). *Creating interdisciplinary campus cultures. A model for strength and sustainability.* Washington, DC: Association of American Colleges and Universities and Jossey Bass.

Kluckhohn, F. R., & Stroedtbeck, F. L. (1961). *Variations in value orientations.* Westport, CT: Greenwood Press.

Kuhn, T. S. (1962). *The structure of scientific revolutions.* Chicago, IL: University of Chicago Press.

Lambert, R. D. (1989). *International studies and the undergraduate.* Washington, DC: American Council on Education.

Marzano, R. J. (2001). *Designing a new taxonomy of educational objectives.* Thousand Oaks, CA: Corwin Press.

Mestenhauser, J. A. (2002). In search of a comprehensive approach to international education: A systems perspective. In W. Gruenzweig & N. Rinehart (Eds.), *Rockin' in red square: Critical approaches to international education in the age of cyberculture.* Muenster, Germany: Lit Verlag.

Mestenhauser, J. A. (2011). *Reflections on the past, present and future of internationalizing higher education. Discovering opportunities to meet the challenges.* Minneapolis, MN: University of Minnesota Office of Global Programs.

Ross, N. (2004). *Culture and cognition: Implications for theory and practice.* Thousand Oaks, CA: Sage.

Schmidt B. C. (2006). On the history of historiography of international relations. In W. Carlesnaes, R. Thomas, & B. A. Simmons (Eds.), *Handbook of international relations* (pp. 3–22). Thousand Oaks, CA: Sage.

Schwartz P., & Ogilvy, J. (1979). *The emergent paradigm: Changing patterns of thought and belief.* Menlo Park, CA: Stanford Research Institute.

Scott, P. (Ed.). (1998). *The Globalization of higher education.* Buckingham, England: SRHE and Open University Press.

Scott, W. R., & Davis, G. F. (2007). *Organizations and organizing: Rational, natural, and open system perspectives.* Upper Saddle River, NJ: Pearson, Prentice Hall.

Sedlacek, T. (2011). *Economics of good and evil. The quest for economic meaning from Gilgamesh to wall street.* Oxford, England: Oxford University Press.

Senge, P. M. (1990). *The fifth discipline: The art and practice of the learning organization.* New York, NY: Doubleday.

Sperber, D. (2008). *Why rethink interdisciplinarity?* Retrieved September 12, 2010 from http://www.interdisciplines.org/interdisciplinary/papers1/25

Thomas, D. C. (2002). *Essentials of international management.* Thousand Oaks, CA: Sage.

Trompenaars, F., & Hampden-Turner, C. (1998). *Riding the waves of culture.* New York, NY: McGraw Hill.

Josef A. Mestenhauser
University of Minnesota

ELENA GALINOVA

2. PROMOTING HOLISTIC GLOBAL CITIZENSHIP IN COLLEGE

Implications for Education Practitioners

GLOBAL CITIZENSHIP EDUCATION IN COLLEGE: SETTING THE SCENE

Global citizenship education is increasingly recognized as an integral part of the movement to internationalize the undergraduate curriculum in North America (Deardorff, de Witt, Heyl, & Adams, 2012; Lewin, 2009; Peters, Britton & Blee, 2008; Shultz, Abdi, & Richardson, 2011). Conceived in response to the pressures of globalization and its contradictory consequences, global citizenship education presents a complex agenda to college educators, ranging from the acquisition of deeper knowledge about the world to the cultivation of empathy for other cultures and a sense of responsibility for the future of humanity. In light of the profound transformations of today's social reality, one of the key messages global educators convey to students is that learning to think and act as citizens of the world is no longer a matter of choice; it is a necessity and a moral imperative. Whether they remain in their local communities upon graduation or choose to live and work in remote places, they will be a part of a community more diverse and integrated with the rest of the world than ever before. Understanding, internalizing, and manifesting the full spectrum of global citizenship characteristics will thus be a primary prerequisite for leading full and productive lives as humans, professionals, and citizens.

Higher education institutions embrace this necessity to promote global citizenship education as integral to the holistic development of college students through a wide range of curricular and co-curricular initiatives (Davies & Pike, 2009; Hill & Helms, 2012; Peterson & Helms, 2013; Schattle, 2008). With the plethora of resources and opportunities available at most colleges and universities in North America, the role of the higher education practitioner in providing guidance and support to students to find and weave diverse experiences smoothly into the unique fabric of their college education becomes critically important. Competent scholar practitioners, versed in the conceptual richness of global citizenship and capable of deliberating on how different aspects of the undergraduate curriculum and co-curriculum fit together in fostering global learning, are indispensable agents of responsible and mindful global citizenship in college. Their primary role is in interpreting the key messages of global citizenship education to students and articulating the essential connections between student interests, academic requirements, and the wider social expectations.

The current chapter seeks to enhance practitioners' expertise in navigating the conceptual intricacies of global citizenship and their facility in incorporating global citizenship themes, discourses, and pedagogies in their work. Its goal is to outline several basic principles and strategies in global citizenship education to help define and enrich the work of education practitioners. An initial discussion of the conceptual foundations and interpretations of global citizenship leads to embracing moral cosmopolitanism as the ideology best suited to promote global citizenship in undergraduate education. The discussion then flows into an inquiry of the distinctive attributes of the cosmopolitan mindset. When transposed to the educational practice domain, these attributes lead to articulating three specific objectives of global citizenship education that constitute a global perspective model, a holistic if somewhat overgeneralized ideal for global educators to aspire to when designing and evaluating different programs. Finally, the discussion identifies several strategies and pedagogies instrumental in cultivating a global perspective and identity in all undergraduate students.

DELINEATING THE CONCEPTUAL TERRAIN OF GLOBAL CITIZENSHIP EDUCATION

The conceptual fluidity and ambiguity of the concept *global citizenship* is among the most salient challenges in formulating a clear and well thought-out global citizenship agenda in college. This fluidity and ambiguity allows for multiple interpretations, and for multiple ideological perspectives to promote their socio-political agendas through it (Mitchell, 2003; Noddings, 2005; Reimers, 2014; Roman, 2003; Schattle, 2008; Shultz, 2011; Stromquist, 2009). In a study of specific educational initiatives, Schattle (2008) identifies four major ideological currents informing the design of different documents and programs deploying a global citizenship discourse: moral cosmopolitanism, liberal multiculturalism, neoliberalism, and environmentalism. From these, he identifies moral cosmopolitanism and neoliberalism as the most prominent yet drastically different outlooks on global citizenship currently circulating in the educational arena.

Two Perspectives on Global Citizenship Education

Unlike the legal and constitutionally defined nature of national citizenship, global citizenship, understood as moral cosmopolitanism, espouses a profoundly ethical imperative of caring about and assuming responsibility for the well-being of other human beings (Dower, 2002). With its focus on social and ethical responsibility, cosmopolitanism is also inclusive of liberal multiculturalism, or the respect and appreciation for diversity, and environmentalism, or the focus on ensuring sustainable development (Schattle, 2008). At the other end of the ideological spectrum is the neoliberal perspective emphasizing human capital and the importance of preparing globally competitive professionals and leaders (Carlin, 2010; Kuisma, 2008).

The overall policy context of higher education most readily aligns with the spirit of neoliberal globalization, with its focus on privatization, marketization, accountability, and entrepreneurship (Bottery, 2006; Slaughter & Rhoades, 2004; Torres, 2011). The higher education policy discourse, on different levels, perpetuates the neoliberal attention to "competition" and "innovation" as well as the skills and competences graduates need to be competitive in a globally integrated society (Matus & Talburt, 2013; Mitchell, 2003; Roman, 2003). This context exerts continuous pressures on educators in meeting goals that "endorse, at least tacitly, the idea of unfettered global markets" (Schattle, 2008, p. 83, see also Carlin, 2010; Matus & Talburt, 2013; Torres, 2011).

Both the neoliberal and the cosmopolitan perspectives are integrated into the higher education experience. From the institutional to the departmental level, strategic plans and different policy documents emphasize the student cognitive skills essential to cultivate within the respective level and field. At the same time, the content of many courses and programs emphasizes the importance of understanding the social consequences of globalization and developing an active civic attitude toward them. The strong traditions of civic engagement and service learning in North America also facilitate an enhanced receptivity to advancing social justice, protecting human life and dignity, respecting diversity, and actively tackling major social issues (Jacoby, 2009). The big challenge for educators is the integration of these two ideologies in an academic context where competition and accountability loom large but students are also educated to be ethical and socially mindful persons capable of confronting the big concerns of today's world. When deliberating this integration, however, educators should keep in mind that the neoliberal and the cosmopolitan outlook are not equally positioned in the world of higher education. Students typically are better attuned to the neoliberal discourse on acquiring knowledge and skills in order to be competitive in the global economy. What is more, through the whole network of influences coming from parents, peers, and the media, many students have adopted a neoliberal mindset by the time they start college. This is why the particular area of global citizenship education in college needs to be developed as a theoretically-grounded, consistent and deliberate educational project founded upon the causes and objectives of moral cosmopolitanism (Papastephanou, 2005). Cultivating a firm grasp of the conceptual foundations and attributes of cosmopolitanism as an educational agenda for 21st century higher education is thus a foundational prerequisite for the implementation of a comprehensive global citizenship college program.

Distinctive Attributes of the Cosmopolitan Mindset

The magnitude of today's globalizing trends has breathed new life into an ancient ideal advocated by the Greek Cynics and the Roman Stoics (Nussbaum, 1996, 1997). One of them, the Roman Stoic philosopher Seneca (4 BC-65 AD) described the cosmopolitan worldview through a comparison between "two commonwealths—the one, a vast and truly common state, which embraces alike gods and men, in which we look neither to this corner of earth nor to that, but measure the bounds of our citizenship by the path of the sun; the other, the one to which we have been assigned by the accident of birth" (Seneca, De Otio 4.1). This sense of oneness with the community of human beings in the entire world, which precedes and embraces any particularistic affiliations, is the essence of the cosmopolitan worldview that modern global educators strive to instill in students.

The revival of cosmopolitanism as an educational agenda in the 21st century is quite logical: the current globalization trends refer not only to an unprecedented rate of integration and interdependence of the world but also to an enhanced awareness of the challenges globalization poses to all humanity, as the human condition "has itself become cosmopolitan" (Beck, 2006, p. 2). As social problems become much more visible on a global scale, more people become aware of the pressing need to confront the existing inequities and injustices in different parts of the world. The complexities of interacting with representatives of immensely different cultures, perspectives, and approaches to specific challenges are also an important aspect of constructing one's identity as a global citizen. In a world where injustices and inequalities have become so much more tangible, cosmopolitanism offers an "ideal of equality, compassion, democracy and care" (Papastephanou, 2002, p. 70). A globally inclusive outlook nurtured by a spirit of oneness with humanity has an immense educational potential to raise awareness of issues of poverty, identity, and cultural differences and cultivate a feeling of empathy and solidarity with the entire humanity in protecting human rights, regardless of any particularistic affiliations (Appiah, 2006, 2008; George-Jackson, 2010; Humes, 2008; Karlberg, 2008; Todd, 2007). Appreciating and critically examining different cultural and ideological perspectives, demonstrating concern for and solidarity with people all over the world, and striving to tackle injustices in a collaborative and cooperative spirit with one's fellow humans are all qualities global educators aim to instill and nurture in students. The cosmopolitan mindset underlying these qualities is predicated on four key attributes: other-orientedness, inclusiveness and empathy, oneness in diversity, and a critical worldview. They are all related to each other, although in different social or educational contexts some may be more visible than others.

Other-orientedness. An essential formative aspect of the cosmopolitan identity is intellectual curiosity, openness and receptivity to Others in their many different guises: as representatives of other countries, cultures, races, or ethnicities. The cosmopolitan spirit is about building bridges, not walls. It is an inclusive and outward driven worldview, appreciative of and receptive to the cultural traditions and values beyond its native community, while also inclusive of its traditions and values (Nussbaum, 1996). As Hall (2002) aptly observes, "it is not that we are without culture but we are drawing on the traces and residues of many cultural systems—and that is precisely what cosmopolitanism means. It means the ability to stand outside of having one's life written and scripted by any one community, whether that is faith or religion or culture—whatever it might be—and to draw selectively on a variety of discursive meanings" (p. 26). Due to the unprecedented rate of transnational migration and linguistic and cultural diversity, cosmopolitanism has become a routine condition for an increasing number of communities and individuals and has given rise to multiple hybrid and multicultural identities (Appiah, 2006, 2008; Beck, 2006; Hiebert, 2002; Merryfield, 2009).

The ability to see oneself as a cosmopolitan, as connected to all human beings by "ties of recognition and concern" (Nussbaum, 1997, p. 10), is a key starting point in any educational discussion with college students. To master this ability, college students must have many opportunities in and out of the classroom for a consistent inquiry into the multiple meanings and consequences of globalization, the significance of cultural differences and ways to overcome cultural barriers, the challenges confronting different human groups and world regions, as well as the opportunities for possible solutions. Of course, the comprehensive effort to instill a lasting interest in Others' lives and problems should not be perceived as advocating for rootlessness and lack of a stable identity, nor with a parasitic elitism that has no respect for established cultural frameworks (Papastephanou, 2005; Skey, 2012; Waldron, 2000). This is why it is important to introduce students to the second essential attribute of the cosmopolitan mindset, its inclusiveness and empathy for other human beings, in a way that affirms certain universal values of life while also cherishing one's native traditions.

Inclusiveness and empathy. The cosmopolitan mindset is not antagonistic to particularistic feelings such as patriotism but only to its extreme manifestations of nationalism and chauvinism (Nussbaum, 1996; Papastephanou, 2008). In this sense, educators should be mindful of Nussbaum's (1996) warning that an emphasis on patriotic pride can be "morally dangerous" since it easily translates into a feeling of superiority to other cultures and nations. "An education that takes national boundaries as morally salient too often reinforces this kind of irrationality, by lending to what is an accident of history a false air of moral weight and glory" (Nussbaum, 1996, p. 11). Therefore, it is critically important that, through specific illustrations, case studies and discussions, global citizenship educators intentionally and persistently refute any extremist interpretations of cosmopolitanism and convey the message that a healthy cosmopolitan outlook is not antagonistic to but "compatible or even complementary" (Papastephanou, 2008, p. 169) with patriotism, and that patriotism should be "globally sensitive" (Nussbaum, 2008) rather than narrowly nationalistic.

An inclusive disposition distinguishes the cosmopolitan mindset not just from extreme manifestations of nationalism and xenophobia but even from an every-day "either/or" view of identity as formed in opposition to what one considers foreign; it embraces a "both/and" type of logic (Beck, 2006, pp. 4–5) and transcends dichotomous concepts such as national and international or ethnic majority and minority. The application of this logic in educational practice warrants that educators emphasize to students that the relationship between the local and the global is not one of contrast and opposition but rather a continuum (Habermas, 1992), a synthesis (Davies and Reid, 2005), or an evolution (Torres, 2002), in which the global/cosmopolitan encompasses the local/national aspects of contemporary citizenship. Being a good citizen to one's region and state does not mean deifying them and deprecating those from the outside; instead, it has a lot to do with caring about democracy, justice and equity, and hence respecting human life and dignity as universal values.

Oneness in diversity. The cosmopolitan worldview is one that respects, appreciates, values, and encourages diversity – this is the third foundational attribute of cosmopolitanism global educators should focus on instilling in students. Asserting the equal value and dignity of different cultural backgrounds has a long and revered tradition in North American higher education (Heilman, 2009). However, until recently, diversity has been conceptualized primarily within a national context. At the same time, in today's world of intense global mobility, national boundaries are no longer a truly meaningful factor when considering issues of cultural pluralism: "Why should we think of people from China as our fellows the minute they dwell in a certain place, namely the United States, but not when they dwell in a certain other place, namely China? What is it about the national boundary that magically converts people toward whom our education is both incurious and indifferent into people to whom we have duties of mutual respect?"(Nussbaum, 1996, p. 14). To add to that argument, even within national boundaries cultural pluralism is an ever increasing trend as a result of increased immigration flows or increased student and professional mobility (Todd, 2007). The novel contribution of cosmopolitan education is in bringing a new focus of attention beyond national specificities, affirming global diversity as a value and a cause to be defended (Heilman, 2009), and emphasizing that "understanding and respect entail recognizing not only difference but also, at the same time, commonality, not only a unique history but common rights and aspirations and problems" (Nussbaum, 1997, p. 69).

Through the methods and materials educators use in and out of the classroom, they must encourage students to identify global social trends and issues beyond their specific enactments in any immediate contexts. They must also encourage the development of attitudinal and emotional skills besides the cognitive ones: only through experiencing with their whole being the trials and suffering of Others will students develop a capacity for a true empathy and compassion. Nussbaum (1997) considers compassion essential for developing civic responsibility and advocates for including it into the undergraduate curriculum, mainly through more courses in literature. She refers to this capacity as the "narrative imagination," a sort of emotional knowledge that lets one experience life through the eyes of the Other. "This requires...a highly complex set of moral abilities, including the ability to imagine what it is like to be in that person's place (what we usually call *empathy*), and also the ability to stand back and ask whether the person's own judgment has taken the full measure of what has happened" (p. 91).

Understanding and respect for global diversity and cultivating empathy for Others demand a focus on dialogue and communication. Therefore, global citizenship education increasingly recognizes *interculturalism* as a more apt term than *multiculturalism*. With the emphasis it places on overcoming cultural isolation and promoting a mutually enriching understanding, dialogue and ideas exchange between different cultures, it conveys more fully the value of diversity in education (Heilman, 2009; Olson & Peacock, 2012).

A critical worldview. Cosmopolitanism is neither a contemplative outlook, nor does it advocate for cultural relativism and uncritical tolerance of morally wrong rules or practices in one's own or in other cultures (Gaudelli, 2003). Cosmopolitanism is a critically inquisitive worldview focused on knowing the wider world for the sake of improving it. It is "simultaneously a skeptical, disillusioned, self-critical outlook" (Beck, 2006, p. 3). It is grounded in what Nussbaum (1997) calls the Socratic disposition: the capacity to critically examine traditional beliefs, to question conventions and put established norms to the test of reason. In higher education it is the effort to encourage students to "reason together about their choices rather than just trading claims and counter-claims" (Nussbaum, 1997, p. 10).

The ability to distance oneself from views, beliefs, and practices taken for granted within one's cultural framework and to examine and understand how they shape one's attitudes and viewpoints is undoubtedly the first step toward gaining "perspective consciousness" (Hanvey, 1976), or realizing the essentially limited nature of any cultural worldview, including one's own. It is the first step toward appreciating and developing empathy for cultural beliefs and norms different from one's own but also a critical appraisal of particular human circumstances and choices. In educational settings, philosophy is considered the discipline most conducive to the cultivation of this self-examining predisposition (Nussbaum, 1997), but other courses in the humanities such as history and literature also offer multiple opportunities to question taken for granted norms and widely held beliefs.

For Appiah (2008), there are two main prerequisites for being a real cosmopolitan citizen: "knowledge about the lives of other citizens, on the one hand, and the power to affect them…The fact is that you can't give real meaning to the idea that we are all fellow citizens if you can't affect each other and you don't know about each other" (p. 87). The cosmopolitan mindset is thus not just other-oriented but also forward looking: it actively strives to combat injustice and inequity in order to improve the human condition in very concrete and specific ways. Therefore, it is of utmost importance for college students to have the opportunity to develop critical experiential knowledge and skills through engaging in projects aimed at improving the lives of different communities, local or distant.

In summary, an open-minded attitude toward the Other, ability to empathize with the less fortunate, a fundamental belief in the common rights and freedoms every human being is entitled to, and a critical stance toward effecting a positive change in the world are all attributes of a cosmopolitan mindset that undergraduate educators should be aiming to instill in students across the undergraduate experience. In the following section some of the specific objectives and strategies that may be instrumental in accomplishing this are discussed.

OBJECTIVES, STRATEGIES AND PEDAGOGIES OF GLOBAL CITIZENSHIP EDUCATION

This section discusses concrete objectives, strategies and pedagogies that global citizenship educators should consider adopting in their daily work. While it does not aspire to provide a fully exhaustive set of guidelines, it highlights the priorities that guide practitioners' efforts in global citizenship education. Good practices will always be shaped in accord with their unique institutional environments and will have their special authentic characteristics.

A Global Perspective Model Informed by Educational Practice

The knowledge, understanding, and empathy for Others and the power to affect their lives constitute the two main focus areas in global citizenship education in college. They are translated into the educational goals of building intercultural competence and cultivating social responsibility in tackling global challenges (Beck, 2006; Landorf, 2009; Stevenson, 2001; Todd, 2007). These two main goals constitute the fabric of the global citizenship pedagogy in college, in and out of the classroom. They guide the educational philosophy behind designing courses, programs, and other initiatives aimed at enhancing the quality of students' knowledge of the world and their capacity to effect social change.

Intercultural competence and global social and ethical responsibility form the foundation of the global perspective model this chapter espouses, a model informed by educational practice. It stems from a summary of several prior research models (Case, 1993; Hanvey, 1974; Karlberg, 2010; Kniep, 1986; Nussbaum, 1997), nationally validated assessment rubrics of students' global and intercultural competences (Association of American Colleges and Universities [AAC&U], n.d.) as well as concrete practitioner observations of different curricular and co-curricular college practices. This two-level model (Figure 1) consists of three main components, equally important in the shaping of student identities. The basic level comprises two sets of cognitive and perceptual skills pertaining to the two big areas of intercultural awareness and social and ethical responsibility.

The two basic sets of cognitive and attitudinal competences merge into a higher level of behavioral competence: student participation and engagement with the World and the Other through research, collaborative learning, and service projects. The focus at this level is on social agency across multiple curricular and co-curricular programs, where the students' global citizenship potential is actualized in constant communication and cooperation across cultural differences and boundaries.

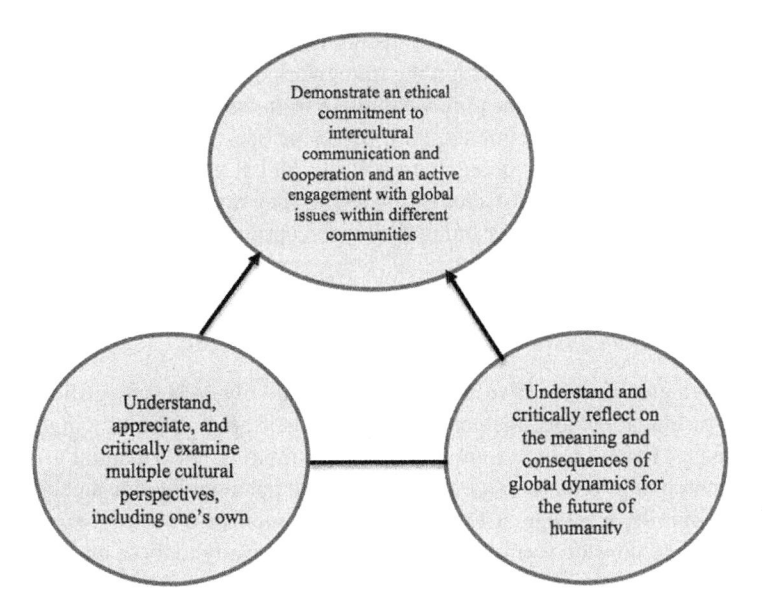

```
                ┌─────────────────────┐
                │  Demonstrate an ethical │
                │     commitment to       │
                │     intercultural       │
                │  communication and      │
                │  cooperation and an active │
                │  engagement with global │
                │  issues within different │
                │     communities         │
                └─────────────────────┘
```

Figure 1. Constituent characteristics of a global perspective: an educational practice model.

(Three circles model: top — "Demonstrate an ethical commitment to intercultural communication and cooperation and an active engagement with global issues within different communities"; bottom-left — "Understand, appreciate, and critically examine multiple cultural perspectives, including one's own"; bottom-right — "Understand and critically reflect on the meaning and consequences of global dynamics for the future of humanity".)

Compared to previous models, the current model offers three novel contributions. First, the inclusion of the "social agency" level is a clear indicator that modern global citizenship education places a strong emphasis on developing pro-active attitudes of engagement and participation and utilizing the whole range of educational experiences, across the curriculum and co-curriculum, to promote global citizenship as a holistic and integrative experience. Acknowledging the organic link between knowledge, skills, attitudes, and their application in practice or research is a key premise in the shaping of this model. Of all previous models, only Karlberg's (2010) also recognized this novel aspect of global citizenship education in college. Second, the multiple discrete literacies and competencies previous studies discuss are now grouped into two major thematic clusters regarding global social dynamics (including global issues, structures and trends, and discourses of inequality, power and privilege) on the one hand, and intercultural competence (i.e., understanding and sensitivity toward cultural differences and collaboration across them) on the other. While the two groups are certainly related to each other, as cross-cultural collaborations are indispensable to tackling any global challenges, they do belong to two distinct spheres of knowledge that could roughly be associated with the dynamics of social structures and the cultural foundations of human behavior respectively. And third, the proposed model departs from Case's (1993) dichotomy of "substantive" and "perceptual" dimensions of global and intercultural competence, where the former referred to factual knowledge and the latter- to an attitudinal and dispositional competence level. While distinguishing the two certainly is helpful, in most educational experiences within the framework of a socially constructed reality, it is not possible to separate the purely cognitive from the perceptual. Any knowledge about social phenomena is imbued with biases as one cannot teach the bare facts without analyzing and critiquing them. While global citizenship educators must encourage the acquisition of factual knowledge, they must be even more persistent in developing the students' reasoning skills, perceptions, emotions, and attitudes in mastering this knowledge.

Strategies and Pedagogies in Cosmopolitan Education

Cultivating a global perspective in college students involves the synergistic enactment of all three global perspective constituents and their application in a diverse range of contexts. However, the cosmopolitan disposition is not a naturally occurring one. Human beings tend to shape their beliefs and behaviors within smaller groups, such as a family, a village, a town, or even a region or a country, so it is much more natural to develop feelings of attachment and loyalty to these more immediate kinship groups than to an abstract global humanity. Historical relationships including frictions and wars further complicate the cosmopolitan impetus toward solidarity with distant and different Others (Papastephanou, 2002). The modern accelerated formation of multicultural and transnational communities and networks often gives rise to different counter-movements subscribing to nationalism, relativism, and fundamentalism (Vertovec & Cohen, 2002). Being a conscious and informed global citizen thus can be a "lonely business" (Nussbaum, 1996, p. 15) indeed. Therefore, the cultivation of a cosmopolitan outlook in students requires laborious and persistent efforts in making the distant, the different, and the unfamiliar more tangible and more deeply and spontaneously experienced.

Promoting a cosmopolitan worldview is a challenging task for any individual, and it is particularly difficult for education practitioners at U.S. colleges and universities. Higher education in the United States has not always been hospitable to the ideals of cosmopolitanism, since they do not mesh with feelings of American superiority and preeminence in the world (Gaudelli, 2003). Additionally, the strong neoliberal focus on human capital, academic achievement, and technical skills is a constant constraint for global citizenship educators (Carlin, 2010). Because of this, higher education institutions should be very explicit in embracing an intentional holistic approach to global citizenship as moral cosmopolitanism, mobilizing the collective expertise of administrators, instructors, academic advisors, and student affairs practitioners, and utilizing all available resources within the curriculum and co-curriculum. Educational practitioners have an essential twofold task of becoming globally competent themselves, committing to the causes of cosmopolitan education and conveying those dispositions to students in a natural way, but also mastering the pedagogic strategies necessary to adopt in educating students to be good global citizens. The four strategies suggested below have a potential to empower educators in the development of effective global citizenship education programs. They can be instrumental in guiding the development of cognitive, attitudinal, emotional, and behavioral skills across the whole spectrum of undergraduate experiences in and out of the classroom.

A comprehensive approach to building global knowledge. Understanding the complex dynamics of the globally integrated world they live in is a necessary prerequisite for the development of ethically competent and socially responsible attitudes in students. Therefore, educators' efforts to incorporate multiple approaches to building global knowledge, including knowledge of cultural diversity and intercultural competence, should be deliberate and consistent across majors, general education requirements, and all other curricular and co-curricular programs. Global education in the 21st century is a truly multidisciplinary and interdisciplinary field, and it has the potential to span the entire undergraduate curriculum and focus on issues ranging from power and privilege and mainstream ideology, to the experiences of marginalized communities, to cross-cultural experiential learning (Merryfield, 2009). However, as prior research shows, the current state of the higher education curriculum at many postsecondary institutions is far from this ideal. References to the meanings, consequences, and challenges of globalization in both institutional documents and the undergraduate curriculum are sporadic, fragmented, and peripheral, focusing primarily on economic processes and not so much on the social implications of processes of global concern (Agbaria, 2011; Fiss & Hirsch, 2005; Matus & Talburt, 2013; Peterson & Helms, 2013; Reimers, 2014). Therefore, higher education administrators and faculty need to ensure above all that courses dealing with global issues (e.g., poverty, migration, human rights violations, sustainability, and global health) are available, recommended and maybe even required across the entire spectrum of undergraduate majors and not just to those focusing on international subject areas. In principle, educators need to consistently develop and promote courses as well as co-curricular programs raising awareness of the challenges globalization creates or augments as well as the opportunities it gives for building alliances across national boundaries to tackle these challenges.

A good number of political and practical considerations come into play when designing an internationally mindful curriculum: as it is not possible to include topics about all cultures or all world regions and nation-states, "knowledge is always inequitable, more representative of some than of others" (Roth, 2007, p. 107). However, finding more and better ways to incorporate non-Western perspectives into curricular and co-curricular initiatives could be an important strategy in overcoming, somewhat, this inequity. Instructors, learning specialists, and experiential project coordinators should also seek to incorporate in their materials and discussions new technologies and modes of communication, such as video illustrations of the issues discussed and Skype sessions with overseas partners. Such approaches will help students experience world issues more immediately and spontaneously, beyond just learning the facts.

Ensuring ethical proximity. A thorough and comprehensive introduction to the many faces of globalization is just a key initial stage in the global citizenship education endeavor. As Nussbaum (1997) notes, one can know all the facts and may still be "not fully equipped for citizenship" (p. 85). It is crucial that the newly gained knowledge of the world is complemented by the appropriate emotional, psychological and ethical dispositions promoting a cosmopolitan mentality (Heilman, 2007). One way to develop such attitudes is through incorporating discussions on how global processes affect the students' own lives, in their immediate communities: how they experience social inequality, prejudice, and cultural tensions, for example. In accord with the values and beliefs of the cosmopolitan mindset, a defining characteristic of a cosmopolitan curriculum is its Other-orientedness and the development of students' understanding of and sensitivity to the cultural complexity of the global society. This capacity should be consciously and purposefully developed via multiple avenues in college. Studying non-Western cultures and global social issues in general education could be complemented with experiential learning during community service projects, internships, and other practical experiences, where students can test their knowledge in real-life, cross-cultural situations. These are all just initial efforts in shaping a new ethos of students who genuinely care about humanity with its many different faces and destinies.

Global citizenship education is a truly transformative education: it helps one divest oneself of irrational particularistic identifications and embrace a new, less egotistical, less ethnocentric, and more altruistic and generous self. It also takes a stand against any lack of interest and curiosity about the Other and against a relativistic and uncritical attitude to different cultures. Students need to not only know about other cultures but be *invested* in them; they need to develop a sophisticated and intimate knowledge of at least one cultural worldview very different from their own. Therefore, just like courses focusing on global social issues, courses that promote this type of deep and critical intercultural knowledge should be widely available, popularized and maybe required. Among these, courses in the humanities are particularly valuable, as they typically focus on the depths of human character and on tangible circumstances and unique experiences in many different social, historical, and cultural contexts. This is why Nussbaum (1997) considers literature to be the discipline most optimally geared toward developing the "narrative imagination" and thus cultivating tolerance and compassion. Many other courses in history, sociology, human geography, anthropology, human development, or business can incorporate descriptive and narrative components such as case studies that can make their content more concrete, powerful, and psychologically effective. Incorporating ethnographic accounts of how cultures respond to or cope with global issues may bring new perspectives and insights (see, for example, Reichman's (2011) compelling ethnography on the devastating effects of globalization on a small rural community in Honduras).

Ensuring ethical proximity should also become a priority for practitioners outside the classroom, especially at schools with considerable numbers of international students and faculty. Killick (2012) makes a strong argument for encouraging live personal encounters between American and international students to counteract a natural tendency to only stick to the familiar. "When we are entrenched in narrow communities of the like minded, there is a strong tendency to stasis—nonlearning" (p. 382). Urban and Palmer's (2014) study confirms that international students are eager to serve as cultural resources for American students; however, institutions do not take full advantage of this potential. At campuses with good numbers of international students and scholars, encountering Otherness could be built into a variety of cross-cultural activities and could become integral to the students' lived experience, contributing to the transformative power of other global citizenship efforts. Let us not forget that global citizenship education can also afford new perspectives on traditional U.S. diversity; in fact, including diverse groups of both American and international students in most intercultural programs on campus could be a healthy and productive strategy. For example, a panel including both international Asian and Asian American students can reveal interesting details about the coexistence and integration across generations of Eastern and Western cultural norms in the broader U.S. society and on a U.S. college campus in particular. Also, encouraging difficult conversations on different types of prejudice and bigotry, including racism and xenophobia, can help American and international students from different ethnic and racial backgrounds share their deepest concerns, deliberate on the universal scope of these evils, and negotiate a common ground of mutual understanding and cooperation toward a goal important to everyone.

Critical self-reflection and deliberation. Ensuring a solid cognitive foundation and introducing an ethical lens in presenting global and intercultural issues is an essential aspect of global citizenship education. However, its potential could never be realized to the fullest without acknowledging and reinforcing the indispensable role of deliberation in connecting social issues to the student's individual consciousness and inner world. The school has long been recognized as a communicative institution (Gaudelli, 2003), and deliberation has been promoted the best strategy of education for democratic citizenship (Gastil, 2008; Lovlie, 2007). Roth (2007) considers deliberation as a more effective approach to citizenship education than knowledge or ethics, since it encourages the synthesis of both and extends the cognitive and ethical disposition to reasoning about one's responsibility for and accountability to Others for one's choices and actions.

Recognizing deliberation as a key component of the pedagogic repertoire in global citizenship education evokes the Socratic dialogue, in which different arguments are presented and issues are examined in their complexity so that conclusions are based on well-informed decisions (Nussbaum, 1997). Deliberation in college can be practiced both in and out of the classroom: it is a demonstration of the students' willingness and capacity to engage in a reasoned reflection and to understand the values, perspectives, and interests of Others. Education for global citizenship should be deliberative in nature and should place the rational justification of different political and ethical decisions at the center of instruction. For example, specific illustrations of the issue of protecting human rights in cultures that consider it a Western norm threatening their traditional way of life may become the subject of a serious classroom deliberation. Deliberation skills need to be emphasized and developed through a continuous focus on classroom discussions and mock debates.

Academic advising is another area especially conducive to deliberative discussions on the meaning and purpose of students' decisions. The Socratic inquiry can and should be cultivated within an advising setting, as academic advisors are the educators situated most strategically to impact student development. As the connecting link for students to all opportunities, resources and experiences in college, and also the persons who can reach out to the greatest number of students through individual, one-on-one discussions, advisors have an immensely important mission to be key educational agents in the shaping of student identities. If modern higher education embraces the goals of global citizenship education, all academic advisors should also consider themselves global educators. Ideally, the "global citizenship" aspect of academic advising would flow smoothly into the advising conversation and would be aimed at both supporting students in their exploration of multiple educational possibilities and challenging them to reflect on the significance and consequences of their academic choices for their own future but also the future of society as a whole.

Focus on student agency. All educators' efforts to instill knowledge, skills, attitudes, and dispositions toward shaping a global identity in students would be futile if they miss the opportunity to directly involve students as active agents in addressing issues of global concern. The transformative power of global education can only be fulfilled through direct student engagement with global issues and intercultural communication in real-world contexts. This strategy should be systematically applied by instructors, academic advisors, and co-curricular educators. Different university programs and initiatives focusing on promoting scholarship in practice, social entrepreneurship and research-based service learning can facilitate the successful inclusion of most students into meaningful global citizenship experiences in and out of the classroom. Courses that alternate more theoretical discussions with breakout sessions dedicated to service projects that address global issues in different local contexts could be particularly effective. A problem-based approach to one's education during advising appointments could also be an excellent opportunity to integrate global themes through combining related curricular and co-curricular experiences.

SUMMARY

Education for global citizenship is a core intrinsic aspect of the 21st century undergraduate experience at North American colleges and universities. As a powerful formative factor impacting overall student development, it should be implemented as a comprehensive institutional effort reaching out to all undergraduate students across multiple curricular and co-curricular areas. The mission of global citizenship education could best be fulfilled through transformative, ethically, and emotionally rich encounters with issues of global concern, such as social inequality, cultural pluralism and intercultural cooperation, and protecting human rights in different regional and cultural contexts. These encounters can happen at multiple points during the entire college experience: through general education courses, capstone projects, majors and minors, research experiences and internships, student organizations conducting service projects, as well as enhanced and deliberative communication on issues of mutual significance with people from different cultural backgrounds from inside or outside the United States. Higher education practitioners are the main engine behind the dynamics of global citizenship education, and as such they need to develop their own global identities in order to best guide students in discovering their personal stakes in global citizenship and in constructing globally competent, responsible, and engaged lives.

REFERENCES

Agbaria, A. (2009). The social studies education discourse community on globalization: Exploring the agenda of preparing citizens for the global age. *Journal of Studies in International Education, 15*(1), 57–74.

Association of American Colleges and Universities. (n.d.). *VALUE: Valid assessment of learning in undergraduate education.* Retrieved from http://www.aacu.org/value/rubrics/index.cfm

Appiah, K. A. (2006). *Cosmopolitanism: Ethics in a world of strangers.* New York, NY: Norton.

Appiah, K. A. (2008). Chapter 6: Education for global citizenship. In G. Fenstermacher (Ed.), *Why do we educate? 107th yearbook of 064the National Society for the Study of Education* (pp. 83–99). Malden, MA: Wiley-Blackwell

Beck, U. (2006). *The Cosmopolitan vision.* Malden, MA: Polity Press.

Bottery, M. (2006). Education and globalization: Redefining the role of the educational professional. *Educational Review, 58*(1), 95–113.

Carlin, P. (2010). Education for social justice or human capital? In J. Zajda (Ed.), *Globalization, education and social justice* (pp. 67–76), Comparative Education and Policy Research 10, Springer Science + Business Media.

Case, R. (1993). Key elements of a global perspective. *Social Education, 57*(6), 318–325.

Davies, I., & Pike, G. (2009). Global citizenship education. In Lewin, R. (Ed.). *The handbook of practice and research in study abroad: Higher education and the quest for global citizenship* (pp. 61–77). New York, NY: Routledge.

Davies, I., & Reid, A. (2005). Globalizing citizenship education? A critique of "global education" and "citizenship education". *British Journal of Educational Studies, 53*(1), 66–89.

Deardorff, D. K., de Witt, H., Heyl, J. D., & Adams, T. (Eds.). (2012). *The Sage handbook of international higher education.* Thousand Oaks, CA: Sage.

Dower, N. (2002). Global ethics and global citizenship. In N. Dower & J. Williams (Eds.), *Global citizenship: Critical introduction* (pp. 146–157). New York, NY: Routledge.

Fiss, C., & Hirsch, P. M. (2005). The discourse of globalization: Framing and sensemaking of an emerging concept. *American Sociological Review, 70*(1), 29–52.

Gastil, J. (2008). *Political communication and deliberation*. Thousand Oaks, CA: Sage.

Gaudelli, W. (2003). *World class. Teaching and learning in global times*. Mahwah, NJ: Lawrence Erlbaum.

George-Jackson, C. E. (2010). The cosmopolitan university: The medium toward global citizenship and justice. *Policy Futures in Education, 8*(2), 191–200.

Habermas, J. (1992). Citizenship and national identity: Some reflections on the future of Europe. *Praxis International, 12*(1), 1–19.

Hall, S. (2002). Political belonging in a world of multiple identities. In S. Vertovec & R. Cohen (Eds.), *Conceiving cosmopolitanism* (pp. 25–31). New York, NY: Oxford University Press.

Hanvey, R. (1976). An attainable global perspective. *The American Forum for Global Education*. Retrieved from http://www.globaled.org/an_att_glob_persp_04_11_29.pdf

Heilman, E. (2007). (Dis)locating imaginative and ethical aims of global education. In K. Roth & I. Gur-Ze'ev (Eds.), *Education in the era of globalization* (pp. 83–104). Springer. Retrieved from http://www.springer.com/education+%26+language/book/978-1-4020-5944-5

Heilman, E. (2009). Terrains of global and multicultural education: What is distinctive, contested, and shared? In T. F. Kirkwood-Tucker (Ed.). *Visions in global education: The globalization of curriculum and pedagogy in teacher education and schools* (pp. 25–46). New York, NY: Peter Lang.

Hiebert, D. (2002). Cosmopolitanism at the local level: The development of transnational neighborhoods. In S. Vertovec & R. Cohen (Eds.), *Conceiving cosmopolitanism: Theory, context and practice* (pp. 209–225). Oxford: Oxford University Press.

Hill, B. A., & Helms, R. M. (2012). Leading the globally engaged institutions: New directions, choices, and dilemmas. American Council on Education. Retrieved from http://www.acenet.edu/news-room/Documents/CIGE-Insights-2013-Trans-Atlantic-Dialogue.pdf

Humes, W. (2008). The discourse of global citizenship. In M. A. Peters, A. Britton & H. Blee (Eds.), *Global citizenship education* (pp. 41–52). Rotterdam/ Taipei: Sense Publishers.

Jacoby, B. (Ed.). (2009). *Civic engagement in higher education: Concepts and practices*. San Francisco, CA: Jossey-Bass.

Karlberg, M. (2008). Discourse, identity, and global citizenship. *Peace Review: A Journal of Social Justice, 20*(3), 310–320.

Karlberg, M. (2010). Education for interdependence: The university and the global citizen. *Global Studies Journal, 3*(1), 129–138.

Killick, D. (2011). Seeing-ourselves-in-the-world: Developing global citizenship through international mobility and campus community. *Journal of Studies in International Education, 16*(4), 372–389.

Kniep, W. M. (1986). Defining a global education by its content. *Social Education, 50*(6), 437–446.

Kuisma, M. (2008). Rights or privileges? The challenge of globalization to the values of citizenship. *Citizenship Studies, 12*(6), 613–627.

Landorf, H. (2009). Toward a philosophy of global education. In T. F. Kirkwood Tucker (Ed.), *Visions in global education: The globalization of curriculum and pedagogy in teacher education and schools* (pp. 47–67). New York, NY: Peter Lang.

Lewin, R. (Ed.). (2009). *The handbook of practice and research in study abroad: Higher education and the quest for global citizenship*. New York, NY: Routledge.

Lovlie, L. (2007). Education for deliberative democracy. In K. Roth & I. Gur-Ze'ev (Eds.), *Education in the era of globalization* (pp. 123–146). Springer. Retrieved from http://www.springer.com/education+%26+language/book/978-1-4020-5944-5

Matus, C., & Talburt, S. (2013). Producing global citizens for the future: Space, discourse, and curricular reform. *Compare: A Journal of Comparative and International Education*, doi: 10.1080/03057925.2013.842682

Merryfield, M. M. (2009). Moving the center of global education; From imperial worldviews that divide the world to double consciousness, contrapuntal pedagogy, hybridity, and cross-cultural competence. In T. F. Kirkwood-Tucker (Ed.), *Visions in global education: The globalization of curriculum and pedagogy in teacher education and schools* (pp. 215–239). New York, NY: Peter Lang.

Mitchell, K. (2003). Educating the national citizen in neoliberal times: From the multicultural self to the strategic cosmopolitan. *Transactions of the Institute of British Geographers, 28*(4), 387–403.

Noddings, N. (2005). Global citizenship: Promises and problems. In N. Noddings (Ed.), *Educating citizens for global awareness* (pp. 1–21). New York, NY: Teachers College.

Nussbaum, M. C. (1996). Patriotism and cosmopolitanism. In M. C. Nussbaum & J. Cohen (Eds.), *For love of country?* (pp. 3–17). Boston, MA: Beacon Press.

Nussbaum, M. C. (1997). *Cultivating humanity. A classical defense of reform in liberal education.* Cambridge, MA: Harvard University Press.

Nussbaum, M. C. (2008). Toward a globally sensitive patriotism. *Daedalus, 137*(3), 78–93.

Olson, C., & Peacock, J. (2012). Globalism and interculturalism: Where global and local meet. In D. K. Deardorff, H. de Witt, J. D. Heyl, & T. Adams (Eds.), *The Sage handbook of international higher education* (pp. 305–322). Thousand Oaks, CA: Sage.

Papastephanou, M. (2002). Arrows not yet fired: Cultivating cosmopolitanism through education. *Journal of Philosophy of Education, 36*(1), 69–86.

Papastephanou, M. (2005). Globalisation, globalism and cosmopolitanism as an educational field. *Educational Philosophy and Theory, 37*(4), 533–551.

Papastephanou, M. (2008). Cosmopolitanism: with or without patriotism? In M.A. Peters, A. Britton, & H. Blee (Eds.), *Global citizenship education: Philosophy, theory, and pedagogy* (pp. 169–185). Rotterdam/Taipei: Sense Publishers.

Peters, M.A., Britton A., & Blee, H. (Eds.). (2008). *Global citizenship education: Philosophy, theory, and pedagogy.* Rotterdam/Taipei: Sense Publishers.

Peterson, P. M., & Helms, R. M. (2013). Internationalization revisited. *Change: The Magazine of Higher learning, 45*(2), 28–34.

Reichman, D. (2011). *The broken village: Coffee, migration, and globalization in Honduras.* Ithaca, NY: Cornell University Press.

Reimers, F. M. (2014). Bringing global education to the core of the undergraduate curriculum. *Diversity & Democracy, 17*(2). Retrieved from http://www.aacu.org/diversitydemocracy/vol17no2/reimers.cfm

Roman, L. (2003). Education and the contested meanings of "global citizenship". *Journal of Educational Change, 4,* 269–293.

Roth, K. (2007). Education for responsibility: Knowledge, ethics and deliberation. In K. Roth & I. Gur-Ze'ev (Eds.), *Education in the era of globalization* (pp. 105–121). Springer. Retrieved from http://www.springer.com/education+%26+language/book/978-1-4020-5944-5

Schattle, H. (2008). Education for global citizenship: Illustrations of ideological pluralism and adaptation. *Journal of Political Ideologies, 13*(1), 73–94.

Shultz, L. (2011). Engaging the multiple discourses of global citizenship education within a Canadian university: Deliberation, contestation, and social justice possibilities. In L. Shultz, A. A. Abdi, & G. H. Richardson (Eds.), *Global citizenship education in post-secondary institutions: Theories, practices, policies* (pp. 13–24). New York, NY: Peter Lang.

Shultz, L., Abdi, A. A., & Richardson, G. H. (Eds.). (2011). *Global citizenship education in post-secondary institutions: Theories, practices, policies.* New York, NY: Peter Lang.

Skey, M. (2012). We need to talk about cosmopolitanism: The challenge of studying openness towards other people. *Cultural Sociology, 6*(4), 471–487.

Slaughter, S., & Rhoades, G. (2004). *Academic capitalism and the new economy.* Baltimore, MD: The Johns Hopkins University Press.

Stevenson, N. (2002). Cosmopolitanism, multiculturalism, and citizenship. *Sociological Research Online, 7*(1). Retrieved from http://www.socresonline.org.uk/7/1/stevenson.html

Stromquist, N. (2009) Theorizing global citizenship: Discourses, challenges, and implications for education. *Interamerican Journal of Education for Democracy, 2*(1), 6–29.

Todd, S. (2007). Ambiguities of cosmopolitanism: Difference, gender, and the right to education. In K. Roth & I. Gur-Ze'ev (Eds.), *Education in the era of globalization* (pp. 65–82). Springer. Retrieved from http://www.springer.com/education+%26+language/book/978-1-4020-5944-5

Torres. C. A. (2002). Globalization, education, and citizenship: Solidarity versus markets. *American Educational Research Journal, 39*(2), 363–378.

Torres, C. A. (2011). Public universities and the neoliberal common sense: Seven iconoclastic theses. *International Studies in Sociology of Education, 21*(3), 177–197.

Urban, E. L., & Palmer, L. B. (2014). International students as a resource for internationalization of higher education. *Journal of Studies in International Education, 18*(4), 305–324.

Vertovec, S., & Cohen, R. (2002). Introduction: Conceiving cosmopolitanism. In S. Vertovec & R. Cohen (Eds.), *Conceiving cosmopolitanism: Theory, context and practice* (pp. 1–22). Oxford: Oxford University Press.

Waldron, J. (2000). What is cosmopolitan? *The Journal of Political Philosophy, 8*(2), 227–243.

Elena Galinova
Division of Undergraduate Studies
Penn State University

MARTA A. SHAW

3. THE CHALLENGES AND IMPLICATIONS OF GLOBALIZATION FOR UNDERGRADUATE PEDAGOGY

Whether in the United States, India, China, or in Poland, today's students in the developed and emerging world construct their identities in a globally interconnected world. It is a world that is increasingly flat (Friedman, 2005), rife with more opportunity than the one inherited by previous generations, but also with more anxiety – a "generalized or unspecified sense of disequilibrium" (Turner, 1988, p. 61, cited by Gudykunst and Nishida, 2001, p. 59). For the lucky and growing minority of the world's youth who get the chance to go to college, the undergraduate years are a prime time to spread their wings in an exciting and interconnected world. Just as importantly, these years are the time to deepen the roots of their own identity – their self-conceptions, or theories of themselves (Cupach & Imahori, 1993). Whether this chance is realized depends to a large degree on the wisdom and mindfulness of those who plan and support their college experience – people who often came of age in circumstances entirely different from those taken for granted by today's college students.

The aim of this chapter is to examine the implications of globalization for college students' identities, and for the role and practice of global citizenship education in the undergraduate years. For this goal, it articulates new questions for the mental models that guide faculty in helping students develop their intercultural and global competencies.

COLLEGE STUDENTS AND GLOBALIZATION 3.0

Many share the sentiment that "we live in rapidly changing and uncertain times, and that the fate of local communities is connected to distant political, economic and cultural happenings" (Singh, 2004, p. 104). Values and habits once passed down from generation to generation are now coming under the pressure of intensifying waves of globalization – "the increased international integration of economic activities" that takes place in the context of a "raising importance of knowledge in economic processes" (Archibugi & Iammarino, 2002, p. 98).

Globalization has reached a stage at which it affects not just nations and companies, but individuals and small groups. According to Thomas Friedman (2005b), "Globalization 1.0" began in 1492 and shrank the world to a smaller size as countries sought resources through conquest. "Globalization 2.0" shrank the world even further, as companies became global in their reach for new markets and labor. What we have witnessed in our lifetime is the rise of "Globalization 3.0," with human knowledge connected and dispersed to a previously unseen and unimagined degree. The acceleration of travel and rise of modern information technologies amounts to what Toffler (1981) described as "the third wave" – the third major shift in the development of human civilization since the invention of agriculture and the Industrial Revolution. Social relations now stretch across significant distances, and "local contexts are increasingly inhabited by the images, surplus labor, ideas, or expertise of people who are not physically present" (Singh, 2004). In the world flattened by the "third wave," the presence of diverse others affects the development of individual identity from the earliest years.

Shifting Identity

The increasing speed of technological change and knowledge accumulation has sped up generational differences, creating what Stone (2010) refers to as "mini-generation gaps" – significant differences in the communication patterns of different age groups, even between people a few years apart. The students who enter today's college classrooms are not only of a different generation than their instructors; they may often represent a generation different than the students one taught three years before.

Technology is transforming the lives of young people and their communities much faster than most realize. The models of intercultural development presented in the previous chapters provide useful road maps for selecting an appropriate point of departure for working with students of new "mini-generations;" but as this chapter suggests, practitioners' mental models must be continuously adapted and extended to reflect the actual experiences and growth trajectories of undergraduate students who enter our classrooms. These trajectories are being shaped by forces changing faster than ever before. As faculty attempt to assist students in their intercultural development, the pace of technological and social change requires that we question the common assumptions of the mental models that frame our understanding of the intercultural journey.

As Ting-Toomey (1999) notes, identity consists of "reflective self-images constructed, experienced, and communicated by the individuals within a culture" (p. 39). For college students today, that culture is no longer defined just by their immediate communities. A high school student in Romania, India, or Vietnam with a computer connected to the Internet grows up in a social system that consists of much more than the immediate family, community, or even nation. His or her identity is shaped by the patterns and trends shared by millions of peers from around the world, present in the home and always just one mouse click away. Indeed, daily experience of young people around the world is shaped as much if not more by mass communication media than by the stable forces that defined the experience of previous generations for hundreds of years (Koschei, 2013). To a young person who grows up connected to the Internet, the idea of functioning in a global world is not a matter of an unknown future, like for those growing up at the dawn of the computer era. It is a matter of the here and now.

Meanwhile, research on student learning leaves little doubt that to assist students' development in the undergraduate years, instructors have to be aware of the developmental stage at which students come to college (Bowman & Brandenburger, 2012). To help students along in their development of global and intercultural competencies, faculty and staff have no other choice but to begin at the stage at which they enter our institutions – a stage that cannot be taken for granted due to the rapid pace of change in contemporary social environments.

New Challenges for Faculty and Student Development Professionals

As recently as 2006, Deardorff and Hunter made a case for the importance of "having an open mind while actively seeking to understand cultural norms and expectations of others, leveraging this gained knowledge to interact, communicate, and work effectively outside one's environment" (p. 74). The arrival of "Globalization 3.0" has all but eliminated the necessity for educators to persuade students or the public that intercultural competence and global citizenship matter – but it has also complicated our task in at least four major ways.

Identity crises. The first major development with considerable implications for undergraduate curriculum and co-curricular programming is the direction of global currents reshaping the role of the individual in society. According to Giddens (1999), we are witnessing "a global revolution going on in how we think of ourselves and how we form ties and connections with others" (p. 17). On the micro-scale of the family and community, technology and globalization are magnifying group differences between generations. Yet on the macro-scale of national culture, globalization has a homogenizing effect, diminishing differences between cultures with regard to how we position the individual within their primary community (Hofstede & Hofstede, 2005).

Culture, described by Spitzberg (2003) as "the sets of behaviors, beliefs, values and linguistic patterns that are relatively enduring over time and generation within a group" (p. 96), is subject to new pressures as societies grow wealthier and individuals gain unprecedented mobility.

In their landmark study of cultural differences across 70 nations, Hofstede and Hofstede (2005) note that the growing wealth resulting from globalization is correlated with a growth in individualism – the primacy of individual interests over collective welfare. Most societies throughout history, and even in this day, have embraced the values associated with collectivism, prioritizing relationships over results, and group values over individual gain (Bordas, 2012). Individualistic cultures are a novel phenomenon in human history. In the early days of human evolution, it was cooperation, reciprocity, and mutual loyalty that constituted the competitive edge over other species, allowing humans to survive and thrive (Baldwin, 2009). Individualism implies greater independence, mobility, and the ability to break with the past to imagine a different future – but these come at the cost of a progressive breakdown of traditional communities, and an attendant sense of rootlessness.

The tension between the values of people-focused collectivism and goal-oriented individualism is especially acute in nations with a recent history of economic and social transformation. Young people grow up in a world where the "behaviors, beliefs, values, and linguistic patterns" (Spitzberg, 2003, p. 96) passed down by their ancestors do not seem adequate for the problems of modern life. In many cases, even the language spoken at home is no longer sufficient to achieve success in life, as English gains ground as the dominant language of business, politics, and science (Phillipson, 2009). As a result, many young people around the world find themselves stretched between the collective values of their past and the independence promised by the winds of the future; between the language of their forebears and the language of their bosses; between the beliefs that sustained their communities for hundreds if not thousands of years, and the worldviews of cultures they admire for their economic success. At times, the tension felt by young people is so intense that it leads them to try extreme means of easing it, either by completely rejecting their native culture, or as completely rejecting the forces of modernity (Giddens, 1999).

In light of these tensions, it is significant to note that researchers believe the first step in intercultural competence is knowing oneself and one's own culture (Bennett, 2009; Ting-Toomey, 1999). Effectiveness in interacting with others requires consciousness of the factors that shaped one's own identity and how they are different from those that shaped others (King & Baxter-Magolda, 2005). Reflecting on the cultural conventions we usually take for granted is the first step towards improving the skills required for intercultural communication (Eisenchlas & Trevaskes, 2007). Yet in the present age, knowledge of oneself becomes less attainable. In pursuit of global opportunities, many people become severed from their roots, embracing "behaviors, beliefs, values and linguistic patterns" unknown to their forebears (Spitzberg, 2003, p. 96). Therefore, faculty and staff in various parts of the world are working with a generation that is at once more knowledgeable about the world than before, and often dramatically less aware or more ambivalent with regard to their own roots and identities – the starting point of all intercultural dialogue (Bennett, 2009; Ting-Toomey, 1999).

Increased knowledge, sustained ethnocentrism. In the 21st century, students come to college with more exposure to, and experience with, difference than at perhaps any other point in history. Thanks to advances in technology, mass communication, and ease of travel, it is increasingly more likely that students arrive on campus with at least some experience with people from other cultures. For a growing number of students, college is no longer the first point of exposure to difference. Such exposure, whether through direct contact or interactions on social media, increases the likelihood that students have knowledge of the differences in behaviors and communication patterns across cultures.

At the same time, recent studies examining the developmental levels of undergraduate students indicate that very few display awareness of their own culture, or the impact it has on how they view the world. In all empirical investigations available to date, over 60% of undergraduate respondents display the characteristics of an ethnocentric stage of development (Durocher, 2007; Medina-Lopez-Portillo, 2004; Pedersen, 2010; Rexeisen, Anderson, Lawton & Hubbard, 2008; Shaw, Lee & Williams, 2014). Increased knowledge of diverse others does not immediately imply the ability to put oneself in their shoes, or to step outside of one's own inherited norms.

Both intercultural theory and the findings of recent studies illuminate an opportunity and a challenge for faculty and staff. Students come to college with a wealth of experience stemming from unprecedented intercultural exposure. At the same time, they often remain unaware of how their own culture shapes the way they perceive and interact with the world.

Research makes it clear that the development of intercultural competence requires more than mere contact with people from other cultures or knowledge about them. In fact, mere contact unaccompanied by a deeper reflective process can actually deepen and perpetuate stereotype. Pettigrew and Tropp (2008) summarize their review of the last 50 years of scholarship in intergroup contact theory with the conclusion that the cognitive mediator (knowledge) reduces prejudice to some degree, but affective mediators (empathy and perspective taking) are much more important for that aim.

What these findings may imply in practical terms is a need for increased focus on personal reflection, drawing on the experience students may already possess when they begin college, providing opportunities for sustained contact with others, and moderating the reflexive process around these experiences. Development of competencies key to global citizenship may be fostered most effectively through the use of techniques such as learning groups, reflective journals, critical case studies, and other tools that require movement towards ethnorelative thinking.

New forms of minimization, simplification and avoidance. Major models of intercultural development also suggest that at the initial stages, ethnocentrism is largely unconscious, and difference is likely to be minimized, simplified, or avoided so as not to provoke a clash with inherited values (Bennett, 1986; King & Baxter-Magolda, 2005). Minimization, simplification, and avoidance serve as defense mechanisms for protecting one's worldview from possible disruption.

In the age of globalization and intense intercultural contact, diversity is both feared and extolled as the cornerstone of a modern democracy. Throughout history, cross-cultural contact was often accompanied by conflict, pointing to the fact that skill in relating to people from other cultures is by no means natural (Bennett, 1993). Today, it can seem at the surface level that difference is so ubiquitous it can no longer be perceived as the same kind of threat it had been to homogenous people groups in history. On college campuses in particular, student bodies have grown more diverse and appreciation towards diversity is far greater than in the past. The opportunity to interact with diverse others is seen as a necessity for learning to interact, communicate, and work effectively with those from outside one's own culture. These competencies are now commonly recognized as essential outcomes of higher education in the 21st century (Lee, Poch, Shaw & Williams, 2012). While ubiquitous, difference still evokes anxiety, triggering the behavioral response of avoidance and the cognitive response of bias (Stephan & Stephan, 1985; Gudykunst, 2005). In the global era, these take on new but strikingly familiar forms.

There is indication in the research literature that students' defense mechanisms against that which is different continue to evolve and robust tensions continue to rumble under the surface even in countries where diversity is strongly valued at the declarative level. For instance, in the United States, Shaw, Lee and Williams (2014) examined the reflective writing of 414 diverse freshmen, and found no signs of open defensiveness towards difference – on the contrary, whenever a value judgment is expressed with regard to difference, it is positive. At the declarative level, difference was not seen as threatening, but rather as interesting, fun, and beneficial. At the same time, respondents employed a host of rhetorical strategies to generalize, simplify, and minimize the difference they declare to value – even if it is through the act of idealizing it. Difference is good, but only as a general idea and not in specific detail. Specific instances of different thinking or behavior are "challenges" or "obstacles" to be "conquered" and "overcome" (Shaw et al., 2014). These findings will likely resonate with faculty members and student development professionals who interact on a daily basis with students who declare to value difference, but minimize or simplify it in practice so as to protect inherited yet unexamined ways of seeing the world. The role of faculty and staff today is often concerned less with overcoming resistance and more with assisting students in rooting their appreciation of difference in deeper experience and reflection.

This point is especially relevant in the United States, where as Bell and Hartmann (2007) observe, diversity has become "the new cornerstone of American democratic idealism" (p. 895). Surrounded by difference and by rhetoric that extols its benefits, young people learn early to perform the prevailing discourse around diversity without necessarily struggling with its complexity in direct and personal encounters with others. Faculty who see global citizenship as an indispensable outcome of college education have a major role to play in moderating student experiences on increasingly diverse campuses in such a way as to deepen the roots of students' positive attitudes in reflective experience.

Inequality, upward mobility, and clashing values. The effects of globalization are not spread equally; higher education is not an exception. Globalization creates a world of winners and losers, evidenced most strikingly in growing income disparities between the rich and poor (Wosińska, 2010). In the 1960s, citizens of the developed world were 30 times wealthier than the bottom 20% of the world's population; by

1996 they were 61 times wealthier, and just two years later, the scale of difference rose to 82. By the turn of the century, the wealth of the three richest men on earth equaled the gross national product of 48 of the poorest countries (Wosińska, 2010). In the United States, globalization has led to a rise in incomes – yet it is there that income inequality has grown especially significantly. In 1995, the wealth of the 1% wealthiest Americans exceeded that of the bottom 95% (Wosińska, 2012). Between 1979 and 2007, the top 1% of households in the United States increased their earnings by ca. 275%, while the middle 60% gained less than 40% (Congressional Budget Office, 2011).

In the context of growing inequality, higher education continues to be seen as the great equalizer and a mediator of opportunity. Since the 1960s, higher education access was expanded to previously excluded groups, such as minorities, lower-status groups – and, notably, women (Bradley & Ramirez, 1996). The expansion of enrollments has led to tensions between the values of the privileged classes that had traditionally dominated universities and those of the classes interested in education primarily for pragmatic ends (Schimank, 2009; Krucken, 2003). The clash continues to be felt in debates over the role of the university as a temple of learning on the one hand, and an engine of economic development on the other.

From an economic perspective, the pursuit of higher education in the industrialized world is one of the most effective means of upward mobility. In 2008, a person with higher education in the developed world earned 58% more than one with a secondary degree (OECD, 2012; cited in Stromquist et al., 2014). With the spread of globalization and the "knowledge economy" of the "third wave," enrollments have skyrocketed. In 1900, there were ca. 500,000 tertiary students in the world, representing 1% of the global cohort. By 2000, the number had grown to over 100 million people, or about 20% of the global cohort (UNESCO, 2004; cited in Shofer and Meyer, 2005).

At the classroom level, global changes in enrollment pools and in the roles ascribed to higher education are evident in the diversity of students and their motivations for coming to college. In the uncertain world of rapid and unpredictable change, the university remains a stable presence offering both continuity with the past and the promise of future opportunities.

Implications for Reflective Practitioners

According to Anthony Giddens (1999), "globalisation is not incidental to our lives today. It is a shift in our very life circumstances" (p. 6). For faculty and student development staff, it shifts the entire framework in which we help young people along their educational paths, especially with regard to the development of citizenship and intercultural competence.

There may not be a way around the "mini-generation gaps" between higher education practitioners and successive cohorts of students, or around the democratization of knowledge in college classrooms. Nevertheless, faculty and student development staff have a crucial role to play in facilitating student development in the uncomfortable terrain of affective process and the formation of identity. As Lee et al. (2012) have shown, the areas of knowledge targeted by individual instructors are just the tip of the iceberg, while below it lie the affective and behavioral foundations of students' development. These foundational areas can and should be addressed on college campuses – not as much through content, but by the structure and facilitation of learning interactions.

The democratization of knowledge and the diversification of college campuses herald the dusk of a traditional, content-focused pedagogy that elevates mere knowledge acquisition as the main objective of undergraduate study (Bennett & Salonen, 2007; Krutky, 2008). A teacher-centered pedagogy emphasizing the cognitive domain alone is insufficient for the kind of transformative learning needed for students to become anchored in a rapidly changing world, and to master the ability to apply knowledge to changing contexts and diverse situations.

Historically, content-focused approaches have been favored as those allowing for the transmission of more material, but in the age of open source publishing and open courses from the world's best learning institutions, with the world's knowledge at one's fingertips, the argument in favor of classroom content no longer holds. There is an increasing amount of evidence and a growing recognition that the value added of higher education is a deeper transformation of "meaning schemes," or what Mezirow (1991) describes as "the process of becoming critically aware of how and why our assumptions have come to constrain the way we perceive, understand, and feel about our world" (p. 167). A crucial role of today's faculty members and student development professionals is "changing these structures of habitual expectation to make possible a more inclusive, discriminating, and integrating perspective; and, finally, making choices or otherwise acting upon these new understandings" (Mezirow, 1991, p. 167). Such outcomes are rarely developed in a large classroom with a distant professor – they require instructional frameworks that foster transformative relationships, both between the instructor and the student, and between students themselves.

The growing recognition of relational processes influencing cognitive outcomes has led to a rising interest in active learning strategies and collaborative learning in higher education (e.g. Summers, Beretvas, Svinicki & Gorin, 2005). A collaborative learning framework redefines the relationship between the teacher and the student, establishing a situation in which knowledge is pursued and created in community of independent and mutually accountable learners. As Johnson, Johnson and Smith (1998) warn, collaborative work understood as mere group projects is not a panaceum – poorly designed group learning can bring in worse results than competitive and individualistic approaches. According to Boekaerts & Minnaert (2006), group learning brings great benefits when the value of the collaborative task is well-established in the context of the classroom, the instructor allows student autonomy and limits intrusion, and classroom agendas are adjusted to students' goals and needs, and students are encouraged to reflect upon the learning process. For these conditions to be met, more is required than the mere goodwill and enthusiasm of faculty and student development professionals. The extent to which redesigning modes of teaching and student development is a real possibility depends to a large extent on the openness of senior administrators towards continuously altering the modes of funding and curriculum design in ways that take into account both the realities of a flat world and the needs of successive generations of students.

One particular type of collaborative practice recognized as effective at the elementary and secondary levels but only rarely tried in higher education is peer tutoring (Falchikov & Blythman, 2001). In the context of the democratization of knowledge and a growing diversity of learners, research has found that a teaching framework in which more advanced students assist those at lower levels brings significant benefits to both groups. While those receiving the tutoring benefit from relating to peers with recent experiences of successful learning, peer tutors improve their own understanding of the key concepts by learning how to explain them to a less advanced audience (Bruffee, 1999; Falchikov & Blythman, 2001; Fougner, 2012).

In the global age, reflective practitioners can aid students in the growth and adaptation of their identities by teaching them the complex dance between continuity and change. Their efforts are not a one-way street; if planned mindfully, collaborative communities can incorporate the knowledge and intrinsic motivation brought by all participants in the learning process. It is the internal change occurring in a collaborative learning community that paves the way for the external symptoms of effective and appropriate communication across difference – the kind of communication needed not only for successful careers, but for a peaceful globe.

REFERENCES

Archibugi, D., & Iammarino, S. (2002). The globalization of technological innovation: Definition and evidence. *Review of International Political Economy, 9*(1), 98–122. doi:10.1080/09692290110101126

Baldwin, C. (2009). *Calling the circle: The first and future culture.* New York, NY: Random House.

Bell, J., & Hartmann, D. (2007). Diversity in everyday discourse: The cultural ambiguities and consequences of "happy talk." *American Sociological Review, 72,* 895–914.

Bennett, J. (2009). Cultivating intercultural competence: A process perspective. In D. K. Deardorff (Ed.), *The Sage handbook of intercultural competence* (pp. 121–140). London, UK: Sage.

Bennett, M. J. (1986). A developmental approach to training for intercultural sensitivity. *International Journal of Intercultural Relations, 10*(2), 179–196. doi:10.1016/0147-1767(86)90005-2

Bennett, M. J. (1993). Towards ethnorelativism: A developmental model of intercultural sensitivity. *Education for the Intercultural Experience, 2,* 21–71.

Boekaerts, M., & Minnaert, A. (2006). Affective and motivational outcomes of working in collaborative groups. *Educational Psychology, 26*(2), 187–208.

Bordas, J. (2012). *Salsa, soul, and spirit: Leadership for a multicultural age.* San Francisco, CA: Berrett-Koehler Publishers.

Bowman, N. A., & Brandenberger, J. W. (2012). Experiencing the unexpected: Toward a model of college diversity experiences and attitude change. *The Review of Higher Education, 35*(2), 179–205.

Bradley, K., & Ramirez, F. O. (1996). World polity and gender parity: Women's share of higher education, 1965–1985. *Research in Sociology of Education and Socialization, 11*(1), 63–91.

Bruffee, K. (1999). *Collaborative learning: Higher education, interdependence and the authority of knowledge*. New York, NY: The John Hopkins University Press

Congressional Budget Office. (2011). *Budgetary estimates for the single-family mortgage guarantee program of the federal housing administration*. Retrieved November 5, 2014, from http://www.cbo.gov/publication/45740

Cupach, W., & Imahori, T. T. (1993). Identity management theory: Communication competence in intercultural episodes and relationships. In R. L. Wiseman & J. Koester (Eds.), *Intercultural communication competence* (Vol. 16). Newbury Park, CA: Sage Publications, Inc.

Deardorff, D. K., & Hunter, W. (2006). Educating global-ready graduates. *International Educator, 15*(3), 72–83.

Durocher, D. O. (2007). Teaching sensitivity to cultural difference in the first-year foreign language classroom. *Foreign Language Annals, 40*(1), 143–160. doi: 10.1111/j.1944-9720.2007.tb02858.x

Eisenchlas, S., & Trevaskes, S. (2007). Developing intercultural communication skills through intergroup interaction. *Intercultural Education, 18*(5), 413–425.

Falchikov, N., & Blythman, M. (2001). *Learning together: Peer tutoring in higher education*. London, England: Psychology Press.

Friedman, T. L. (2005a). *The world is flat: A brief history of the twenty-first century*. New York, NY: Farrar, Straus and Giroux.

Friedman, T. L. (2005b). It's a flat world, after all. *The New York Times, 3*, 33–37.

Giddens, A. (1999). *Runaway world: Reith lectures*. London, England: British Broadcasting Company.

Gudykunst, W. B. (2005). An anxiety/uncertainty management (AUM) theory of effective communication: Making the mesh of the net finer. In W. B. Gudykunst (Ed.), *Theorizing about intercultural communication* (pp. 281–349). Thousand Oaks, CA: Sage.

Gudykunst, W. B., & Nishida, T. (2001). Anxiety, uncertainty, and perceived effectiveness of communication across relationships and cultures. *International Journal of Intercultural Relations, 25*(1), 55–71.

Hofstede, G., & Hofstede, G. J. (2005). *Cultures and organizations: Software for the mind*. New York, NY: McGraw Hill Professional.

Johnson, D. W., Johnson R. T, & Smith, K. A. (1998). Cooperative learning returns to college: What evidence is there that it works? *Change, 30*(4), 27–35. Retrieved from http://www.wsac.wa.gov/sites/default/files/2014.ptw.%2849%29.pdf

King, P. M., & Baxter Magolda, M. (2005). A developmental model of intercultural maturity. *Journal of College Student Development, 46*(6), 571–592.

Koschei, J. (2013). The growing technological generation gap. *The Industry*. Retrieved from http://theindustry.cc/2013/02/12/the-growing-technological-generation-gap/

Krücken, G. (2003). Learning the 'new, new thing': On the role of path dependency in university structures. *Higher Education, 46*(3), 315–339. doi:10.1023/A:1025344413682

Lee, A., Poch, R., Shaw, M., & Williams, R. (2012). Engaging diversity in undergraduate classrooms: A pedagogy for developing intercultural competence. *ASHE Higher Education Report, 38*(2).

McKenzie, R. M. (2010). *The social psychology of english as a global language: Attitudes, awareness and identity in the japanese context*. Springer Science & Business Media.

Medina-Lopez-Portillo, A. (2004). Intercultural learning assessment: The link between program duration and the development of intercultural sensitivity. *Frontiers: The Interdisciplinary Journal of Study Abroad, 10*, 179–199.

Mezirow, J. (1991). *Transformative dimensions of adult learning*. New York, NY: John Wiley & Sons.

Pedersen, P. J. (2010). Assessing intercultural effectiveness outcomes in a year-long study abroad program. *International Journal of Intercultural Relations, 34*(1), 70–80. doi:10.1016/j.ijintrel.2009.09.003

Pettigrew, T. F., & Tropp, L. R. (2008). How does intergroup contact reduce prejudice? Meta-analytic tests of three mediators. *European Journal of Social Psychology, 38*(6), 922–934.

Phillipson, R. (2009). *Linguistic imperialism continued*. New York, NY: Routledge.

Rexeisen, R., Anderson, P., Lawton, L., & Hubbard, A. (2008). Study abroad and intercultural development: A longitudinal study. *Frontiers, XVII*, 1–20.

Schimank, U. (2009). Humboldt in Bologna – falscher Mann am falschen Ort? In *Fachtagung Studienqualitat*. Hannover, Germany: HIS GmbH. Retrieved from http://www.fernuni-hagen.de/imperia/md/content/soziologie/sozii/humboldt_in_bologna_-_falscher_mann_am_falschen_ort_.pdf

Schofer, E., & Meyer, J. W. (2005). The worldwide expansion of higher education in the twentieth century. *American Sociological Review, 70*(6), 898–920.

Shaw, M., Lee, A., & Williams, R. (2014). Formative journeys of first-year college students: tensions and intersections with intercultural theory. *Higher Education Research & Development*, (ahead-of-print), 1–17.

Singh, P. (2004). Globalization and education. *Educational Theory, 54*(1), 103–115.

Spitzberg, B. H. (2003). Methods of skill assessment. In J. O. Greene & B. R. Burleson (Eds.), *Handbook of communication and social interaction skills* (pp. 93–134). Mahwah, NJ: Lawrence Erlbaum.

Stephan, W. G., & Stephan, C. W. (1985). Intergroup anxiety. *Journal of Social Issues, 41*(3), 157–175.

Stone, B. (2010, January 9). The children of cyberspace: Old fogies by their 20s. *The New York Times*. Retrieved from http://www.nytimes.com/2010/01/10/weekinreview/10stone.html

Stromquist, N. P., & Monkman, K. (2014). Defining globalization and assessing its implications for knowledge and education, revisited. In N. P. Stromquist & K. Monkman (Eds.), *Globalization and education: Integration and contestation across cultures* (pp. 1–38). Lanham, MD: R&L Education.

Summers, J. J., Gorin, J. S., Beretvas, S. N., & Svinicki, M. D. (2005). Evaluating collaborative learning and community. *The Journal of Experimental Education, 73*(3), 165–188.

Ting-Toomey, S. (1999). *Communicating across cultures*. New York, NY: Guilford Press.

Toffler, A. (1981). *Future shock: The third wave*. New York, NY: Bantam Book.

Tomlinson, J. (1991). *Cultural imperialism: A critical introduction*. Edinburgh: A&C Black.

United Nations. (2014). *UN global education first initiative – United Nations Secretary General's global initiative on education*. Retrieved September 10, 2014 from http://www.globaleducationfirst.org/about.html

Wosińska, W. (2010). *Oblicza globalizacji (The faces of globalization)*. Sopot: Smak Slowa.

Marta A. Shaw
Institute of Public Affairs
Jagiellonian University, Poland

KRISTA M. SORIA

4. INSTITUTIONAL AND INSTRUCTIONAL TECHNIQUES TO PROMOTE UNDERGRADUATES' INTERCULTURAL DEVELOPMENT

Evidence from a Multi-Institutional Student Survey

In response to increasingly globalized environments, many higher education institutions are actively seeking to internationalize their curricular and co-curricular efforts to foster students' development of intercultural competencies—competencies necessary to thrive in a multicultural and global workforce (Lee, Poch, Shaw, & Williams, 2012; Soria, Snyder, & Reinhard, in press; Soria & Troisi, 2014). In order to achieve those aims, institutions have traditionally focused their efforts on promoting students' engagement in study abroad. Indeed, the extant literature has demonstrated the many powerful effects of study abroad on students' development of intercultural competencies (Norris & Gillespie, 2009; Stebleton, Soria, & Cheney, 2013; Twombly, Salisbury, Tumanut, & Klute, 2012); however, given the persistent disparities in study abroad rates among low-income students and students of color (Brux & Fry, 2010; Otero, 2008; Salisbury, Paulsen, & Pascarella, 2011), emergent scholarship has shifted toward examining the benefits of internationalization at home efforts, which can provide opportunities for students to gain intercultural skills on campus (Nilsson, 2000; Osfield, 2008; Otten, 2000; Paige, 2003; Soria & Troisi, 2014). These on-campus internationalization efforts warrant future study because they can be integrated into existing curricular and co-curricular structures, may be less expensive for students to pursue than study abroad, offer opportunities for faculty and practitioners to collaborate in internationalization efforts, and can be utilized by a wide variety of higher education practitioners in several different outlets—all of which potentially widens access to a greater number of diverse learners.

Although internationalization at home practices hold the potential to positively support students' development of intercultural knowledge and skills, the effectiveness of these practices remains relatively unexplored in multi-institutional contexts in the United States. The purpose of this chapter is therefore to examine whether on-campus instructional and institutional curricular practices are associated with undergraduate students' self-reported development of intercultural skills. By discovering which practices are affiliated with students' development of intercultural skills, higher education practitioners in many different capacities—faculty, advisors, supervisors, or mentors—can be better positioned to include these practices in their daily work

R. D. Williams & A. Lee (Eds.), Internationalizing Higher Education, 47–59.
© *2015 Sense Publishers. All rights reserved.*

or direct students to engage in opportunities to stimulate their development. The multi-institutional perspective of this study demonstrates the utility of large-scale institutional data to inform not only future research, but also daily practice. Furthermore, given the focus of this chapter is to examine instructional and institutional practices beyond the traditional measures of study abroad, the results of the analysis undertaken here can potentially inform institutional change efforts to internationalize campuses.

The *instructional* practices examined include encouraging interpersonal connections between international and domestic students (both in class and outside of class in social settings), embedding themes of diversity or global content in courses, asking students to attend international/globally-themed events on campus, and collaborating with undergraduates on internationally-themed research—these are all strategies that instructors can include in their classrooms. The *institutional* curricular practices examined include common book reading programs, living-learning programs, learning communities, service-learning, and first-year seminars. Although faculty are necessarily vital elements of those institutional strategies, these programs typically require institutional collaboration, organization, resources, and support to establish and are not often within the immediate purview of faculty to initiate on their own, which is why I have categorized those activities as *institutional* in nature. Below, I briefly describe the potential for these instructional and institutional activities to promote college students' intercultural competencies.

Instructional and Institutional Practices to Promote Intercultural Skills

There are several ways in which faculty and practitioners can engage students with the multicultural diversity already present on college and university campuses. Indeed, there is ample evidence regarding the many benefits to be garnered from students' interactions with diverse peers and their participation in initiatives focused on diversity (Gurin, 1999; Gurin, Dey, Hurtado, & Gurin, 2002; Gurin, Nagda, & Lopez, 2004; Hurtado, 2001; Nagda, Gurin, Sorensen, & Zuñiga, 2009; Pascarella & Terenzini, 2005). Several scholars have noted that structural diversity—the representation of diverse individuals on campus (Bowman, 2011)—does not directly impact student outcomes. Instead, structural diversity provides college students with more opportunities in which interactions with peers from diverse backgrounds can occur (Denson & Chang, 2009; Gurin, 1999; Gurin et al., 2002). Faculty can capitalize upon the structural diversity present in their classrooms to formally and informally connect students with their peers in collaborative assignments, group projects, or research opportunities.

The majority of students' interactions with diverse peers frequently occur in informal contexts outside the classroom, such as informal social interactions, intramurals, and co-curricular events (Bowman, 2011; Gurin et al., 2002). Students who experience positive and informal interactions with diverse peers have higher cultural and social awareness and perspective-taking skills (Hurtado, 2007). Extending these lines of research, Dugan and Komives (2010) discovered that peer *conversations* across a wide array of differences (e.g., lifestyles, political ideologies), not just *interactions* with peers, provided a platform for clarification of personal values and social perspective-taking. Furthermore, Soria and Troisi (2014) discovered that domestic college students who had developed a friendship with an international student were significantly more likely to develop intercultural competencies over their peers who did not develop those friendships. Faculty and practitioners who work to connect their students with others from diverse backgrounds can promote the development of friendships that persist outside of the classroom and beyond one semester—and thereby positively influence students' acquisition of intercultural skills.

In collaboration with other campus officials, faculty are influential players in the development and execution of institutional practices that can promote the development of college students' intercultural skills. Faculty also play a vital role in providing structured opportunities for students to participate in formal diversity experiences or in initiatives spanning curricular programs (Bowman, 2011; Denson, 2009; Hurtado, 2007). Formal diversity experiences can include providing students with opportunities to enroll in classes on diversity-related subjects (e.g., women's studies, ethnic studies, international studies), participate in cultural awareness workshops or campus events, or attend globally-themed programs developed by academic departments. Students who enroll in globally-themed courses or attend lectures, symposia, workshops, or conferences on international/global topics are more likely to develop intercultural competencies compared with their peers who do not engage in these formal curricular experiences (Soria & Troisi, 2014). Faculty can encourage their students to participate in those lectures, conferences, or workshops by promoting these events in classes, asking students to attend these events to meet the requirements of class assignments, serving as advisors to students interested in hosting their own workshops, or helping students to locate and secure funding to attend.

Additional institutional practices also present venues in which students can develop intercultural skills; for example, many institutions engage students in common book reading programs, which often feature texts along multicultural themes and cultural events associated with the common book, including films, performances, panel discussions, or exhibits (Ferguson, 2006). Soria (in press) found that students who participate in common book reading programs were significantly more likely to develop multicultural appreciation and competence compared to their peers. Similarly, King and Baxter Magolda (2005) described the potential for living/learning programs to engage students at varying levels of intercultural maturity, emphasizing the importance of reflection, validation, and experiential experiences in facilitating intercultural maturity within cognitive, intrapersonal, and interpersonal domains. Service-learning has also been positively associated with diminished ethnocentrism among college students and is hypothesized to be effective in providing students with meaningful opportunities for students to interact with others from diverse cultures (Borden, 2007).

Some of the activities cited above—living-learning programs, service-learning, and common book reading programs—are known in the literature as high-impact educational practices (Kuh, 2008). Those practices, in addition to participation in undergraduate research with faculty, learning communities, and courses based upon themes of diversity, are known to be powerful opportunities to promote students' personal and social development (Kuh, 2008); however, the effect of some of those practices in promoting students' development of intercultural skills is presently unknown. Specific institutional conditions may also make these practices more effective in helping students to acquire intercultural skills; for example, Salisbury and Goodman (2009) stressed that, when students participate in high-impact practices that provide them with substantive interactions with individuals different from themselves, engage in activities to integrate their knowledge and skills in disparate contexts, and enroll in classes featuring clear and organized instruction across disciplines, they are better positioned to develop intercultural competencies.

In the sections that follow, I explore the effectiveness of instructional and institutional practices to develop college students' intercultural competencies, which I define as inclusive of the ability to appreciate cultural diversity, experience comfort working with people from other cultures, develop self-awareness, and understand different perspectives—a definition based upon prior scholarship in this area (Deardorff, 2009; Soria & Troisi, 2014; Stebleton, Soria, & Cheney, 2013), with the addition of self-awareness, which has been identified as important in developing cross-cultural relationships (Wedding, 2013). I utilized a multi-institutional student survey—the Student Experience in the Research University (SERU) survey—to investigate the association between students' participation in instructional and institutional practices and their self-reported development of intercultural skills in the consideration of additional demographic and environmental factors.

METHODOLGY

The SERU survey is based at the Center for Studies of Higher Education at the University of California-Berkeley. In the SERU survey, students answer a set of core questions related to their academic engagement, research experiences, satisfaction, and demographic information. Students are also randomly assigned one of several modules containing items focused specifically on a research theme, including one module assessing their academic and global experiences. The survey was administered in spring 2013 to all undergraduate students enrolled in 14 large, public universities in the United States classified by the Carnegie Foundation as having very high research activity. The institutional response rates for the SERU survey ranged from 15% to 62% ($n = 95,000+$). The survey items used in this analysis were located in a module that was randomly assigned to between 10% and 30% of students depending upon institutional preferences ($n = 13,483$). Within the sample used in the present analysis, 60.17% of students were female ($n = 8,113$), and 39.83% male ($n = 5,370$),. 20% American Indian or Alaskan Native ($n = 27$), 4.1%

African American ($n = 546$), 7.91% Hispanic ($n = 1,067$), 11.01% Asian ($n = 1,484$), 5.86% multiracial ($n = 790$), 3.67% international ($n = 495$), and 64.76% White ($n = 8,743$). Additionally, 2.45% of students declined to state their race/ethnicity ($n = 331$).

DATA ANALYSIS AND MEASURES

I utilized a hierarchical linear regression analysis to investigate the relationship between students' participation in institutional and instructional practices and their self-reported development of intercultural skills. I entered the data into three blocks: block one included demographic variables (sex, race, and social class, which was self-reported by students) and students' self-reported intercultural competencies when they started college; block two included students' cumulative grade point average, academic level, academic major, level of academic engagement, interest in pursuing academic majors along international themes and in studying abroad, and frequency of following international and global news events; block three included students' participation in 13 different instructional and institutional practices.

In the first block, I utilized students' rating of their intercultural skills when they started college at their institutions. Rather than using change or growth scores in regression models, Pascarella, Wolniak, and Pierson (2003) suggested the inclusion of a statistical control for the pretest measures. When a statistical control for the pretest measure is included in the analysis, the impact of the independent variables on the posttest scores is functionally the same as the impact of the same independent variables on the growth or gains made from the pretest to the posttest; consequently, the dependent measure reflects students' development of intercultural skills between the time they enrolled at their institutions and their current assessment of skills.

Before I ran the regression analysis, I first developed four factors from survey items: academic engagement (four items), frequency of following international/global news and events (six items), interest in pursuing academic majors along international themes (two items), and intercultural skills (six items). Academic engagement included items asking students to rate the frequency with which they had contributed to class discussions, asked insightful questions in class, integrated course concepts, and interacted with faculty during lectures. Students rated the frequency with which they followed international and global news and events including global politics, international conflicts or business, global climate, and global health issues. Students also indicated whether they selected their academic majors because the majors completed their desire to study abroad and provided international opportunities. Finally, students rated their current abilities in appreciating and understanding race, ethnic, cultural, and global diversity, comfort in—and ability to—work with people from other cultures, current self-awareness and self-understanding, and ability to understand international perspectives.

The 13 different areas of instructional and institutional participation were measured in two primary ways. First, students rated the frequency with which they had

51

interacted with international students both in class (e.g., through class discussions) and in social settings, developed a friendship with an international student, attended lectures/workshops/conferences on international/global topics, worked with faculty on an international/globally-themed project, attended an international/globally-themed performance, or presented a paper at a conference along an international/global theme. Those items were scaled 1 = never to 6 = very often. Students also indicated whether they had ever—or were currently—participating in a first-year seminar, living-learning program, learning community (two or more courses linked across a common theme), common book reading program, service-learning or community-based learning, or courses involving themes relating to diversity or global learning. Those items were measured 0 = never or 1 = had previously or were currently participating.

RESULTS

The results of the hierarchical linear regression suggest the internationalization at home variables entered into the third block explained a significant amount of variance in students' self-reported development of intercultural skills after accounting for the variance explained by the variables entered in the first and second blocks ($R = .717$, $R^2 = .514$, $F(43, 13,439) = 330.730$, $p < .001$; R^2 *Change* = .033). These results suggest that the instructional and institutional practices chosen in this analysis are important in predicting students' development of intercultural skills above and beyond other factors, lending weight to the potential for these practices to spur students' appreciation of different cultures, comfort working with others from different cultures, self-awareness, and the ability to understand different perspectives.

Ten of the instructional and institutional practice areas were significantly and positively associated with students' self-reported development of intercultural skills controlling for students' demographic variables, intercultural skills when they started college, academic majors, interest in international and global activities, academic engagement, academic level, and grade point average. The results suggest college students who more frequently interacted with international students in classes, interacted with international students in social situations, or developed a friendship with international students reported significantly higher development in intercultural skills compared to their peers ($\beta = .022$, $p < .01$, $\beta = .074$, $p < .001$, and $\beta = .063$, $p < .001$, respectively). An examination of those standardized coefficients suggests that, of the three ways in which students interact with international students, the social interactions are more important predictors of students' intercultural skills development.

Additionally, the results suggest a significant and positive relationship between the frequency with which students attended lectures, symposia, or workshops along international or global themes ($\beta = .033$, $p < .001$) or attended a performance along an international/global theme ($\beta = .039$, $p < .001$) and students' development of intercultural skills. Students who participated in a first-year seminar ($\beta = .015$, $p < .05$), a common book reading program ($\beta = .021$, $p < .001$), a service-learning or community-learning program ($\beta = .040$, $p < .001$), or in courses following global/international themes ($\beta = .060$, $p < .001$) were significantly more likely than their peers to report higher development of intercultural skills. One area of participation was negatively associated with students' self-reported development of intercultural skills: students who presented a paper at a conference on international/global themes ($\beta = -.057$, $p < .001$) reported significantly lower development of intercultural skills compared to their peers.

While the focus of this chapter is on the relationships between students' participation in instructional/institutional practices and students' development of intercultural skills, I believe it is also important to highlight additional results of the regression analysis that may be important for faculty and other campus staff to consider when planning efforts to promote students' intercultural skills. For example, males and transfer students reported significantly lower development of intercultural skills compared to females and non-transfer students; however, Hispanic and multiracial students reported significantly higher development of intercultural skills compared to females. As students progressed in their education by continuously earning credits, they were also more likely to report developing intercultural skills. Students' academic engagement, frequency in following international/global news and events, and interest in pursuing international opportunities were also positively associated with their development of intercultural skills. Finally, students enrolled in STEM degrees reported significantly lower development of multicultural skills compared to their peers while students enrolled in social science degrees reported significantly higher development of intercultural skills compared to their peers. The implications of these findings will be discussed below.

DISCUSSION AND IMPLICATIONS

The results of this analysis suggest there are several instructional and institutional practices that faculty can undertake to help students develop comfort working with individuals from other cultures, an appreciation of cultural diversity, and the ability to understand different perspectives. First, students who interacted with international students in social situations or who developed friendships with international students were significantly more likely to report development in their intercultural skills. The particular importance of social interactions with international students in elevating intercultural skill development resonates with prior scholarship indicating college students with international friendships are more open-minded and experience less apprehension in intercultural communication (Williams & Johnson, 2011). Subsequently, faculty are encouraged to promote increased opportunities for their students to engage with the intercultural diversity already found on college campuses by thoughtfully and meaningfully connecting domestic and international students in social contexts (Williams & Johnson, 2011). Domestic students are not the only ones to gain from these social interactions: international students with social networks in their host country are less likely to experience acculturative stress, more likely to experience a successful adjustment to their host country, and have higher grades and retention (Hendrickson, Rosen, & Aune, 2011; Ingman, 2003; Perucci & Hu, 1995; Westwood & Barker, 1990; Yeh & Inose, 2003).

Additionally, the results of the analysis suggest students who attend international and cultural performances, enrolled in diversity-themed academic courses, or attended workshops/conferences on international and global themes are more likely to report development in intercultural skills compared to their peers. These findings are also supported by prior research which suggests diversity courses are beneficial for a variety of student outcomes including attributional complexity (Hurtado, 2004), intellectual engagement (Gurin et al., 2002), and cognitive skills (Bowman, 2009), although the effects accrue when students take multiple courses (Bowman, 2010). The expressive arts—including international and global performances—can introduce college students to visible elements of cultural differences and serve as a way for students to develop awareness of other cultural differences that are not as visible, including values, norms, and patterns of relationships (Neuner, 2012). Faculty can encourage their students to take advantage of these workshop, performance, and conference opportunities—both on-campus or off-campus in local communities—by encouraging students to attend for course credit, developing assignments encouraging students to reflect upon these cultural experiences (King & Baxter Magolda, 2005; Kumagai & Lypson, 2009; Lee et al., 2012), and engaging students in critical classroom dialogues about culture, learning, and development (Quaye & Harper, 2009). Interestingly, students who presented a paper at an international/globally-themed conference reported significantly less intercultural skill development compared to their peers—a finding that may be reflective of students' awareness of their intercultural limitations amid their more expansive international/global experiences. In other words, when students learn about the complexity of global and international cultures, they may become more cognizant of how much more there is yet to be learned about different cultures across the world.

Faculty also play a vital role within many of the high-impact institutional practices in this text; for example, faculty are integral in teaching first-year seminars, integrating common books into their courses, facilitating students' involvement in service-learning endeavors, and in leading courses embedded with global and international themes. While not all instructors can teach first-year seminar courses, they can incorporate many common features of first-year seminars into any course; for example, if smaller class sizes cannot be achieved, faculty are encouraged to develop smaller discussion groups of students to encourage students' interactions with diverse peers in a collaborative and cooperative learning environment (Lee et al., 2012). Service-learning opportunities can be incorporated into most college courses and new evidence also suggests these opportunities are beneficial for students enrolling in distance education courses as well (Soria & Weiner, 2013). Finally, faculty in a number of disciplines can incorporate common book programs by assigning readings and encouraging students to attend common book events on campus to benefit students' appreciation of diversity and elevate their multicultural skills (Soria, in press). Reflection in all of those opportunities is crucial to helping students connect their new-found experiential knowledge to their attitudes, beliefs, and perspectives about other social groups (Boler, 1999; Lee et al., 2012)—and how those beliefs may have shifted as a result of their experiences.

Implications for Research and Praxis

Overall, the results of this study suggest the importance of internationalization at home activities in promoting college students' self-reported intercultural competencies above and beyond the intercultural competencies students perceived they had before they entered college, students' demographic characteristics, students' academic major, academic achievement and academic level, academic engagement, and interest in international and global pursuits. Ten of the thirteen internationalization at home practices emerged as significant predictors of students' intercultural skill development, suggesting internationalization at home instructional and institutional activities are promising practices for faculty and practitioners to consider implementing on their own campuses. Many of these practices can easily be incorporated at little or no expense to institutions; for example, the results of the analysis suggest students who interacted with international students in academic and social contexts are likely to benefit from enhanced intercultural skill development. As institutions consider policies and programmatic efforts to increase students' intercultural development, it is important to recognize that broad, sweeping changes—such as requiring all students to study abroad—may not be necessary given it may be strategically more feasible to capitalize upon existing intercultural diversity on campus for the benefit of students' intercultural skills development (Soria & Troisi, 2014).

The results of this study also point toward programmatic strategies that may be effective in promoting students' intercultural skills development—strategies that are, in some cases, already present on college campuses or could easily be added to existing curricular or co-curricular structures. For example, students who participated in international/global performances, workshops, or conferences, first-year seminars, service-learning, and common book reading programs were more likely to report development in intercultural skills than their peers who did not participate in these activities. These instructional and institutions practices hold a large degree of promise in promoting students' development of intercultural skills above and beyond other college experiences. I therefore encourage faculty and practitioners to consider incorporating some of these elements in their courses, expanding programmatic offerings to students across campus, and collaborating with other campus partners to develop similar opportunities for their students.

As a researcher, I am struck by the results of this study that suggest relatively commonplace programmatic activities (e.g., common book programs, first-year seminars, etc.) are positively associated with students' development. In other words, no grand, complicated measures need to be undertaken to foster students' development of intercultural skills; instead, institutions can easily leverage programs that currently exist on their campuses and encourage more students to take part in those activities. Furthermore, students can more easily participate in those internationalization activities without incurring the expenses of formal travel and study abroad. As a researcher, this study was revealing in that it suggests the importance of assessing the constellation of students' participation in a wide variety of institutional programs rather than assessing only the "usual suspects" that have traditionally been linked to students' intercultural outcomes (e.g., study abroad, travel abroad).

As a faculty who currently teaches several graduate and undergraduate courses across disciplines (humanities, education, and leadership) at three different types of institutions—a large public research university, a mid-size regional comprehensive university, and a small private liberal arts university—I am struck by the importance of fostering interpersonal dialogue and academic collaboration between international and domestic students in classes. These conversations may be already occurring between students in my classes; however, given the results of this study, I am increasingly motivated to offer more structured opportunities for students to engage in collaborative assignments or small/large group discussions that enhance their awareness of their peers' cultural backgrounds.

Furthermore, even though I teach in multiple disciplines, each university at which I teach has a common book reading program, a community engagement office, and several opportunities for students to participate in international/globally-themed presentations, workshops, and performances; therefore, as a faculty member, the results of this study inspire me to more actively collaborate with existing offices and integrate their best-practices and programs into my own curriculum. Additionally, as a supervisor of undergraduate and graduate researchers, I am more actively seeking to provide my students with opportunities to dive deeper into global and international topics and present their findings at regional and national conferences. I am also increasingly mindful of learning and understanding my students' strengths to help them increase their self-awareness and appreciation of others' differences as well (Soria, Roberts, & Reinhard, in press; Soria & Stubblefield, in press).

Overall, the results of this study support the critical need for faculty and practitioners to consider the importance of on-campus curricular and co-curricular strategies in promoting students' intercultural skills development. These efforts can operate in isolation—such as individual faculty building connections between international and domestic students in their courses; however, many of these programs also provide rich opportunities for faculty and practitioners to collaborate together for the benefit of all students. I also recommend future collaborations between practitioners and researchers to continually investigate the potential of internationalization efforts on campuses to promote students' development of critically important intercultural skills.

REFERENCES

Boler, M. (1999). *Feeling power: Emotions and education.* New York, NY: Routledge.

Borden, A. W. (2007). The impact of service-learning on ethnocentrism in an intercultural communication course. *Journal of Experiential Education, 30*(2), 171–183.

Bowman, N. A. (2009). College diversity courses and cognitive development among students from privileged and marginalized groups. *Journal of Diversity in Higher Education, 2*(3), 182–194.

Bowman, N. A. (2010). Dissonance and resolution: The non-linear effects of diversity courses on well-being and orientations toward diversity. *Review of Higher Education, 33*, 543–568.

Bowman, N. A. (2011). Promoting participation in a diverse democracy: A meta-analysis of college diversity experiences and civic engagement. *Review of Educational Research, 81*(1), 29–68.

Brux, J. M., & Fry, B. (2010). Multicultural students in study abroad: Their interests, their issues, and their constraints. *Journal of Studies in International Education, 14*(5), 508–527.

Deardorff, D. K. (Ed.). (2009). *The SAGE handbook of intercultural competence.* Thousand Oaks, CA: SAGE Publications, Inc.

Denson, N., & Chang, M. J. (2009). Racial diversity matters: The impact of diversity-related student engagement and institutional context. *American Educational Research Journal, 46*, 322–353.

Ferguson, M. (2006). Creating common ground: Common reading and the first year of college. *Peer Review*, 8–10.

Gurin, P. (1999). Selections from "The compelling need for diversity in higher education," Expert reports in defense of the University of Michigan. *Equity and Excellence in Education, 32*(2), 36–62.

Gurin, P., Dey, E. L., Hurtado, S., & Gurin, G. (2002). Diversity and higher education: Theory and impact on educational outcomes. *Harvard Educational Review, 72*(3), 330–366.

Gurin, P., Nagda, B. A., & Lopez, G. (2004). The benefits of diversity in education for democratic citizenship. *Journal of Social Issues, 60*(1), 17–34.

Harper, S. R., & Quaye, S. J. (2009). Beyond sameness, with engagement and outcomes for all: An introduction. In S. R. Harper & S. J. Quaye (Eds.), *Student engagement in higher education: Theoretical perspectives and practical approaches for diverse populations* (pp. 1–12). New York, NY: Routledge.

Hendrickson, B., Rosen, D., & Aune, R. K. (2011). An analysis of friendship networks, social connectedness, homesickness, and satisfaction levels of international students. *International Journal of Intercultural Relations, 35.* 281–295.

Hurtado, S. (2001). Linking diversity and educational purpose: How diversity affects the classroom environment and student development. In G. Orfield (Ed.), *Diversity challenged: Evidence on the impact of affirmative action* (pp. 187–203). Cambridge, MA: Harvard Education Publishing Group and the Civil Rights Project at Harvard University.

Hurtado, S. (2004). *Preparing college students for a diverse democracy: Final report to the U.S. Department of Education, Office of Educational Research and Improvement, Field Initiated Studies Program.* Ann Arbor, MI: Center for the Study of Higher and Postsecondary Education, University of Michigan.

Hurtado, S. (2007). Linking diversity with the educational and civic missions of higher education. *The Review of Higher Education, 30*(2), 185–196.

Ingman, K. A. (2003). An examination of social anxiety, social skills, social adjustment and self-construal in Chinese and American students at an American University. *Dissertation Abstracts International, 63*(9-B), 4374.

King, P. M., & Baxter Magolda, M. B. (2005). A developmental model of intercultural maturity. *Journal of College Student Development, 46*(6), 571–591.

Kumagai, A. K., & Lypson, M. L. (2009). Beyond cultural competence: Critical consciousness, social justice, and multicultural education. *Academic Medicine, 84*(6), 782–787.

Kuh, G. D. (2008). *High-impact educational practices: What they are, who has access to them, and why they matter.* Washington, DC: Association of American Colleges and Universities.

Lee, A., Poch, R., Shaw, M., & Williams, R. (2012). Engaging diversity in undergraduate classrooms: A pedagogy for developing intercultural competence. *ASHE Higher Education Report, 38*(2).

Nagda, B. A., Gurin, P., Sorensen, N., & Zuñiga, X. (2009). Evaluating intergroup dialogue: Engaging diversity for personal and social responsibility. *Diversity & Democracy*, *12*, 4–6.

Neuner, G. (2012). The dimensions of intercultural education. In J. Huber (Ed.), *Intercultural competence for all: Preparation for living in a heterogeneous world* (pp. 11–49). Strasbourg: Council of Europe.

Nilsson, B. (2000). Internationalising the curriculum. In P. Crowther, M. Joris, M. Otten, B. Nilsson, H. Teekens, & B. Wächter (Eds.), *Internationalisation at home: A position paper* (pp. 21–27). Amsterdam: European Association for International Education, Drukkerij Raddraaier.

Norris, E. M., & Gillespie, J. (2009). How study abroad shapes global careers: Evidence from the United States. *Journal of Studies of International Education*, *13*(3), 382–397.

Osfield, K. J. (2008). *Internationalization of student affairs and services: An emerging global perspective*. Washington, DC: NASPA.

Otero, M. S. (2008). The socio-economic background of Erasmus students: A trend towards wider inclusion? *International Review of Education*, *54*(2), 135–154.

Otten, M. (2000). Impact of cultural diversity at home. In P. Crowther, M. Joris, M., Otten, B. Nilsson, S. Teekens, & B. Wächter (Eds.), *Internationalisation at home: A position paper* (pp. 15–20). Amsterdam: European Association for International Education, Drukkerij Raddraaier.

Paige, R. M. (2003). The American case: The University of Minnesota. *The Journal of Studies in International Education*, *7*(1), 52–63.

Pascarella, E. T., & Terenzini, P. T. (2005). *How college affects students: A third decade of research* (Vol. 2). San Francisco, CA: Jossey-Bass.

Pascarella, E. T., Wolniak, G., & Pierson, C. (2003). Explaining student growth in college when you don't think you are. *Journal of College Student Development*, *44*(1), 122–126.

Perrucci, R., & Hu, H. (1995). Satisfaction with social and educational experiences among international graduate students. *Research in Higher Education*, *36*(4), 491–508.

Salisbury, M. H., & Goodman, K. (2009). Educational practices that foster intercultural competence. *Diversity and Democracy*, *12*, 12–13.

Salisbury, M. H., Paulsen, M. B., & Pascarella, E. T. (2011). Why do all study abroad students look alike? Applying an integrated student choice model to explore differences in the Factors that influence white and minority students' intent to study abroad. *Research in Higher Education*, *52*(2), 123–150.

Soria, K. M. (in press). Common reading, learning, and growing: An examination of the benefits of common book reading programs for college students' development. *Journal of the First-Year Experience and Students in Transition*.

Soria, K. M., Roberts, J., & Reinhard, A. (in press). Undergraduate students' strengths awareness and leadership development. *Journal of Student Affairs Research and Practice*.

Soria, K. M., & Stubblefield, R. (in press). Knowing me, knowing you: Building strengths awareness and belonging in higher education. *Journal of College Student Retention: Research, Theory, and Practice*.

Soria, K. M., Snyder, S., & Reinhard, A. (in press). Strengthening college students' capacity for integrative leadership by building a foundation for civic engagement and multicultural competence. *Journal of Leadership Education*.

Soria, K. M., & Troisi, J. N. (2014). Internationalization at home alternatives to study abroad: Implications for students' development of global, international, and intercultural competencies. *Journal of Studies in International Education*, *18*(3), 260–279.

Soria, K. M., & Weiner, B. (2013). A "virtual fieldtrip": Service learning in distance education technical writing courses. *Journal of Technical Writing and Communication*, *43*(2), 179–198.

Stebleton, M. J., Soria, K. M., & Cherney, B. (2013). The high impact of education abroad: College students' engagement in international experiences and the development of intercultural competencies. *Frontiers: The Interdisciplinary Journal of Study Abroad*, *22*, 1–24.

Twombly, S. B., Salisbury, M. H., Tumanut, S. D., & Klute, P. (2012). Study abroad in a new global century: Renewing the promise, refining the purpose. *ASHE Higher Education Report*, *38*(4), 1–152.

Wedding, D. (2013). Improving international multicultural competence by working and studying abroad. In R. L. Lowman (Ed.), *Internationalizing multiculturalism: Expanding professional competencies in a globalized world* (pp. 289–300). Washington, DC: American Psychological Association.

Westwood, M. J., & Barker, M. (1990). Academic achievement and social adaptation among international students: A comparison groups study of the peer-pairing program. *International Journal of Intercultural Relations, 14,* 251–263

Williams, C. T., & Johnson, L. R. (2011). Why can't we be friends? Multicultural attitudes and friendships with international students. *International Journal of Intercultural Relations, 35*(1), 41–48.

Yeh, C. J., & Inose, M. (2003). International students' reported English fluency, social support satisfaction, and social connectedness as predictors of acculturative stress. *Counseling Psychology Quarterly, 16*(1), 15–28.

SECTION 2

DEVELOPING INTERCULTURAL PROGRAMS AND PRACTITIONERS

GAYLE WOODRUFF, KATE MARTIN
AND MARY KATHERINE O'BRIEN

5. INTERNATIONALIZING TEACHING AND LEARNING

Transforming Teachers, Transforming Students

FRAMING THE INSTITUTIONAL CONTEXT

In 2009, the University of Minnesota established initiatives to internationalize the curriculum on all five of its system campuses. These efforts began and have continued as a direct response to the University's strategic educational goal to graduate lifelong learners, leaders, and global citizens.

The University of Minnesota defines "internationalizing the curriculum and campus" as including all of the learning experiences in which students gain global and intercultural competencies. These experiences may be curricular or co-curricular. The learning may happen in classrooms on-campus, on study abroad programs, in local communities via service learning programs, on campus in informal settings, or by technology with students and communities in other countries. This broad definition allows for academic departments and student affairs units to envision and implement a range of learning experiences that span the entire student population, from first-year undergraduates to doctoral-level students.

In order to guide academic departments and student affairs units with developing global learning experiences, we enlisted the help of professors and staff in developing a definition of "global competency" for the entire University. We elicited responses from 225 faculty, staff, and students to the question: *What does global competency mean to you?* The results were crafted into a working definition of global competency for the institution.

> Globally competent University of Minnesota faculty, staff and students will demonstrate the skills, knowledge and perspectives necessary to understand the world and work effectively to improve it.

Specifically with regard to internationalising the curriculum, pivotal change happened in 2009 when we discovered the work of Gavin Sanderson on the "internationalization of the academic self" (Sanderson, 2008). Upon consultation with Sanderson, we realized that this principle was central to our goal of internationalizing the curriculum. We thought about the skills, knowledge, and attitudes that instructors have when they engage with teaching. How cosmopolitan or globally minded are our educators? What values and biases do our educators bring to the construction of curricula and teaching methods? What can educators learn from others around the world regarding approaches to teaching and learning? What work do our educators need to do on the "academic self" in order to further "internationalize" the experiences of our students?

Reframing our efforts to internationalize the curriculum as an initiative to "internationalize teaching and learning" addresses a institutional gap by providing for faculty development within an interdisciplinary setting. Putting faculty first has led to success in developing new and innovative courses and revamping existing ones. Expanding the mindset of faculty has been driven in part by their own motivation and also by incentives of professional development stipends and opportunities to present and publish on their work.

This chapter focuses on efforts by the University of Minnesota's international education offices and teaching and learning services units to partner on a unique faculty development program aimed at transforming the curriculum and how it is taught. The chapter establishes the rationale for an internationalized curriculum within the institutional context, and then highlights the development, implementation, and evaluation of the University's *Internationalizing Teaching and Learning (ITL) Faculty Cohort Program*. We refer to this program in short as the *ITL Cohort Program*. In the chapter, we will use the terms "faculty," "faculty members," and "ITL cohort participants" to refer to those individuals who are participants in the *ITL Cohort Program*. We are the ITL team of facilitators from the international offices and teaching and learning services units that develop and facilitate the program. The ITL team has expertise in global and intercultural learning, course design, and assessment.

INTERNATIONALIZING TEACHING AND LEARNING FACULTY COHORT PROGRAM

This chapter focuses on the *ITL Cohort Program*, an intensive initiative to support faculty with course design or re-design for the integration of international, global, and intercultural elements into their course content and pedagogical approaches. Internationalizing Teaching and Learning (ITL), in general, is a continuum of professional development offerings for faculty on all five University of Minnesota campuses. The continuum ranges from the least to most intensive experiences for faculty. Under the ITL umbrella there are web-based resources, consultations for faculty with teaching and learning specialists, workshops, a faculty cohort program, and a faculty fellows program, the latter of which provides *ITL Cohort Program* alumni with an opportunity to further their internationalization work on their campuses.

Historically, the University of Minnesota has had several models for internationalizing on-campus courses. A notable innovation that was the precursor to the *ITL Cohort Program* ran from 2001 to 2004 and in 2007–2008, called *Internationalizing On-Campus Courses* (IOCC). For more details see O'Donovan and Mikelonis (2005) and Smith and Mikelonis (2008). This precursor enrolled forty faculty members from two of the campuses, Duluth and Twin Cities. These faculty members were called upon to serve as mentors for the re-envisioned *ITL Cohort Program* launched in 2010.

Since 2010, fifty-three faculty members have participated in the *ITL Cohort Program*. They have represented all five campuses, a wide range of disciplines (Figure 1) and levels of courses taught, from freshman biology to doctoral classes in nursing. ITL cohort participants range from having no international experience to those who were born and raised outside of the United States and now reside in Minnesota.

Agricultural Education	Leadership
Agriculture and Natural Resources	Music
Anthropology	Nursing
Art	Philosophy
Biology	Political Science
Business	Postsecondary Teaching and Learning
Communication Studies	Public Affairs
Design	Public Health
Education	Social Work
Electrical and Computer Engineering	Spanish
English	Veterinary and Biomedical Sciences
Family Social Science	Women's Studies
French and Francophone Studies	Writing Studies
History	

Figure 1. Academic units or disciplines of ITL faculty.

The *ITL Cohort Program*, and all faculty support under the ITL umbrella, is developed and administered by a team of professional education specialists and international educators at the University of Minnesota. We refer to ourselves as the ITL team or ITL facilitators. We play an active role in the delivery of this program as experts in course design and assessment, effective teaching strategies, and curriculum internationalization.

As part of their course design process, faculty members consider how they will adjust for student diversity in the classroom environment and how they will provide content that will challenge students' intercultural development and worldviews. Emphasis is placed on promoting multiple perspectives. The concepts of "international", "global", and "intercultural" are developed for the class through disciplinary lenses.

In the program model, seasoned faculty members who have been successful with internationalizing their curriculum serve as mentors. These faculty alumni share their successes and failures with expanding teaching strategies and the process of developing materials and activities for an internationalized curriculum. Communities of practice emerge across disciplines in this model as evident in collaborative research and publications initiated by the ITL cohort participants.

Evaluation and assessment of the program outcomes occurs in three phases. First, we evaluate program level outcomes. We then assess the impact that the program has made on faculty members, and, ultimately, the outcomes that students demonstrate in the internationalized courses. We share the evaluation and assessment model in this chapter. The chapter concludes with discussion of the transferability of the model beyond the case of the University of Minnesota.

METHODOLOGY: INTERNATIONALIZING TEACHING & LEARNING COHORT PROGRAM

The *ITL Cohort Program* focuses on three primary goals and subsequent tasks for participants: to develop a sense of the academic self (Sanderson, 2008); to articulate discipline-specific and course-appropriate global learning outcomes; and, to develop assessments and teaching activities that align with the new outcomes. These program goals are grounded in broadly applicable principles of course design (Fink, 2003, 2005) and in Sanderson's (2008) call for faculty to engage in a reflective process to internationalize the academic self. Given their broad scope, the goals are appropriate for working with faculty across disciplines regardless of the type, level, size, or modality of the courses they teach. Similarly, these goals enable us to meet faculty "where they are" in terms of their international and intercultural experiences both professionally and personally.

This is not to suggest that internationalizing teaching and learning is a one-size-fits-all program. Indeed, the way in which we operationalize these goals through our program design and delivery challenges faculty to uncover the ways in which their own cultural and epistemological perspectives inform their teaching and the learning environment. This enables each participant to customize the internationalization of their teaching and learning to fit their discipline, their courses, and their entry point in the process of reflecting on and transforming their instructional roles in internationalized courses.

The current program format consists of three stages that take place over a period of approximately nine months. Each stage is scaffolded around a curriculum of readings, video lecturettes, and written assignments. The program structure and duration supports the on-going nature of course design, as well as the gradual transformation of participants' pedagogy and academic self.

First, ITL participants complete assignments in an asynchronous online course. This work begins the self-reflection process and establishes a common understanding of conceptual frameworks and core knowledge that will be applied during and after the workshop. The online work encourages participants to uncover responses to the questions, "What do I know and believe?" and "What new knowledge and attitude shifts might benefit me as I internationalize my courses?"

Next is an experiential, face-to-face, three-day intensive workshop that is facilitated by the ITL team and the faculty alumni. Here, participants consider numerous possibilities to address the questions, "How might I redesign my course?" and "How might I change my pedagogy and myself?" Past participants demonstrate teaching activities and discuss the developmental process of internationalizing their courses.

After the intensive workshop, participants return to the online course environment to reflect upon, revise, and extend what they have learned in the program. They post an annotated syllabus for feedback from their peers and the facilitators. The essential questions they answer during this period are, "What specific changes will I design into my course?" and "How have I changed as a result of being in this program?"

Upon completion of the formal *ITL Cohort Program*, most participants continue deepening their involvement by engaging in ongoing activities offered through the ITL continuum. These opportunities include attending workshops, seeking consultations with ITL facilitators, joining the *ITL Fellows Program*, and disseminating their work both on their campuses and at national and international conferences.

In keeping with the ever-strengthening call across higher education for program evaluation and assessment, international educators face increased demand to document outcomes related to internationalized learning (Astin & Antonio, 2012; Braskamp et al., 2010; Deardorff, 2009). Demonstration of *ITL Cohort Program* effectiveness includes documenting program-level outcomes as well as looking for evidence of ongoing changes in teaching and learning. The following sections highlight aspects of the evaluation model with examples of the data collected to document program efficacy and faculty impact. Discussion of student outcomes, the third phase of the evaluation model, concludes the chapter.

THREE-PHASED EVALUATION MODEL

The model for evaluating the ITL Cohort Program is comprised of three distinct phases: *program evaluation, faculty impact assessment, and student impact assessment*, guided by the overarching question *How do we know that the ITL Cohort Program is making a difference in teaching and learning at the University of Minnesota?* This three-phased approach (Figure 2) provides a framework to focus on the value of the program through *program evaluation* (Scriven, 1967) as well as the outcomes of the program through *assessment* (Fitzpatrick, Sanders & Worthen, 2010). We refer to the model as "phased" because it was rolled out over a three-year time period, with each phase building upon the lessons learned in the previous evaluation or assessment activities.

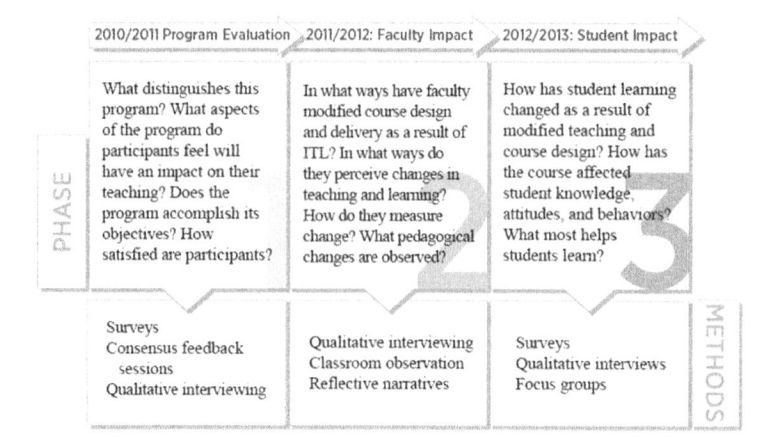

	2010/2011 Program Evaluation	2011/2012: Faculty Impact	2012/2013: Student Impact
PHASE	What distinguishes this program? What aspects of the program do participants feel will have an impact on their teaching? Does the program accomplish its objectives? How satisfied are participants?	In what ways have faculty modified course design and delivery as a result of ITL? In what ways do they perceive changes in teaching and learning? How do they measure change? What pedagogical changes are observed?	How has student learning changed as a result of modified teaching and course design? How has the course affected student knowledge, attitudes, and behaviors? What most helps students learn?
METHODS	Surveys Consensus feedback sessions Qualitative interviewing	Qualitative interviewing Classroom observation Reflective narratives	Surveys Qualitative interviews Focus groups

Figure 2. Evaluation model of ITL Cohort Program.

Program Evaluation

Program evaluation is rooted in continuous program and process improvement. The questions outlined in Figure 2 detail an approach that is designed to understand the participant experience during the three-day intensive session and throughout the course revision process. Data collection is conducted via on-line surveys, in-person feedback sessions, and follow up interviews.

Written reflection is considered a key element of the program evaluation model. Cohort participants write guided reflections during and immediately after the program regarding their initial perceptions of impact. Their responses are revisited later in semi-structured interviews so that faculty may further reflect on their changing experiences and perspectives throughout the program. Evaluation activities such as this lay the foundation for faculty impact assessment.

Assessing Faculty Impact

To document curricular change during the *ITL Cohort Program*, faculty participants use syllabus annotation, creating a pre-/post-picture of their internationalized course. Building upon the syllabus or course proposal submitted with their ITL program application, cohort members write reflective annotations explaining curricular changes and the rationales for doing so. This is submitted approximately three months after the conclusion of the intensive three-day workshop.

Members of the ITL team conduct in-person, semi-structured interviews and classroom observations during the semesters in which the cohort members teach their internationalized courses. Consultations are also done via phone, email and video conference to minimize the challenges of working system-wide and with busy faculty schedules.

These conversations and visits also serve to familiarize ITL team members with the cultures of varying disciplines, the teaching environments in which ITL faculty work, and the students they are instructing and, in some cases, advising. A partnership for understanding the work of internationalizing the curriculum is forged where the basis of the assessment is to understand impact rather than to evaluate teaching quality.

Assessing Student Impact

First and foremost, the ITL team works with cohort faculty to develop course assessments aligned with learning goals and activities, per the Fink (2003) model for course design for significant learning. In addition to training during the intensive workshop, ITL team members provide ongoing consultation to cohort members regarding course assessments and broader questions about assessing learning goals.

Recognizing the need for broader assessment of international, global, and intercultural learning, the ITL team also developed a set of student assessment questions that are administered at the conclusion of each semester, alongside the University's standard reviews of teaching. The assessment is comprised of five quantitative questions, answered with Likert-scale options of *strongly agree, agree, disagree, and strongly disagree*:

- The course materials and assignments encouraged me to consider global perspectives.
- The instructor integrated global perspectives into the course.
- This course encouraged me to question assumptions surrounding global perspectives in my field.
- This course increased my interest in studying international or global issues and concerns.
- This course motivated me to have new international experiences (work, study, travel abroad).

The assessment also includes two open-ended, qualitative questions:

What was/were the most important thing(s) you learned in this course in relation to global/international/intercultural issues? and What most helped you to learn the global/international/intercultural elements in this course?

OUTCOMES

Since the first group of ITL faculty began teaching their internationalized courses in fall term 2011, multiple sections of forty-three distinct courses have been internationalized. Figure 3 shows a small sample of those courses. According to official University system-wide enrolment headcounts, these courses have reached nearly 5,000 students at all levels of study.

Agriculture & Natural Resources	
AFEE 5111W	Methods of Teaching Agricultural Education
NATR 3344	Land Use Planning

Business & Marketing	
MKTG 3300	Principles of Marketing

STEM	
BIOL 1009H	Honors Biology
BIOL 3420	Ecotoxicology

Humanities	
WRIT 2506	Introduction to Writing Studies
PHIL 1003	Ethics and Society
HUMS 1435	Introduction to History: Trouble Spots in Today's World

Social Sciences	
COMM 3525	Deciding What's News
FSOS 3104	Global and Diverse Families
PA 5311	Program Evaluation

Nursing	
NURS 7500	Health Care of Children for the Family Nurse Practitioner

Figure 3. Example courses that have been internationalized through ITL program.

The next section of this chapter aims to illustrate the gradual process of teacher transformation through the use of excerpts from participants' written reflections and course (re)design work, particularly as these changes align with the overarching program goals: to develop the academic self (Sanderson, 2008), to articulate discipline-specific and course-appropriate global learning outcomes, and to develop assessments and teaching activities that align with the new outcomes.

Development of an Internationalized Sense of "Academic Self" (per Sanderson, 2008)

> Throughout the ITL Cohort Program, participants engage in numerous written reflection activities that focus on their evolving sense of academic self (Sanderson, 2008). Specifically, we ask them to identify their current teaching perspectives and assumptions about learning, and to explore new ways of thinking about how they teach an internationalized course. Sanderson (2008) writes "Critical reflection and self-reflection are important mechanisms by which individuals can become aware of the context in which they live and work. These processes have the potential to assist in the development of an authenticity that allows individuals to genuinely engage with others in teaching and in life in general" (p. 287). Faculty members are challenged to acknowledge

the ways in which their own cultural and epistemological standpoints inform their teaching and the learning environment.

The following quotes exemplify the range of participants' initial insights, critiques, and concerns regarding Sanderson's call for self-examination and self-knowledge in order to effectively design and teach an internationalized course:

> I found it interesting that one of the things that makes a good instructor also makes a good intercultural/international content teacher; which is critical reflection and self reflection. It seemed that one of the most important concepts was to know thyself, and then analyse your values/beliefs to determine where they came from – what makes you who you are. Cosmopolitanism, to me, is a term loaded with trouble – with echoes of (a) Europeans who manage to convert other cultures into aesthetic objects, marketable goods, or Oriental imaginings, and (b) a certain connection, then, to global capitalism that makes me queasy. ... I'm still a little hazy on whether I like this as a position for internationalizing my curriculum [because] I am desperately anxious about anything that leads to arguments about making writers (I teach in a writing major) better tools for multinational corporations. I don't want my students to better understand other cultures in order to sell to them more effectively. (Name withheld, ITL Cohort participant)

> I am on board with the cosmopolitanism idea but will need to be persuaded with regard to this idea of authenticity. I fall under the category of "introverted thinking" on personality tests. However, my teaching style does not reflect this. I tend to entertain and provide an active learning environment. I don't think students would ever guess that I have a tendency to avoid crowds. The disconnect between me and my teacher self seems suggestive of non-authenticity? I've taught for over 10 years and think I know myself, my limitations, and how my personal perspectives are being articulated. (Name withheld, ITL Cohort participant)

Consistently over time, ITL cohort participants state that the Sanderson article and reflective writing is a catalyst for shifting their mindset about teaching and learning.

Identification of Global Learning Outcomes

As ITL cohort members conclude their initial reflections on Sanderson's (2008) internationalization of the academic self, they are guided through the process of writing discipline-appropriate outcomes that reflect global, international, and/or intercultural student learning. Similar to other aspects of the *ITL Cohort Program*, the writing of these goals is process-driven and developmental in its approach.

In the "Global Ready Student" activity (Woodruff, Martin, & Smith, 2010), participants articulate program-level learning outcomes by describing the knowledge, skills, and attitudes a student in their discipline will need to have once they graduate from college. Participants respond to the following prompt:

> Please complete the following statement: "'A global ready student from my discipline **knows. is able to. cares about.**' Please submit at least one response for each prompt."

Two examples of participants' responses to the Global Ready Student Activity are in Figure 4.

A global ready student in nursing...

Realizes there are many, many effective systems of healing and just because one system doesn't align with bio-medicine or science-based medicine doesn't mean it should be totally disregarded.

Is prepared to work around the world wherever the need for nursing arises.

Is able to create culturally relevant healing environments for individuals and communities.

Recognizes that the health care system in the United States has a great deal to learn from systems in other countries.

A global ready student in biology...

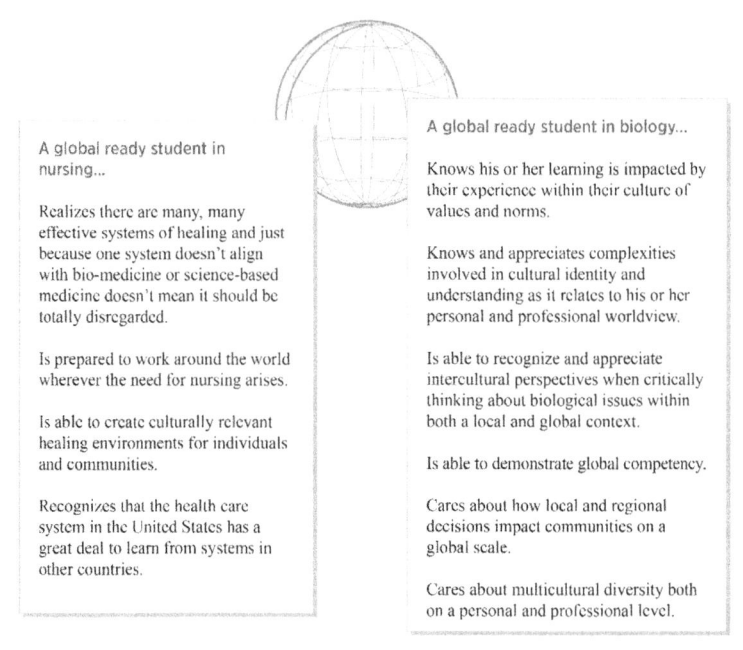

Knows his or her learning is impacted by their experience within their culture of values and norms.

Knows and appreciates complexities involved in cultural identity and understanding as it relates to his or her personal and professional worldview.

Is able to recognize and appreciate intercultural perspectives when critically thinking about biological issues within both a local and global context.

Is able to demonstrate global competency.

Cares about how local and regional decisions impact communities on a global scale.

Cares about multicultural diversity both on a personal and professional level.

Figure 4. Examples of ITL participants' responses to the Global Ready Student Activity.

After articulating broad outcomes for "global-ready" students in their disciplines, participants drill down to specific learning goals for their internationalized courses. To assist in this process, we provide a grid that maps two learning frameworks. The first is Fink's (2003) taxonomy for significant learning, which proposes six types of learning that stimulate and interact with one another to result in long-term transformational *significant* learning: foundational knowledge, application, integration, human dimension, caring, and learning how to learn. The other framework is the AAC&U Global Smart Grid (2010) which proposes five dimensions of global learning: knowledge-building, social responsibility, intercultural competencies, experiential engagement, and human capital.

Each of the AAC&U dimensions articulates a set of potential student abilities and experiences that, when mapped to the Fink taxonomy of significant learning, can spark ideas for global learning outcomes for ITL faculty members' classes. This is the case particularly for Fink's learning to learn, caring, and human dimensions, as the relevance of these dimensions becomes more evident when paired with aspects of global learning. Figure 5 illustrates how to use these two frameworks to move from broadly thinking about *significant learning,* to more specifically imagining *global learning,* to very concretely articulating *significant global learning goals for my course.* The sample course goals in Figure 5 are excerpted from University of Minnesota - Crookston assistant professor Katy Nannenga's course ENSC 3124: Environmental Science and Remediation Techniques.

Significant Learning	Global Learning	Course-Specific Learning
Fink Taxonomy of Significant Learning (2003)	AAC&U Dimensions of Global Learning (2010) mapped to Fink Taxonomy	EnSc 3124 course goals mapped to Fink Taxonomy and AAC&U Dimensions
Course design questions to guide the articulation of learning goals in the *Application domain* What kinds of thinking are important for students to learn? Critical thinking (analyze and evaluate) Creative thinking (imagine and create) Practical thinking (solve problems and make decisions) What important skills do students need to gain? Do students need to learn how to manage complex projects?	Students are able to... Work respectfully and effectively with others to address shared concerns Have practical, hands-on experiences that foster deeper expertise in intercultural learning Develop capacities to listen carefully to others and to share imaginatively in what it might mean to see the world from a different vantage point and historical experience Capacity to use a multiplicity of lenses for interpreting the world Using global frameworks as a means of posing additional questions and defining areas of inquiry	Students will... Possess the skills to apply Standard Remediation Technique strategies, alternative remediation strategies and approaches people may take to contaminated lands depending on their values and cultural backgrounds Be able to collaborate and communicate with various stake holders regardless of cultural differences to negotiate and mediate a remediation plan to resolve the environmental issue and sustain the health of that environment post-remediation Suggest measures that can be taken to prevent problems such as this particular contamination issue from arising in the future
Course design questions to guide the articulation of learning goals in the *Human Dimension domain* What should students learn about themselves? What should students learn about understanding others and/or interacting with them?	Students are able to... Describe the diversity and complexity of one's own country with greater knowledge and awareness Examine their own knowledge, perspectives, and values through engagement and partnerships with a variety of less familiar communities Interpret aspects of others' cultures and countries with sophistication and accuracy	Students will... Describe how environmental risk is perceived by themselves and others outside the U.S. Mediate those perceptions when developing remediation goals, making remediation decisions, and writing environmental laws and regulations

Figure 5. Example of excerpts from Fink's taxonomy and AAC&U grid with EnSc3124 learning goals.

Participants make various kinds of modifications to their course learning goals. Some add global content and non-U.S. perspectives where none existed previously, as in Nannenga's case above. Others, like James T. Ford, a lecturer from the Rochester campus, integrate a wider palette of expectations for global learning that include aspects of culture and ethnocentrism:

> The ITL program has broadened my understanding of the "global". Heretofore I've largely (but not exclusively) focused on international relations between countries. I've discussed diplomacy and role of international organizations in resolving a crisis. I still discuss these "big picture" events, but I now give equal weight to cross-cultural encounters, the intercultural experience, discrimination, and prejudice. – James T. Ford, lecturer, History (Rochester campus)

Many faculty, through the process of drafting and revising course goals, realize that they hold certain unarticulated aspirations for student learning:

> The program brought important focus on the course learning objectives for my course. The use of Fink's model to address multiple dimensions of learning was helpful and useful to me as I examined my course and thought about changes I needed to make. As a result, I expanded my objectives, giving specificity to goals I was trying to accomplish but hadn't named for myself or for my students. – Catherine Solheim, associate professor, Family Social Science (Twin Cities campus)

With their discipline-specific and course-appropriate learning goals in hand, participants come together for the intensive three-day workshop to experience activities that develop, stimulate, support, and perhaps challenge their initial thinking about course design and learning goals in particular. Across the three days, participants are immersed in activities and discussions that stimulate thinking about, "How might I redesign my course to achieve these new learning goals?" and "How might I need to change my pedagogy and myself?"

Expansion of Teaching Strategies and Development of Course Materials, Activities and Assessments

Building upon their articulated course goals, faculty next begin to identify appropriate assessments and learning activities to fill in their internationalized course design. Assessments demonstrate students' progress toward accomplishing the global learning goals and ideally increase global, international, and cultural knowledge, attitudes, and skills through focused and thoughtful feedback. As part of the overall learning strategy to accomplish the learning goals, course content is more inclusive of international, global, and intercultural perspectives and learning activities encourage students to integrate new international, intercultural and global knowledge, skills, and attitudes.

Empirical evidence from classroom observations and individual course consultations support the conclusion that participants from the ITL cohort have operationalized Fink's (2003) course design principles and integrated new strategies for international, intercultural, and global learning. The following section provides concrete examples regarding the ways in which ITL faculty cohort members have incorporated educative assessments and new learning activities into their courses to accomplish their revised goals.

In the previously mentioned course ENSC 3124: Environmental Science and Remediation Techniques, assistant professor Katy Nannenga wanted her students to use the scientific method—rather than their intuition or biases—to evaluate sites for environmental health. She articulated this goal as part of the "application" domain of Fink's (2003) taxonomy, relating it to the development of critical thinking skills.

During the cohort program, Nannenga and other participants experienced the intercultural learning exercise "Describe-Interpret-Evaluate" (D.I.E.), the purpose of which is to illustrate the tendency of human beings to interpret and evaluate what is unfamiliar based on prior knowledge, experiences, and worldviews. The activity teaches participants to recognize what is unknown and unfamiliar to us and seek to understand it before rushing to interpret and evaluate it.

Nannenga adapted the D.I.E. format and principles to create a learning activity to introduce students to a fundamental mindset for those in her discipline: to recognize their preconceived ideas about the subject matter, and to gather data before making judgments. In Nannega's adaptation of the activity, students view images of ten rivers and decide whether or not they would swim in each river. Some images are serene and picturesque, while others show discolored water and floating waste. After going through all ten images, she reveals that these are the ten most contaminated rivers on the planet, describing the location and contaminates of each. Invariably, the most contaminated river in the world is one that students misjudge and elect to swim in. Through this activity, Nannenga illustrates to students that judging a river for water quality and "safeness" by its appearance alone is a mistake. Instead, they must learn to put aside their preconceived ideas, and base their judgments on scientific information.

Like Nannenga, many faculty participants succeed in adapting the activities and materials that are modeled and presented during the cohort program to their own disciplinary context. In his NatR 3374: Ecology course, assistant professor Matthew Simmons uses an activity incorporating images from Istvan Banyai's wordless picture book *Zoom* (1995) to underscore the importance of scale, perspective, and interconnectedness in the discipline of Ecology. Each page of the book contains an engaging scene followed by a zoomed out perspective on that same scene which alters one's interpretation of the prior page. For example, one image shows two children looking out the window at a rooster. Subsequent pages unveil that the children and rooster are but toy figurines being played with by a child. Within a couple more pages, the reader realizes that the girl playing with the figurines appears on a magazine cover being held by a woman.

The *Zoom* activity, modelled during the cohort program and used by Simmons during the first week of his course, provides each student with a page from the book *Zoom*. He instructs students to mingle with their classmates, compare images, and seek to uncover the relationships and patterns among the pictures. He eventually instructs them to line up at the front of the room in a manner reflecting the pattern that they have uncovered – that of scale – from smallest to largest.

Simmons impresses upon students how ecological systems form a hierarchy (i.e., from smallest to largest: individual organism, population, metapopulation, community, ecosystem, landscape, biome, and biosphere). He explains how ecologists study these different levels of hierarchy, asking different questions and studying different patterns and processes that occur at these different ecological levels. He refers back to the *Zoom* activity during the semester to remind students that it is essential for ecologists to choose the right scale when studying ecological processes and patterns and to see how those patterns and processes might relate to those that are occurring at different hierarchical levels. Simmons threads throughout his course that viewing life from different perspectives helps to improve ecologists' understanding of nature, and he regularly asks students to discuss course material from both their own perspective and that of others.

Another teaching tool that is frequently adapted after being modeled during the cohort program is the Global Village Activity (Falk, 2010). In the original design of this activity, each student is assigned a unique "global villager" identity (e.g. age 55, male, rural, India) in proportion to the actual demographics of the world. Students then examine and report on course content through the lens of their villager. By researching their own global villager and geographic location, as well as learning about those of their classmates, students broaden their knowledge of the world. They also develop skills in recognizing and taking on other perspectives.

Associate professor Sarah Buchanan from the Morris campus has designed the "global villager" concept into the very fabric of her course FREN 3605: Cinema du Maghreb francophone (Maghrebian Cinema), modified to focus on francophone North Africa (Algeria, Morocco and Tunisia). Her aim is that students have a deep understanding of the diversity within that geographic region, rather than consider the Maghreb as monolithic and culturally undifferentiated. She refers to her adaptation of the Global Village Activity as "The Intercultural Village."

In Buchanan's adaptation, students assume the identity of characters representing various demographic groups from North Africa and complete a series of assignments with this assumed worldview. They create a profile of their character, including the type of family structure, education, socio-economic class, politics, culture and art that would likely be a part of that individual's experience. Characters are encouraged to have a culturally relevant name and appearance. To establish the authenticity of the profile they create, students are encouraged to collaborate, in French, with a student from Algeria, Morocco, or Tunisia to confirm or revise the information. The students share these during class presentations.

As Buchanan's is a film class, the students are asked to respond to structured reflection questions on each film the class watches recording their own and their character's reactions to the movie's cultural and political themes. Buchanan underscores that the reactions should be honest and need not be politically correct, framing the assignment as an "intercultural journey" where students can feel free to ask questions and where she, as the instructor, can provide feedback on any stereotyping or broad generalizations she sees emerging from the narratives. Peer-to-peer feedback also takes place in intercultural debates among the students at periodic intervals through the semester.

Through her use of the Intercultural Village concept, Buchanan exemplifies strong alignment among her learning goals, teaching activities, and assessments. She has articulated a particular learning goal (that students deeply understand diversity in the Maghreb). She has designed multiple learning activities throughout the course to move students toward the achievement of that goal (by researching, modifying, and adapting the viewpoint of their character). Finally, she has created multiple ways to provide feedback and assess student success (through interviews with students from the Maghreb, debates, and a final exam question that promotes students' synthesis of what they have learned during the Intercultural Village exercise).

Hilary Kowino, associate professor of English on the Duluth campus, uses the case study method in his World Literatures course to aid students in interrogating the implications of culture and context as they read and analyze texts. The case, "A Tragedy in Santa Monica" (Reese, 1985), presents the story of Fumiko Kimura, a Japanese immigrant who drowned her two children and was herself rescued from drowning as she attempted to carry out a suicide attempt. Kimura had learned that her husband was having a long-term extra-marital affair and that the couple's financial difficulties were compounded by his support of this second partner.

The case focuses on the cultural significance of *oyako-shinju*, an act of taking one's own life to preserve dignity. In Kimura's homeland of Japan, *oyako-shinju* carries legitimacy and honor, but not in California where the infanticide and attempted suicide case occurred. The difficult themes of the case study raise "a crisis of culture and law", providing rich opportunities for students to examine the impact of cultural values and their intersection with societal institutions and systems (Kelley, Kowino & Woodruff, 2012, p. 9).

"The case of Fumiko becomes quite complex when we contextualize it; that is, contextualizing this case study grants us an international perspective that would have been outside of our view, and thus allows us a more complex reading of Fumiko", states Kowino, "Simply put, this…lens provides a different light. We don't necessarily excuse Fumiko's crime, but we recognize its complexity. And it is this complexity that we are trying to cultivate in our students; without it, our students would be tempted to judge Fumiko because they would only see her crime through one angle (through mainstream American lens/ through the letter of the American law). The mere appreciation of a diversity of perspectives that this case study promotes is critical, but also pivotal is what the case study does not say" (Kelley, Kowino & Woodruff, 2012, p. 9–10).

In addition to the intercultural dimension, Kowino asserts that the case prompts his students to examine family dynamics, poverty, and the immigrant experience in the United States as global issues. Kowino says that he hopes that through the process of examining and debating these themes in the classroom, students will refine and apply this type of thinking to their out-of-class lives.

Integrating Multiple Perspectives

Given the *ITL Cohort Program's* focus on the intentional integration of multiple perspectives into the learning environment, the experiences and viewpoints of international students are regarded as particularly valuable and potentially impactful for all students' intercultural learning. As Mestenhauser (2011) writes: "There can be no global citizenship without taking into account people from other countries and, in this case, without foreign students being a part of this" (p. 275).

In the report *Finding Common Ground: Enhancing Interactions Between Domestic & International Students* Australian researchers Arkoudis et al. (2010) speak to the power that faculty can play in enhancing students' exposure to differing perspectives and cultural traditions, and the accomplishment of more complex learning outcomes. Further research suggests that these types of student interactions are "important to developing cognitive understandings and offer opportunities for learning. Peer interaction can provide learners with a greater sense of belonging and support, which may have a positive impact on student retention and learning achievement" (Eames & Stewart, 2008; Huijser & Kimmins, 2008).

There are two critical assumptions at the core of the *ITL Cohort Program's* approach to integrating international students. In keeping with the literature on student engagement (e.g. Coates, 2005; Kuh, 2005; Kuh et al., 2007), the first assumption is that the engagement of international students is both *student driven* and *institution driven*. Andrade (2010) argues: "with varying cultural, ethnic, and linguistic backgrounds as well as academic preparation, support for student learning is a critical concern, as well as an opportunity to expand pedagogical approaches. Institutions must be accountable for serving those they admit and for adjusting methods of instruction and support systems to address learners' needs" (p. 221). The *ITL Cohort Program* thus focuses on the role faculty play in creating inclusive environments to support international students in their transitions to the University of Minnesota. ITL participant Louis Porter II, a lecturer on the Twin Cities campus, reflects on his role in engaging the international students in the classroom:

> I am searching for ways to empower the international students in my class and create ways to respectfully share from their own culture. As I think about my past sections, students from outside the United States can consider themselves disadvantaged in this [public speaking] course and one of the things I plan

to do is to dispel that mythology. – Louis Porter II, lecturer, Communication Studies (Twin Cities campus)

The second assumption is the benefit for all students of intentional efforts to increase the clarity of the "hidden curriculum"—the culturally-informed, unarticulated aspects of the learning environment (Leask, 2009). Aligned with Scott, McGuire and Embry's (2002) universal design for instruction, it is assumed that modifications to course delivery, materials, feedback, interactions, and class environment can increase learning accessibility and effectiveness for both international and domestic students.

Each of these principles is evident in the way that Laura Bloomberg, associate dean and professor in the Humphrey School of Public Affairs (Twin Cities), restructured her graduate-level PA 5311 Program Evaluation course after participating in the ITL program. After hearing from several international students that they often felt reluctant or unable to speak to their expertise within group settings, Bloomberg asked each student to use an on-line forum to describe their expertise related to a policy issue. Moving this framing discussion to a guided, asynchronous forum post took a negligible amount of time, but opened a new means by which all students had an opportunity to participate and share their backgrounds. International students in the course reported a sense of deeper inclusion in the course, expressing appreciation at having more time to write and edit their introductions. U.S. students reported the value of the non-U.S. perspectives coming from the international students and extensive course evaluation shows increased satisfaction from all students in the class.

Assistant professor Christina Clarkson from the Twin Cities campus' College of Veterinary Medicine developed an overarching goal for the students in her CVM 6013 Professional Development III: Applied Communication course to recognize that "they have a perspective that they bring to all communication encounters and that others come to those situations with their own perspectives, as well" (Clarkson, Bjarnadottir & O'Brien, 2013). In her syllabus, these broad objectives translate to the following specific learning goals: "review and reaffirm your current communication skill sets through professional interactions and outreach with diverse client populations", "recognize the value of continuing to develop professional and effective communication skills with a diverse client base", and "develop a respectful form of inquiry (i.e., a questioning route) to elicit information from clients of diverse backgrounds".

This last goal reflects a learning activity that has grown from Clarkson's iterative course modification process. In her search for strategies to help students have authentic intercultural communication encounters, Clarkson enlisted the help of the University of Minnesota's Culture Corps, an initiative on campus that helps faculty to connect with international students and scholars as learning resources for their courses. Through Culture Corps, Clarkson was able to invite 17 international students from various areas of veterinary medicine and practice to visit the course and work with her students to understand effective communication strategies for interacting with diverse clients.

Clarkson's students receive an interactive talk by a guest lecturer about communication styles and the ways that culture may (or may not) be a factor in one's approach to interpersonal interaction. The students then develop an intake interview procedure that would be responsive to a client of a different national background. In the final step, Clarkson's students conduct small group interviews with Culture Corps students to practice their interview protocols and to gain insights on the content of the interviews, strategies for recognizing a diversity of communication preferences, and also to become more aware of culturally-specific beliefs on animal ownership and veterinary practice. After this activity is conducted, students write guided reflections about their experiences and the connections they se between the activity and their future lives as veterinary professionals. Follow up course evaluation data show that after this activity 82% of the students strongly agree that veterinarians need to be aware of the different cultures that exist within their practice and 71% of the students strongly agree that the international student interview gave them insight into cultural differences in animal care.

During the ITL program, faculty participants to share in an online forum their own backgrounds, challenges, and the opportunities they see for more effectively working with international students. Commenting on the role of international students in the classroom, Njoki Kamau, a Kenyan scholar and faculty participant from the Duluth campus wrote to her ITL peers, "Silence and lack of active participation in the classrooms does not always mean that the students are intellectually weak and desiring remedial work, but is a reflection of many things, including cultural differences in how we speak, when we speak, how to engage a professor, what to speak about, avoidance of conflict, fear of being not being heard, perception of power differentials and of course perceptions of the other."

EMERGENT PROGRAM OUTCOMES

As faculty have become more comfortable in teaching their internationalized courses and as the *ITL Cohort Program* has gained momentum, the ITL team also documents "emergent outcomes." These are examples of program impact that were not anticipated in the program design but have been articulated as program impacts by faculty cohort members themselves.

Evidence of ongoing curricular change is particularly evident at the Crookston campus, where professors Katy Nannenga and Brian Dingmann are working to internationalize the courses they teach and team-teach, as well as working with their colleagues to set internationalized program-level outcomes for biology and environmental science majors. Encapsulating this expansion of internationalized teaching and learning, Dingmann recently said in a conference presentation:

Once you do it and you see the impact on the students, it's like, "Why don't I do it with this [other] class or with this assignment?" And so it starts building. You quickly realize that you want to completely throw out your old curriculum, and build a new curriculum. ...Nobody has time to that, but you have to basically commit to it. It's a lot of fun, and I think students get a lot out of it.

I teach microbiology so I think it's somewhat viral and it just spreads—you sort of get an infection when you start this work. You become motivated, passionate. When you are trying to change something, you have to be really passionate about it. So I think it just slowly spreads [into all that you do]. – Brian Dingmann, associate professor, Biology (Crookston campus)

Dingmann is not alone in his ongoing interest in internationalizing teaching and learning. Thirteen *ITL Cohort Program* alumni participated in the 2013–14 *ITL Fellows Program*, a structured opportunity to give faculty with a background in course-level internationalization further support to deepen their work around internationalizing the curriculum and campus. Fellows' projects ranged from strategies to deepen course-based assessment to campus conversations about existing structures and support required for further internationalized teaching and learning. For example, professor Jiann-Shiou Yang, department head of electrical engineering on the Duluth campus, has begun conversations with his faculty about internationalization and curricular innovations such as using technology to connect students across borders.

ITL alumni have started to publish articles on their internationalized teaching and research activities in publications such as the *Journal of Research in International Education* and *Landscape Architecture Record*. Conference sessions have been presented institutionally at the University of Minnesota's Academy of Distinguished Teachers Conference and the Internationalizing the Curriculum and Campus Conference, and as far away as the AC21 Conference at the University of Adelaide in Australia. Faculty have actively spoken to the benefits of their internationalization work to the promotion and tenure process and the ITL team has documented several academic units on campus that value these scholarly contributions.

Evidence of Student Impact

While the evidence of curricular and pedagogical changes are critical in documenting program outcomes, the ITL team recognizes that success cannot be achieved until there is also evidence of internationalized student learning. Understanding *what* students are learning and *how* they are learning it has, therefore, become the focus of the course-level assessments and the ITL team's broader effort to assess students' international, intercultural and global learning.

The previously mentioned end-of-semester course assessment provides preliminary information about the student experience in ITL faculty's internationalized courses. Aggregate response data (n = 309) for Spring 2013, Fall

2013, and Spring 2014 show that 92.5% of students either agreed (n = 157) or strongly agreed (n = 129) with the statement *The course materials and assignments encouraged me to consider global perspectives.* In response to the statement *This course encouraged me to question assumptions surrounding global perspectives in my field,* 88.9% of students either agreed (n = 147) or strongly agreed (n = 128). A majority of students (72.4%) also agreed (n = 107) or strongly agreed (n = 117) with the statement *This course increased my interest in studying international or global issues and concerns.* The Cronbach's alpha for the instrument's internal reliability is (α): 0.893.

Thematic analysis of students' responses to the open-ended questions on the end-of semester course assessment showed that students identified the most important global, international, and intercultural learning outcomes from their courses as: developing new ways of thinking, seeing, and understanding, contextual understanding, and personal growth and awareness.

A student on the Rochester campus in lecturer James T. Ford's course HUMS 1435: Introduction to History—Trouble Spots in Today's World wrote the following: "I learned that there are definitely more than one side to an issue or crisis and the resolution is more difficult and intertwined with greater complex issues. I think that this course instilled in me a greater need to explore the historical perspective of issues rather than what the current issue is."

Other student reflections on the end-of-term course assessment more closely reflected the "how" dimension of learning:

Reading the memoirs helped me learn most about issues because I'm the kind of person who really remembers things when they strike me emotionally, and survivor accounts do this for me in a way that reading a textbook...cannot. (Anonymous student)

I think that class discussion helped me learn the most about international issues. There were so many different viewpoints within the class that it helped for a better understanding overall. (Anonymous student)

The last exam had a question about how a contaminant reached a part of the world that was not originally exposed to the contaminant. This helped me to think about how everything is connected in the world even if we don't intend for it to be. (Anonymous student)

Other qualitative evidence of student learning has been collected via course-based assignments, classroom observations and student interviews. In the Twin Cities' College of Veterinary Medicine's course CVM 6013: Professional Development III: Applied Communication assistant professor Christina Clarkson created student learning goals "to develop increased understanding of one's own cultural orientations and to develop awareness of and communication skills to interact with a diverse client base". In response to an intercultural learning activity in the CVM 6013 classroom, one student wrote the following:

I became much more aware of the individuality each person has. I never really took the time to think about the values or cultural qualities my own family has. I suppose I took them for granted and never took the time to appreciate or identify them... This activity allowed me to learn things about my classmates I never would have known. ...I think culture will have varying impacts on interactions depending on the situation. But no matter what, I think our culture impacts the way we view the world and it's important to remember that each person sees through a different lens. (Anonymous student)

FUTURE CONSIDERATIONS AND TRANSFERABILITY

A program of this nature is only possible because of the partnership between the teaching and learning services units and the international education offices on our campuses, which allows each unit to bring its expertise into the program development, as well as the commitment of motivated faculty participants who are willing to do the hard work of redesigning their courses, learning new teaching techniques and exposing themselves to new ways of thinking about their roles as teachers. In a 2013 external review of the Global Programs and Strategy Alliance, the *ITL Cohort Program* was praised and a recommendation was made to continue such support for faculty. The University of Minnesota provost placed a focus on deepening the strategy for internationalization into the University's plan in 2013. In 2014, the Center for Teaching and Learning and the Office of e-Learning merged to become the new Center for Educational Innovation to serve the entire university system. All of these developments, on top of the concrete impact data of the *ITL Cohort Program*, provide a strong foundation for the program's future.

A community of practice for faculty and staff has emerged as a result of the program. The ITL participants refer to this community as one of the most important program outcomes, as they have found a group of peers who share similar goals and to whom they can turn for advice and ideas. Developing a community of practice around teaching and learning would be our first suggestion to other institutions attempting such models.

An overarching goal regarding internationalizing the curriculum at the University of Minnesota continues to serve all faculty members who are interested in curriculum internationalization, not just the ITL cohort faculty. A long-term goal is to develop less-intensive options for those faculty members who may not be able to participate in the *ITL Cohort Program*. With this mind, those faculty members who have participated in the cohort program must continue to serve as mentors and role models for educational reform in their academic departments. These professors, through their scholarly publications on how this program has changed their courses, their teaching and their students' learning outcomes will deepen the literature base on curriculum internationalization and on teaching in their disciplines. These professors, through their direct communication with their peers, will influence the nature of international education in their academic units. It is their experiences with internationalizing their courses that will be shared with other faculty members who seek to engage in this process.

Despite the positive outcomes, challenges exist for a program of this structure. Scope is the prime challenge. Given the size of the institution, it will take many years to reach a critical mass of faculty members if we just use the cohort model to engage faculty. Our goal must be maximize gains made by individual faculty members' curricular changes toward broader discipline outcomes. Each ITL faculty member is partially responsible for moving beyond simply internationalizing their own classes to considering their role as educational reformers in their disciplines. The institution bears the rest of the responsibility for supporting these faculty members then as role models for educational innovation.

Unique institutional contexts will determine the extent of transferability of the *ITL Cohort Program* model described in this chapter. For those whose context limits their ability to implement the type of faculty program on the scale we describe here, we offer the following starting points for consideration. *Involve faculty in defining internationalizing teaching and learning at your institution.* Use or adapt the *global-ready student* exercise described in the methodology section of this chapter to stimulate thinking about discipline-specific learning outcomes that are global, international, and/or intercultural. *Reward and bring together faculty who are already internationalizing their teaching and learning.* Know who these faculty are, and learn how they have been successful in their work. Invite them to lead or collaborate on establishing an interdisciplinary community of practice to internationalize teaching and learning that includes a formal course design process. Formalize a reward structure and raise the visibility of their work. *Think creatively about potential partners when building a collaborative support team.* In addition to collaborating with expert faculty at your institution, consider potential partners whose work supports the teaching and learning mission, such as those who have expertise in the global, international, and intercultural realms (e.g., instructional designers, librarians, ESL teachers).

CONCLUSION

The *Internationalizing Teaching and Learning Faculty Cohort Program* brings to the forefront the cognitive skill of self-reflection that Mestenhauser (1998) deems critical to international educational reform. This principle is applied directly to the teaching environment by focusing on the teachers themselves as critical factors in the design and delivery of internationalized courses. As members of the academy who are responsible for teaching begin to engage in self-reflection about their own experiences and transfer what they learn from that self-reflection to their course design and delivery, they begin to shift the nature of the student learning experience. It is the act of transforming teachers in order to transform students that we argue is paramount to shifting the educational landscape to be more conducive to the goals of internationalizing the curriculum.

ACKNOWLEDGEMENTS

The authors wish to thank the members of the ITL team who have helped to shape this program since its inception: Shelley Smith, Barbara Kappler, Thorunn Bjarnadottir, Jeff Lindgren, Amanda Allers, Cristina Lopez, Elizabeth Schwartz, Beth Isensee and Alison Link, in addition to the ITL faculty alumni who have served as mentors.

REFERENCES

Andrade, M. S. (2010). Increasing accountability: Faculty perspectives on the english language competence of nonnative english speakers. *Journal of Studies in International Education, 14*(3), 221–239.

Arkoudis, S., Yu, X., Baik, C., Borland, H., Change, S., Lang, I., Pearce, A., & Watty, K. (2010). *Finding common ground: Enhancing interaction between domestic and international students.* Melbourne, Australia: Australian Learning & Teaching Council.

Association of American Colleges and Universities. (2010). *The global smart grid, global institutional inventory.* Washington, DC: Author. Retrieved from http://www.aacu.org/value/rubrics/globallearning.cfm

Astin, A. W. & Antonio, A. L. (2012). *Assessment for excellence: The philosophy and practice of assessment and evaluation in higher education* (2nd ed.). Lanham, MD: Rowman & Littlefield.

Banyai, I. (1995). *Zoom.* New York, NY: The Penguin Group.

Braskamp, L. A., Deardorff, D. K., Paige, R. M, Briggs, P., Gladding, S., & Sutton, R. (2009). *Assessment and evaluation for international educators.* Washington, DC: NAFSA, Association of International Educators. Retrieved May 23, 2014 from http://www.nafsa.org/uploadedFiles/NAFSA_Home/Resource_Library_Assets/Publications_Library/Assess%20and%20Eval%20in%20IE.pdf

Clarkson, C., Bjarnadottir, T. & O'Brien, M. K. (2013, October). *Internationalizing the curriculum: A professional communication course for veterinary medicine students.* Presented at the Academy of Distinguished Teachers conference, University of Minnesota-Twin Cities, Minneapolis MN.

Coates, H. (2005). The value of student engagement for higher education quality assurance. *Quality in Higher Education, 11*(1), 25–36.

Deardorff, D. K. (2009). Implementing intercultural competence assessment. In D. K. Deardorff (Ed.) *The SAGE handbook of intercultural competence* (pp. 121–140). Thousand Oaks, CA: Sage.

Eames, C. & Stewart, K. (2008). Personal and relationship dimensions of higher education science and engineering learning communities. *Research in Science & Technological Education, 26*(3), 311–321.

Falk, D. (2010). Global village activity. In D. Falk, S. Moss, & M. Shapiro (Eds.), *Educating globally competent citizens* (p. 86). Washington, DC: Center for Strategic and International Studies.

Fink, L. D. (2003). *Creating significant learning experiences.* San Francisco, CA: Jossey-Bass.

Fink, L. D. (2005). *A self-directed guide to designing courses for significant learning.* Retrived September 15, 2010 from http://www.deefinkandassociates.com/GuidetoCourseDesignAug05.pdf

Fitzpatrick, J. L., Sanders, J. R., & Worthen, B. R. (2004). *Program evaluation: Alternative approaches and practical guidelines* (3rd ed.). Boston, MA: Pearson Education.

Harari, M. (1992). Internationalization of the curriculum. In C. B. Klasek (Ed.), *Bridges to the future: Strategies for internationalizing higher education* (pp. 52–79). Carbondale, IL: Association of International Education Administrators.

Huijser, H. & Kimmins, L. (2008). Peer assisted learning in fleximode: Developing an online learning community. *Australasian Journal of Peer Learning 1*(1), 51–60.

Kelley, S., Kowino, H., & Woodruff, G. (2012). *Educating globally competent citizens through transformational learning: Diverse case studies.* Paper presented at AC21 conference in Adelaide, Australia.

Kuh, G. D. (2005). Student engagement in the first year of college. In M. L. Upcraft, J. Gardner, & B. Barefoot (Eds.), *Challenging and supporting the first-year student: A handbook for improving the first year of college* (pp. 86–107). San Francisco, CA: Jossey-Bass.

Kuh, G. D., Kinzie, J., Buckley, J., Bridges, B., & Hayek, J. C. (2007). *Piecing together the student success puzzle: Research, propositions, and recommendations. ASHE Higher Education Report, 32(5)*. San Francisco, CA: Jossey-Bass.

Leask, B. (2009). Using formal and informal curricula to improve interactions between home and international students. *Journal of Studies in International Education, 13*(2), 205–211.

Mestenhauser, J. (1998). Portraits of an international curriculum. In J. Mestenhauser & B. Ellingboe (Eds.), *Reforming the higher education curriculum: Internationalizing the campus*. Phoenix, AZ: Oryx Press.

Mestenhauser, J. (2011). *Reflections on the past, present, and future of internationalizing higher education: Discovering opportunities to meet challenges*. Minneapolis, MN: Global Programs and Strategy Alliance, University of Minnesota.

O'Donovan, K. & Mikelonis, V. (2005). Internationalizing on-campus courses: A faculty development program to integrate global perspectives into undergraduate course syllabi. In L. C. Anderson (Ed.), *Internationalizing undergraduate education: Integrating study abroad into the curriculum*. Minneapolis, MN: University of Minnesota.

Reese, M. (1985, May 6). A tragedy in Santa Monica. *Newsweek, 105*, 10.

Sanderson, G. (2008). A foundation for the internationalization of the academic self. *Journal of Studies in International Education, 12*(3), 276–307.

Scott, S., McGuire, J. M., & Embry, P. (2002). *Universal design for instruction fact sheet*. Storrs, CT: University of Connecticut, Center on Postsecondary Education and Disability.

Scriven, M. (1967). The methodology of evaluation. In R. E. Stake (Ed.), *Curriculum evaluation*. (American Educational Research Association Monograph Series on Evaluation, No. 1, pp. 39–83). Chicago, IL: Rand McNally.

Smith, S. & Mikelonis, V. (2008). Internationalizing technical communications courses. In B. Thatcher & K. St. Amant (Eds.), *Teaching intercultural rhetoric and technical communication: Theories, curriculum, pedagogies, and practices*. Amityville, NY: Baywood Publishing.

Woodruff, G., Martin, K., & Smith, S., (2009). *Global ready student classroom activity*. Internationalizing teaching and learning cohort program, University of Minnesota, MN.

Gayle A. Woodruff
Global Programs and Strategy Alliance
University of Minnesota

Kate Martin
Center for Teaching and Learning
University of Minnesota

Mary Katherine O'Brien
Global Programs and Strategy Alliance
University of Minnesota

JILL E. BLONDIN

6. STRATEGIES FOR THE DEVELOPMENT OF AN INTERCULTURAL ENVIRONMENT

One way that institutions of higher education in the United States have responded to the need to foster global competence in undergraduate students is by creating living-learning communities (LLCs) that take global studies or international interests as the focus. Such intercultural environments, frequently planned around area studies or core curriculum courses, study abroad experiences, or residence halls that house international students, differ in curriculum, co-curriculum, and length of program. Often these programs have little in common beyond the initial motivation to create intercultural experiences for students (McClanahan, 2014). For institutions seeking to develop such programs, specifically global education LLCs, information and resources are scant, and there remains no blueprint or model. VCU Globe, a high-capacity global education LLC hosting an innovative curriculum that fosters intercultural learning through sustained and structured interactions among program participants, international students and scholars, and community members at Virginia Commonwealth University (VCU), can serve as a model or case study for examining strategies for the development and implementation of a multifaceted intercultural environment. The VCU Globe Model (VGM) facilitates global competence and creates an intercultural environment at the intersection of three distinct, yet interrelated areas: curriculum; the co-curriculum and residential experience; and global and community engagement.

As a hybrid academic-residential program, the VGM uses a holistic approach to develop global competence in its participants. Global competence is defined as "having an open mind while actively seeking to understand cultural norms and expectations of others, and leveraging this gained knowledge to interact, communicate, and work effectively in diverse environments" (Hunter, White, & Godbey, 2006, p. 277).

Critical thinking skills as well as an apprehension of intercultural communication concepts also characterize a globally-competent person (Shams & George, 2006; Olson, Green, & Hill, 2005). Other wide-ranging definitions, including global, international, and intercultural (GII) competencies (Soria & Troisi, 2014) and more narrowly defined terms, such as global engagement competency (Kennesaw State University, 2014), are useful for identifying the skills and ways of thinking that globally-astute students should have.

This chapter examines the VGM, including the programmatic structure, along with the contexts and vision that informed its development. Additionally, specific strategies for the creation of this intercultural environment will be considered. For practitioners seeking to implement this type of programming, this chapter provides concrete ways in which the VGM can be adapted.

THE CONTEXT OF VCU GLOBE

Students are increasingly interested in developing global competencies as well as their abilities as culture brokers, those who are able to bridge, link, or mediate "between groups or persons of differing backgrounds for the purpose of reducing conflict or producing change" (Jezewski & Sotnik 2001, p. 21). As the integration of international, global, intercultural, and comparative perspectives into teaching and program content has increased, academic institutions must be prepared to provide intercultural environments to support the learning process (Altbach & Knight, 2007). This is the context out of which the VGM was developed at VCU, an urban, public research university in the Eastern region of the United States with more than 31,000 students.

Traditionally the way to acquire global competency skills has been through study abroad programs. At VCU, in the last five years, overall study abroad participation numbers have increased by 46%, and the number of VCU faculty-led programs has increased by 37.5%. (*VCU Global Education Office Annual Report*, 2013–14). Yet 90% to 95% of college students will not have a firsthand international experience (Urban & Palmer, 2014). At most institutions, study abroad is the only opportunity for students to participate in global engagement, which is defined as meaningful cross-cultural interaction between individuals and groups that exposes them to the languages, culture, and customs of world populations. In fact, global engagement is often missing entirely from students' undergraduate experiences.

As the number of international students on American college campuses continues to grow, an environment must be created in which these learners can succeed. Efforts have included making the college campus more "international friendly" (Redden, 2014) and considering affordability and financial concerns that also impede retention rates for international students (Fischer, 2014). The presence of growing numbers of international students on campus and the proximity to communities of recently-arrived residents of diverse languages, cultures, and experiences are enormous assets for global education (Urban & Palmer, 2014; Leask, 2009). Underscoring the principle that "international diversity can enrich the learning experience and social interaction of domestic students who might not have opportunities to travel or live abroad" (Urban & Palmer, 2014, p. 307), the VGM prepares students as culture brokers while creating a campus that welcomes and enriches the experiences of international students and scholars. While cultural activities enrich campus life, there have been very few structured programs organized around specific global learning objectives through which students can engage in sustained interaction with peers from other cultures and document their learning (*Global Education Curriculum Document,* 2012). These considerations provide the external context and the motivation for the development of an effective intercultural environment at VCU.

In fact, VCU's desire to bring global competency to the fore is a charge that comes directly from the institution's strategic plan, *Quest for Distinction* (Reimers, 2014; Whitt et al., 2008). The *Quest for Distinction* (2011) includes the pledge to increase "the global engagement of students, faculty, and staff that transforms lives and communities," and the subsequent distillation of three global priorities: improve recruitment and retention of international students and scholars; increase global engagement of students and faculty; and expand VCU's global footprint through research, teaching, and service (p. 14). VCU's commitment to increasing the global engagement of the institution's diverse faculty and student population resulted in the subsequent creation of the Task Force for Comprehensive Internationalization to expand growth in the areas of international students and scholars; teaching and curriculum/education abroad; strategic partnerships and research; and campus culture and community (VCU Global Education Office, 2014; Brown, 2014). To ensure the full engagement of University stakeholders in the process, fifty members, including students, faculty, and staff comprised the Task Force. The Task Force, supported by participation in the 10th cohort of the ACE Internationalization Laboratory, identified the need to create a campus culture that supports the growing number of international students and enriches intercultural experiences for faculty, students, and staff (VCU Global Education Office, 2014; Brown, 2014). Creating a more internationalized campus culture also meant increasing the opportunities for faculty, staff, and students to participate in intercultural opportunities that enhance their understanding and appreciation of cultural differences as well as their abilities to demonstrate these competencies (Reimers, 2014).

VCU Globe serves as both an outcome and a microcosm of these campus-wide internationalization efforts, and the development of this intercultural environment has been intentional and coordinated. VCU Globe is a campus-wide initiative, and one that recognizes, understands, and attends to institutional culture (Whitt et al., 2008). Designed and developed by an interdisciplinary team of faculty, students, and community partners, VCU Globe boasts intersecting curricular, co-curricular, and extra-curricular components made possible by the rich and vibrant learning environment of a newly-constructed, purpose-built residence hall that features designated instructional space.

Utilizing Peter Stearns' assertion that "leadership in global education can and should come from a variety of sources," (Stearns, 2009, p. 151) the structure and administration of the VGM is shared by Global Education Office (GEO) and the Division of Student Affairs. The centralized organizational structure of GEO optimizes global educational initiatives and is fundamental to the success of such a student-centered initiative (Stearns, 2009). VCU Globe is administered by a director, who works with a team of three assistant directors to manage the three components of the VGM.

THE VCU GLOBE MODEL (VGM)

From the various contexts that led to the development of the VGM, including reflecting on and advancing the institution's mission, a vision of the holistic, structured, intercultural environment as a way to develop global competence was paramount (Whitt, Elkins Nesheim, Guentzel, Kellogg, McDonald, & Wells, 2008). The design of the VGM is ambitious: coordinated curriculum, residential programming, and global engagement both on campus and in new communities locally and abroad, form three distinct, yet interrelated components that overlap and prepare students to navigate within and between global communities at home and abroad, in professional and personal contexts. Students expand their identity as global citizens by developing their skills in leadership and teamwork both in global education and in their academic majors. In VCU Globe's classes and programs, students are exposed to the impact of global migration and become more aware of globalization's role in the lives of people around the world. Through global engagement efforts, such as English-language support in the form of conversation partners, the VGM addresses some of the challenges that both domestic and international students face in participating fully in a globalized community. Through co-curricular activities and the residential experience, this sustained interaction and engagement between program participants and international students is encouraged.

The LLC itself, regardless of its focus, is a hybrid residential-academic experience that provides students with an integrated program of both curricular and co-curricular requirements. Defined as a "seamless learning environment," in which the boundaries between in- and out-of-class experiences are blurred, LLCs are places where students can learn most effectively (Pascarella & Terenzini, 2005; Wawrzynski et al., 2009, Whitt et al., 2008). Global education LLCs have their roots in international houses, the first of which was established in 1908 by Dr. Waldo Stevenson at Pennsylvania University (McClanahan, 2014). Since that time, numerous, more complex global education and international studies LLCs have been developed on campuses around the United States. These communities range from those that focus on the social sciences (Global Communities at University of Maryland) or the core curriculum (Global Awareness through Education (GATE) at the University of Texas at Tyler) to programs that require only a semester or academic year commitment (Global Village at Indiana University; Global Scholars Program at the University of Michigan) to communities designed for incoming first-year students (Global Crossroads at the University of Illinois at Urbana-Champaign; Global Village at Oregon State University) or programs that focus on study abroad (Global Citizens LLC at the University of South Florida).

The VGM takes a more all-encompassing approach. Launched in January of 2013, VCU Globe is a carefully-designed, six-semester program, open to students in all disciplines, that is centered on global competency. Students enter the program in the spring of their first year as part of a cohort, the cohort moves through the program together and shares common courses and experiential learning activities. After successfully completing the requirements of the program, students earn a certificate of completion in global education. When designing the VGM, administrators adapted the programmatic structure of another LLC at the same institution, ASPiRE (Academic Scholars Program in Real Environments), which has a community-engagement focus. ASPiRE's four-semester curriculum includes program-centered seminars and core courses as well as community engagement service along with a multi-faceted co-curriculum, which includes coordinated residential activities and leadership training.

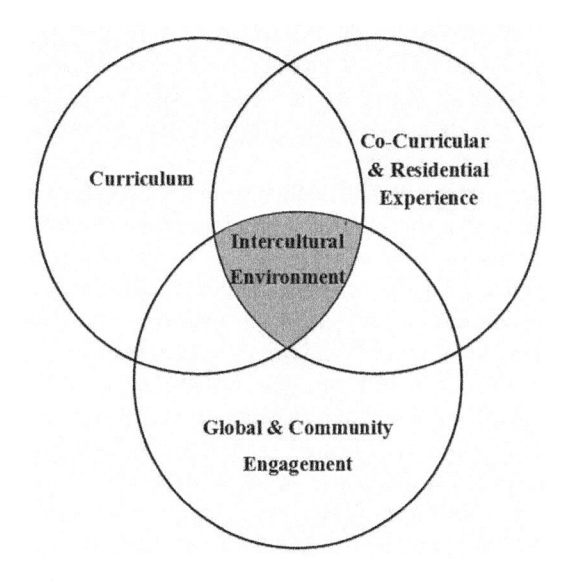

Diagram 1. The VCU Globe Model (diagram byChristina Marino).

The VGM includes three integrated components (Diagram 1) designed to prepare students for the skills needed for a successful life in an increasingly globalized world: 1) curriculum: students complete twelve credits of specialized coursework in intercultural competence, global leadership, and related topics, and are able to demonstrate critical thought in reference to issues and topics in global contexts; 2) co-curricular and residential experience: international and domestic students share apartments in a residence hall designed for the program in which frequent co-curricular activities provide opportunities for sustained, intentional, intercultural communication and learning; and 3) global and community engagement: students engage in a minimum of forty hours of service with and for members of other cultures on campus and in communities locally.

The learning outcomes for the VGM are clearly defined. After participating in the program, students are expected to demonstrate abilities to serve as culture brokers across personal and cultural borders; to demonstrate critical thought in reference to issues and topics in global contexts; to demonstrate an understanding of the causes and impact of global migration on people and communities; to engage local, national, and global communities to affect positive outcomes, including greater access to cultural resources; and to demonstrate abilities in leadership and teamwork.

Having developed clear learning outcomes informs the formative and summative assessments used to measure student learning and program success. The complexity of the VGM requires various assessment methods. As students (rising sophomores) begin the program, they are given a pre-assessment designed by the GEO specifically for VCU Globe that assesses their knowledge as they enter the program. Questions are based on the learning outcomes; for instance, students are asked about their understanding of global migrations and definitions of culture. The pre-test establishes a baseline of the students' knowledge, and is compared to subsequent cohorts. As students complete the program, they take the same survey as a post-test to measure learning

The staff uses the quantitative and qualitative information to improve the program as well as to report on the success of the program to the Global Education Office. Not only does the director report monthly on the program's progress, but an annual report is compiled that links the program's learning outcomes and student success to university-level initiatives outlined in the *Quest for Distinction*. Feedback is solicited from international students and campus and community partners in order to improve the global and community engagement component.

Students regularly evaluate their experience and progress in the program. Feedback from orientation is collected each fall, and a Study Abroad Interest Survey is administered (In the spring of 2014, 85% of VCU students indicated that they were interested in study abroad during their undergraduate career). In the second-semester of the program, students are given a specially-designed Program Outcomes Survey, at mid-semester, to determine the success of the intercultural environment through an evaluation of each program component (as it related to learning outcomes). Specifically students are asked about the introduction of key global learning concepts in class as well as impressions of co-curricular activities, global engagement experiences, and the living environment. Each semester students evaluate the performance of their instructors in a standardized evaluation form.

Curriculum

Through the VGM, global education content is integrated into students' area of study. The twelve-hour VCU Globe curriculum includes six 1-credit globally-focused seminars, a special globally-focused section of the university's 200-level research and writing course, and one 3-credit upper-level globally-themed elective course. Students take a 1-credit seminar each semester of the program. Through these courses, students learn about the challenges and opportunities caused by globalization and the importance that global competency plays in helping to address these issues

(Blondin, Bozeman, & Russell, 2013). In the first year, students are introduced to core concepts, including global education as a learning paradigm, the role of the culture broker in professional fields, and the idea of global citizenship. Students then explore definitions of culture and community, intercultural communication, emerging ideas of global leadership, and the global commons. VCU Globe students are exposed to the impact of global migration and become more aware of globalization's role in the lives of people around the world. The interdisciplinary curriculum fosters students' awareness of the skills required of a global citizen and culture broker, while the applied dimensions of the courses are intended to expose students to a wide range of individuals and groups of people, and to have direct and substantive contact with worldviews and experiences different from their own. The global and community engagement components are infused throughout the coursework.

Global and Community Engagement

The applied dimensions of the VGM complement the theoretical concepts examined in classes. As students learn about intercultural communication and the challenges of globalization in the first full year of the program, they serve as peer mentors to international students. In the second year, students serve in new communities in the local area, and put their knowledge and skills in practice as they gain experience in service across cultural boundaries. Demonstrating the ability to serve as culture brokers, or mediators, across personal and cultural borders and the ability to engage local, national, and global communities to affect positive outcomes is a learning outcome of the program.

VCU Globe prepares skilled culture brokers to welcome and support international students. VCU Globe is the one of the first programs to employ a credit-bearing curricular platform for students to provide peer mentoring and support to incoming international students. In fact, the global engagement component is designed to link VCU Globe participants and international students, scholars, and visitors on campus and to provide students with opportunities to practice and enhance culture brokering skills (Bozeman, 2013). The global engagement component is the structured and sustained way in which program participants interact with international students, scholars, and visitors (Leask, 2009). The VGM's global engagement links these groups together, both in-person and virtually, primarily for the exchange of cultural knowledge and language practice (Patterson, Botero Carrillo, & Solano Salinas, 2012). Participants must complete at least ten hours of service each semester during the first full year of the program.

Focus is on the success of VCU's international student participants and VCU Globe students in developing cross-cultural competencies, which is assessed relative to intercultural skills outcomes. According to Leask (2009), "cultural diversity on campus and intercultural learning are linked through internationalization of the curriculum only if there is a strong emphasis on carefully structured and designed interactive and collaborative learning processes" (p. 208). Specifically, the VGM is interested in assessing students' abilities to serve as culture brokers, to engage global communities to affect positive outcomes, and to lead and work as a team.

Recognizing the need among VCU's diverse domestic student population to develop global awareness and among international students to adapt to American culture on and off campus, as well as the demand for cross-cultural competencies in both groups, the VGM provides many opportunities for engagement. The integrated academic and residential experience provided by VCU Globe enables both domestic and international participants to enhance global competency and to gain success as global citizens. For example, program participants design and lead interactive sessions on American culture and on academic skills and resources (International Student Learning Labs); provide English language support under the guidance of ESL faculty (English Language Program Cultural Ambassadors), assist international students with English language acquisition and practice in a semi-structured environment (GEO Conversation Partners); and work with native speakers in order to improve their abilities in a foreign language (Native Speaker Connection). Other more structured initiatives are designed to encourage the exchange of cultural knowledge between international populations and program participants, and to give students leadership experience in a structured intercultural context. These include orienting students to the library (International Student Library Tours) and facilitating roundtable discussions with international visitors on campus (Global Engagement Series Facilitators). Participants can also support international students in the design and implementation of a required course project (Focused Inquiry E-Portfolio Support), interact in an informal environment with international students (GEO Global Cafes) and learn from international students, visitors, and faculty (Global Engagement Series).

VCU Globe exposes students directly to globalization in the local community and abroad. Students entering the second full year of the program work with community partners within the local area. The community engagement component is designed to strengthen the partnership between VCU and the local and global communities. In the context of VCU Globe, community engagement refers to engagements with members of diverse cultures and communities who reside off campus, both in the local area and abroad. Students participate in service-learning by working with members of immigrant and/or refugee populations at selected, off-campus sites with the purpose of improving outcomes for at-risk populations and increasing students' civic and academic learning. The overall goal of the community outreach component of VCU Globe is to gain a better understanding of the forces of global migration and the migrant experience as well as to apply theory to real-world situations, to improve intercultural competency, and to develop the role as culture broker.

Community partner opportunities are diverse, and represent an attempt to serve the local community needs while accommodating the program's needs and student schedules. The four strategic community partners include a public middle school with a large population of immigrant, refugee, and first-generation English-language learners; a community center that serves the city's Latino community, particularly recent arrivals from rural indigenous communities); adult refugees and immigrants in Civics and English as a Second Language classes; and a clinic that serves the uninsured. Participants also have the opportunity to engage in service with communities abroad, often communities represented by recently-arrived immigrants in the Richmond area.

Co-Curricular and Residential Experience

The co-curricular and residential experience with the VGM takes advantage of the residence hall's capacity to be a "twenty-four-hour-a-day setting for intellectual engagement" (Schoem, 2004, p. 132). Co-curricular requirements are designed purposefully to integrate with and significantly enhance learning that occurs through the program's academic curriculum (Davis, Blondin, Erwin, Reed, & Slade, 2014). Program participants, comprised primarily of domestic and in-state students (nearly 90% of program participants), live together and with international students. Living together in the residence hall facilitates structured and spontaneous interactions. Students participate in a variety of co-curricular activities together on campus and off, including visits to local museums, poetry readings, dance and music instruction, interactive cooking demonstrations, workshops on global health practices, lectures, and films. In fact, program participants are encouraged and supported in interacting with international students, as international students are encouraged and supported in their interactions with program participants (Leask, 2009). This specialized, multicultural programming enhances the undergraduate students' sense of community and belonging (Spanierman, Soble, Mayfield, Neville, Aber, Khuri, & De La Rosa, 2013), and increases social ties for the international students (Kashima & Loh, 2006; Urban & Palmer, 2014).

Study Abroad

Studying abroad is not a mandatory component of VCU Globe, but making program-specific opportunities available is paramount. VCU Globe-specific opportunities are distinctive and have been strategically designed to expose students to a wide range of individuals and groups of people, and for students to have direct and substantive contact with worldviews different from their own. All three components of the VGM overlap in the program-generated study abroad courses in Oaxaca, Mexico and Doha, Qatar; an intentional intercultural environment is created abroad.

VCU Globe piloted a program in Oaxaca, Mexico, in the summer of 2013. The Oaxaca program immerses students in rural communities, and provides a simulacrum of extended international development work, such as Peace Corps service. Under the direction of VCU Globe's Assistant Director of Community Outreach, students work with a locally-based nonprofit community partner, Fundación En Vía, which provides no-interest microloans to Zapotec women in communities near Oaxaca. Participants teach English to Zapotec villagers in Teotitlán del Valle, and use intercultural competencies and skills to adjust their teaching to challenging situations and to their learners' needs and behaviors. As a result of the experience, one participant wrote, "I learned many valuable skills [among them]: never to assume something or give in to stereotypes and to remember cultural details [such as] personal space, greetings and gestures that may or may not be appropriate," while another reflected, "This experience has taught me to ... assess the needs of the culture I am working with so I can identify community service projects that could be tackled through nonprofit organizations" (Ingber, 2014, p. 13). The experience also elicited empathy from a student who observed: "I expect to interact with international students on a deeper level. I now understand the struggle of being in another culture, learning a new language, and trying to make friends" (Ingber, 2014, p. 15). In the pilot year of the program (summer 2014), the diversity of participants was notable: 88% were first-time study abroad participants and 50% were African-American.

With VCU Globe's spring break program to Qatar, students have the opportunity to visit VCU's campus in Doha. This short-term program offers further opportunities for students to build their awareness of the skills required of a global citizen and to have direct and substantive contact with worldviews and experiences different from their own. This program offers a unique opportunity for global engagement through participation in campus activities at VCUQ, including an art and design conference, an Arabic language workshop, and other social and academic activities coordinated with VCUQ students. Students meet with educators, professionals, expatriates, and immigrants and others to discuss life and education in Qatar, and in doing so, examine the concept of culture broadly and study communication styles across cultures as well as the characteristics of the cultural communities in Doha, Qatar.

Significance of VCU Globe

The VGM's learner-centered environment, designed around collaboration at all levels, benefits program participants, international students, and the campus overall as well as the local community. From its inception, VCU Globe has been a campus-wide initiative that brings together the academic and student life divisions of the campus (West, 2012). The VGM engages interdisciplinary teams of students, faculty, and staff around its programmatic theme and supports high levels of student, faculty, and staff engagement (Davis et al., 2014). Many units work together in order to create a learner-centered environment that support the program's curriculum and co-curriculum, and encourages inquiry and discovery with a global perspective (West, 2012).

Furthermore, the VGM specifically creates cross-functional, interdepartmental linkages that combine resources and expertise to address the learning needs of students (Whitt et al., 2008). Specifically faculty members can apply to teach specially-designed upper-level seminars in the faculty's area of expertise that count toward the twelve hours of the VCU Globe curriculum. These experiences dramatically enhance the experiences of students and faculty and maximize the internationalization of VCU's campus and curriculum. These faculty members, from disciplines as varied as Anthropology and Health and Human Performance, are encouraged to engage in research and other scholarly endeavors with VCU Globe.

The campus impact of VCU Globe continues to grow. In 2014, program enrollment increased 233.33% from the first year of the program. VCU Globe students represent 34 different majors, with Biology (10.8%), International Studies (9.2%), Political Science (8.5%), Psychology (7.7%), and Mass Communications (6.2%) as the most popular (*VCU Globe Annual Report*, 2014). The diversity of majors, particularly STEM students, is noteworthy and indicates the ease of fitting the program into other coursework. Research has found that LLCs have a positive effect on students' social development, overall satisfaction with their university experience, and academic achievement (Spanierman et al., 2013; Wawrzynski, Jessup, Anger, Stolz, Helman, & Beaulieu, 2009). The mean GPA for program participants is consistent with this research (Stassen, 2003), as the mean GPA for program participants is .37 higher than the mean GPA for undergraduates at VCU.

The greatest impact, though, is from the contact that program participants have with international students. Fuller engagement of international students and scholars on campus can be linked to the implementation of VCU Globe, which creates an effective intercultural environment, but also allows for an "open, tolerant, and cosmopolitan university experience" for all (Kalantzis & Cope, 2000, p. 31; Leask, 2009). The synergy of these elements provides a transformative high-impact educational opportunity that develops culture brokering skills for VCU Globe participants. In 2013-2014, students devoted more than 860 hours to global engagement activities. Through collaborations and the design of the program, the VGM advances student learning dynamically and in a way that contributes to campus-wide internationalization and, above all, results in a high-impact academic and residential experience.

Adapting the VCU Globe Model

The VGM, which benefits domestic and international students by effectively utilizing campus collaborations and resources, can be extracted for use at other institutions. Not every institution will have the resources, the administrative oversight, the residence hall space, the centralized international office, faculty participation and buy-in, the potential for collaboration, or the institutional interest to create an international LLC or to adapt the VGM in its entirety. It is critical, however, along with emphasizing the shared and multiple manifestations of the leadership of the LLC that the perception of the intercultural environment remains clear for faculty, staff, and students to be in accord (McClanahan, 2014).

In fact, in extracting the VGM, one must consider how an intercultural environment can serve as a resource to foster international perspectives among the campus community. Intercultural skills training programs can help prepare staff to model and to guide students' intercultural competence development (Deardorff &

Jones, 2012). VCU Globe staff members, for instance, offered an intercultural communication course designed to enhance intercultural communication knowledge and to introduce tools and strategies to faculty and staff members so they may be more proficient communicators in intercultural settings, both inside and outside of the classroom.

The VGM can be changed in part, and could be used for smaller cohorts of students, or for shorter lengths of time. The programmatic structure can be simplified to include only co-curricular activities or limited global and community engagement opportunities. The VGM can be adapted for a study abroad experience; for instance, practitioners can capitalize on already-established strategic partnerships with international universities to form the foundation of expanding program-specific education abroad opportunities. As far as global engagement activities, practitioners are encouraged to capitalize on and to incorporate pre-existing initiatives, such as workshops for international students, language-partner programs, and other outreach activities.

Even with resources and the support of academic and student affairs divisions, creating an intercultural environment on any campus has challenges. The integration of the global education curricula into certain disciplines, particularly ones in which there is little room for electives or course selection, can make it difficult to attract certain undergraduate students. The curriculum itself, along with the rigidity of students' course schedules, can be a challenge. Finances must always be a consideration as one considers adapting the VGM. Costs of living on campus in the designated residence hall of the LLC will be a factor. Although the LLC does not cost more than other residence halls on campus, some students perceive on-campus housing to be more expensive than off-campus housing. If a study abroad experience is offered, the costs and length of time must be taken into consideration. Additionally, financial aid plays an important role in helping to facilitate experiences. The cost of tuition must be considered as well.

The community outreach component of the VGM allows students to demonstrate global learning. Managing the expectations of partners, on campus and off, and working closely to sustain these relationships, is paramount to success. The challenge to practitioners is how to connect global learning in the classroom to work in the community, both locally and abroad, as well as how to leverage resources as well as identify and cultivate community partners. Realizing how to identify and to integrate students' academic, career, and scheduling demands with the genuine needs of the community in an effort to initiate meaningful interactions and to increase the intercultural competencies of students is critical.

CONCLUSION

This chapter examined strategies for developing and implementing an intercultural environment for undergraduate students at an institution of higher learning by using VCU Globe, a global education LLC at Virginia Commonwealth University, as a case study. The program prepares students to become "culture brokers" by developing their global competencies, skills and experiences needed to navigate the complexities of globalization. The VGM establishes the intercultural environment at the intersection of three interrelated, but distinct components. The programmatic structure, which consists of the curriculum, co-curriculum and residential experience, and global and community engagement activities, employs intentional interactions between program participants, international students, visitors, and community members in locally and abroad to help participants become effective culture brokers and mediate across difference. This model can be applied at other institutions through an understanding of external and institutional contexts. The program's implementation as well as the vision that informs the VCU Globe Model allows practitioners to adapt aspects of the program at their own institutions.

REFERENCES

Altbach, P. G. & Knight, J. (2007). The internationalization of higher education: Motivations and realities. *Journal of Studies in International Education, 11*(3–4), 290–305. doi:10.1177/1028315307303542

Blondin, J., Bozeman, L., & Russell, R. (2013). *VCU Globe: The synergy of collaboration across the campus and in the community*. Unpublished manuscript, VCU Globe, Virginia Commonwealth University, Richmond, VA.

Bozeman, L. (2013). *The global engagement component of VCU Globe*. Unpublished manuscript, VCU Globe, Virginia Commonwealth University, Richmond, VA.

Brown, R. M. (2014). *Global Priorities Report*. Unpublished manuscript, Global Education Office, Virginia Commonwealth University, Richmond, VA.

Davis, M., Blondin, J., Erwin, C., Reed, T., & Slade, M. (2014). *Living-learning communities guidelines*. Unpublished manuscript, Virginia Commonwealth University, Richmond, VA.

Deardorff, D., & Jones, E. (2012) Intercultural competence: An emerging focus in international higher education. In D. K. Deardorff, H. de Wit, J. Heyl, & T. Adams (Eds.), *The Sage handbook of international higher education* (pp. 283–303). Thousand Oaks, CA: Sage.

Fischer, K. (2014). *Retention is a growing issue as more international students come to U.S. Chronicle of Higher Education*. Retrieved from http://chronicle.com/article/Retention-Is-a-Growing-Issue/146807/.

Global education curriculum document. (2012). Unpublished manuscript, Global Education Office, Virginia Commonwealth University, Richmond, VA.

Hunter, B., White, G., & Godbey, G. (2006). What does it mean to be globally competent? *Journal of Studies in International Education, 10*(3), 267–285.

Ingber, B. (2014). VCU globe in Oaxaca: Outcomes, evaluations, suggestions. Unpublished manuscript, VCU Globe, Virginia Commonwealth University, Richmond, VA.

Jezewski, M., & Sotnik, P. (2001). *Culture brokering: Providing culturally competent rehabilitation services to foreign-born persons*. Buffalo, NY: Center for International Rehabilitation Research Information and Exchange.

Kalantzis, M., & Cope, B. (2000). Towards an inclusive and international higher education. In R. King, D. Hill, & B. Hemmings (Eds.), *University and diversity: Changing perspectives, policies and practices in Australia* (pp. 30–53). Wagga, Australia: Keon.

Kashima, E. S. & Loh, E. (2006). International students' acculturation: Effects of international, conational, and local ties and need for closure. *International Journal of Intercultural Relations, 30*(4), 471–485. doi:10.1016/j.ijintrel.2005.12.003

Kennesaw State University. (2014). *Global engagement competency*. Retrieved from https://web.kennesaw.edu/sacs/global_engagement.

Leask, B. (2009). Using formal and informal curricula to improve interactions between home and international students. *Journal of Studies in International Education, 13*(2), 205–221. doi: 10.1177/1028315308329786

McClanahan, S. (2014). The global neighborhood: Programming initiatives with international living-learning communities. *Journal of International Students, 4*(2), 191–95. Retrieved from http://jistudents.files.wordpress.com/2013/12/2014-4-2-7-global-neighborhood-programs.pdf

Olson, C. L., Green, M. F., & Hill, B. A. (2005). *Building a strategic framework for comprehensive internationalization*. Washington, DC: American Council on Education.

Pascarella, E. T., & Terenzini, R. T. (2005). *How college affects students, volume 2, a third decade of research*. San Francisco, CA: Jossey-Bass.

Patterson, L. M., Botero Carrillo, P., & Solano Salinas, R. (2012). Lessons from a global learning virtual classroom. *Journal of Studies in International Education, 16*(2), 182–197. doi:10.1177/1028315311398665

Redden, E. (2014). The international-friendly campus. Inside Higher Ed. Retrieved from https://www.insidehighered.com/news/2014/05/30/international-educators-discuss-ways-make-campus-more-international-student-friendly.

Reimers, F. M. (2014). Bringing global education to the core of the undergraduate curriculum. *Diversity & Democracy, 17*(2). Retrieved from http://www.aacu.org/diversitydemocracy/vol17no2/reimers.cfm

Schoem, D. (2004). Sustaining living-learning programs. In J. L. Laufgraben & N. S. Shapiro (Eds.), *Sustaining and improving learning communities* (pp. 130–156). San Francisco, CA: John Wiley & Sons, Inc.

Shams, A. & George, C. (2006). Global competency: An interdisciplinary approach. *Academic Exchange Quarterly, 10*(4).

Soria, K. M. & Troisi, J. (2014). Internationalization at home alternatives to study abroad: Implications for students' development of global, international, and intercultural competencies. *Journal of Studies in International Education, 18*(3), 261–280. doi:10.1177/102831531349657

Spanierman, L. B., Soble, J. R., Mayfield, J. B., Neville, H. A., Aber, M., Khuri, L., & De La Rosa, B. (2013). Living learning communities and students' sense of community and belonging. *Journal of Student Affairs Research and Practice, 50*(3), 308–25. doi:10.1515/jsarp-2013-0022

Stearns, P. M. (2009). *Educating global citizens in colleges and universities*. New York, NY: Routledge.

Urban, E. L. & Palmer, L. B. (2014). International students as a resource for internationalization of higher education. *Journal of Studies in International Education, 18*(4), 305–324.

VCU Global Education Office. (2014). *Task force for comprehensive internationalization (2014)*. Richmond, VA: Virginia Commonwealth University.

VCU Global Education Office Annual Report 2013–14. (2014). Unpublished manuscript, Virginia Commonwealth University, Richmond, VA.

Virginia Commonwealth University (2011). *Quest for distinction*. Richmond, VA: Virginia Commonwealth University.

Wawrzynski, M. R., Jessup-Anger, J. E., Stolz, K., Helman, C., & Beaulieu, J. (2009). Exploring students' perceptions of academically based living-learning communities. *The College Student Affairs Journal, 28*(1), 138–158.

West, C. (2012). Engaging stakeholders in internationalization: Strategies for collaboration. NAFSA, 1–7.

Whitt, E. J., Elkins Neshaim, B., Guentzel, M. J., Kellogg, A. H., McDonald, W. M., & Wells, C. A. (2008). "Principles of good practice" for academic and student affairs partnership programs. *Journal of College Student Development, 49*(3), 235–249.

Jill E. Blondin
Director VCU Globe
Virginia Commonwealth University

DIANA RAJENDRAN, JANET BRYANT,
PATRICIA BUCKLEY AND RYAN JOPP

7. GLOBAL CITIZENSHIP

*Surfacing the Gap between Rhetoric and Reality
in Internationalization of Management Curricula*

INTRODUCTION

Supporting students' in their development of global citizenship (GC) is recognised as an integral part of higher education (Aneas & Montané, 2009; Brigham, 2011; Shiel, 2007; Thanosawan & Laws, 2013; Zahabioun, Yousefy, Yarmohammadian, & Keshtiaray, 2013). As such, universities in many parts of the world today are attempting to institutionalize GC by way of engaging in a process of internationalizing their curricula, and increasingly appear to be promoting 'Global Citizenship' as a core graduate outcome (Thanosawan & Laws, 2013). Indeed the academic literature is awash with research articles promulgating the benefits of, and necessity for, internationalization of the curriculum (IoC); and for developing students as global citizens (see, for example, Aneas & Montané, 2009; Childress, 2010; Clifford, 2014; Shiel, 2007; Zahabioun et al., 2013). Yet, given the complexity of the workplace and world today, the range of interpretations used by practitioners in unravelling the term global citizenship is challenged by 'conceptual fuzziness' (Hicks, 2003).

The lack of clarity around what global citizenship means in terms of student learning within our particular disciplines is troubling when many universities' vision and mission statements mandate that we 'internationalize the curriculum.' If faculty fail to have a clear conceptual picture of 'what' comprise attributes of a global citizen, then how can they be expected to develop an internationalized curriculum supported by appropriate intercultural pedagogy to develop students as global citizens? How can faculty bridge the gap between the institutional rhetoric on internationalization and intercultural classroom pedagogy to better develop the global citizenship attributes frequently espoused in higher education institutions? What might this process look like within a departmental unit?

As a group of four management educators from the Swinburne Business School at Swinburne University of Technology in Victoria, Australia, we shared a joint interest in exploring intercultural pedagogical practice for Internationalizing the Curriculum (IoC) to support development of global citizenship attributes. To achieve this we believed that besides just adding international content, IoC must integrate intercultural pedagogical approaches with the broad aim of developing an inclusive, cross-culturally sensitive, co-operative, and collaborative learning community within our department. However in order to accomplish this, the development of a shared understanding of GC attributes was deemed essential in order to accomplish our vision of an internationalized management curriculum and globally mindful graduates.

This chapter highlights the process used among a group of four management educators to conceptualize the IoC process. We agreed to use the OXFAM GC attributes (for details see – Stage 2 – Our approach section of the chapter) as a vehicle to elicit ratings of the importance of the OXFAM global citizenship attributes; and, to initiate conversations with eight other faculty on how they rated the extent to which they embedded GC attributes into curriculum they developed for the management program.

Why Internationalization of the Curriculum?

The process of internationalizing the curriculum is a key factor in developing attributes of global citizenship in the domain of higher education. IoC as a process is created and negotiated as a means for developing students global citizenship attributes. Our examination of the literature brought forward many interesting and challenging issues about the relationship between IoC and GC. For the purpose of this chapter we focus on differing rationales for IoC, and how these impact on definitions and interpretations of these terms.

The range of rationales for why institutions support faculty engagement in IoC process include economic, political, and social perspectives. From an economic standpoint for example, Shiel (2007) posits that employers prefer graduates who are culturally sensitive, aware, appreciative, and understanding of diversity, and who have an international outlook. Thanosawan and Laws (2013) also point to an increasing demand for multi-lingual graduates for positions in international organisations. In contrast, Aneas and Montané (2009), take a more political perspective, and reframe GC attributes as an asset for employability in terms of social cohesion. They see this as integral for providing services to a multi-cultural society built largely on immigration.

In contrast to such economic and political understandings of what constitutes an employable graduate, with GC attributes, Andrezejewski and Alessio (1999) approach the connection between jobs and global citizenship from a primarily ethical standpoint. They stipulate that "global citizenship requires an understanding of ethical behaviour in one's personal and professional life, their philosophical and cultural values and understanding of the interrelationship of personal and professional decision/actions on society and the environment" (Andrezejewski & Alessio 1999, p.8). Shiel (2011) adds to the economic perspective that global perspectives should equally be considered as 'Education for Sustainable Development'. More recently, Shiel (2013) stipulates that the global university "will seek to ensure that global perspectives and sustainable development permeate all aspects of university systems and extends to embrace the community" (p. 44).

Thus, from a normative standpoint, the primary agenda of education is not just about employability and enhancement of the profits of global corporations, but should mandatorily encompass consideration of ethics and sustainability. Such normative assertions that education be directed to students becoming 'stewards of the earth' and participants in the pursuit of global social justice, serve to illustrate the tension between treating IoC as the means for procuring skill sets to enhance employability, and the ideals of liberal education.

IoC as an Outcome of Process Based Intercultural Pedagogy

The reform agenda across the higher education sector reflects the many tensions generated between perspectives on internationalization of the curriculum, as outlined above. The extant literature indicates that the forces of globalisation are currently driving a reform agenda across the higher education sector globally. For example, Thanosawan and Laws (2013) argue that global forces have facilitated transnational exchange not only of consumer goods, but also of human resources, intellectual capital, knowledge, and ideas. In addition, others argue that it is imperative to encourage student development which involves an understanding of global consciousness, connectivity, and responsibility (Zahabioun et al., 2013).

Unquestionably, then, as a consequence of globalisation and modernisation, the concept of GC has become more visibly entrenched into higher education agendas. It is "an intriguing term appealing to current advocates of a wide range of movements from world peace, to sustainability, to social equity and justice" (Clifford & Montgomery, 2014, p.28). Therefore, in terms of course design and pedagogy while investigating a range of definitions of IoC, it emerged that earlier understandings were often content rather than process focused. The definitions were often modelled on the OECD (1995) prescription that "curricula with an international orientation in content [*should be*] aimed at preparing students for performing (professionally/socially) in an international and multicultural context and designed for domestic students as well as foreign students" (p. 4).

Given that globalisation impacts upon economic, political, and social domains of human life, significant for higher education, IoC may be better understood not just from a curriculum content standpoint, but also dependent on a process oriented intercultural pedagogy to support development of GC.

For instance, Brigham (2011) explores GC in relation to higher education in Canada identifying several key themes including values, ethics, identity, a social justice perspective, intercultural skills, and a sense of responsibility to act with a global mindset. For Brigham then, GC represents a way of understanding how the world works. The focus is on links between our own lives and those of people throughout the world, and is thus primarily relational. If GC is understood more as a way of seeing, based on understandings of social justice and equity, other people's reality, diversity, inter-connectedness, and ways that people can make a difference, then process based intercultural pedagogy becomes fundamental. This means including international content alone will not be sufficient. If, as Brigham suggests, GC entails ways of seeing and acting including the exercising of political rights, critical thinking, and challenging injustice (Brigham, 2011), the content orientations set out earlier by the OECD clearly need to be revisited.

This shift in focus from a content approach to internationalised curriculum to an outcome and learner centered focus on what constitutes a global citizen is reflected in the definition given by Shiel (2007). Accordingly a global citizen is defined "as a person who operates effectively in the context of diversity, and who is empowered to bring about change to enhance society" (Shiel, 2007, p. 153). Haigh (2008) too, in positioning GC alongside the discourse on sustainability, challenges a neo-liberal approach to IoC, thus giving rise to healthy debates on curriculum design. Internationalization of the curriculum therefore entails "incorporation of an international and intercultural dimension into the preparation, delivery and outcomes of a program of study" (see Leask 200, p. 209). Ninnes and Hellstén (2005) recognise that in many higher educational institutions IoC agendas are effectively a site for exchanges and conflicts, suggesting that interfacing IoC with discourses on GC remains inherently problematic.

Crosling, Edwards, & Schroder, (2008) in their analysis of implementation issues, point out that, although some Australian universities have revised their aims and objectives to incorporate international skills and knowledge as core graduate attributes, that "little work has been done to translate this priority into curriculum documents and teaching practice" (p. 118). This finding is indicative of a gap between institutional rhetoric on IoC in higher education and teaching practice, in the Australian case.

The upshot of our review of current definitions made it increasingly apparent that, despite great academic interest in both IoC and GC, no singular definition exists for either construct. Rather a wide array of student attributes and outcomes are put forward as a vehicle for including GC in the curriculum. To this end we explored a number of learner-centred approaches and practical strategies used internationally for achieving GC by means of IoC.

Strategies for Implementing IoC and Development of GC Attribute

Interventions by international scholars that exemplify the implementation of teaching strategies designed to develop GC attributes include a learner-centred focus used by Kroesen, Klaassen, & Enserink (2012) which leverages on the challenges and benefits of global student diversity in the classroom. 'The 1000 Flowers Project', implemented in the faculty at Delft University of Technology (TU Delft), Netherlands (2012), provides examples of cross-cultural initiatives from both process and content perspectives to open up "the black box of the abstract notion of GC" enabling consideration of "the concrete values and behavioural patterns of which it is composed" (p. 74). As an outcome, Kroesen et al. (2012) claim that egalitarian and dialogical forms of communication and cooperation become embedded into traditionally hierarchical relationships, thus representing a cultural transition for many students by providing insights into the universal nature of human feelings common across generations, and cultures.

In addition, Aneas and Montané (2009) explored the need to develop intercultural education in the Spanish university sector, in order to empower students with cross-cultural competences aimed to reduce culture-shock and improve their intercultural experiences. Whilst in Thailand, the government has put forward GC as a desirable graduate attribute in their higher education reform program, whilst acknowledging that GC within the Thai context differs from understandings held by Western institutions (Thanosawan & Laws, 2013). Nevertheless, Thailand's higher education reforms are designed to create graduates who are equipped to deal with an increasingly complex and interconnected world.

The rapid increase in courses claiming to internationalize their curriculum for the purposes of supporting student development of GC attributes should, from a strategic standpoint, also embrace a shift of focus from treating curriculum as the province of external regulatory frameworks to consideration of the more subjective/psycho-social domains of intercultural competence and identity. Cultural intelligence is an individual's capability to function effectively (see Earley & Ang, 2003) in culturally diverse settings. According to Kim, Kirkman, and Chen (2008) effective participation in such contexts requires four factors critical to cultural intelligence: cognitive skills, metacognitive skills, a motivational dimension, and a behavioural dimension. Eisenberg et al. (2013) investigate *how* business schools contribute to making students culturally competent by documenting the effects of educational interventions on students' cultural competencies, specifically Cultural Intelligence (CQ). They found that academic training through cross cultural management courses were effective in increasing students' overall CQ. Importantly, such courses had pronounced effects on the cognitive and metacognitive aspects of CQ, although effects on motivational CQ were mixed, and on behavioural CQ not significant. Their findings confirmed that international experience positively affects CQ (Eisenberg et al., 2013, p. 618).

Other theorists such as Simms (2006) see that global citizenship, although dynamic, is embedded and "shaped by conditions of time and place" and is thus neither a unitary condition, nor necessarily a fixed identity (p. 171). Simms (2006) raises critical questions vis-à-vis designing curriculum for business programs: "When living and working in a country other than one's own, whose rules apply? ... Does one oblige the host country, or does one presume to apply one's own cultural values, management principles and ethics?" (p. 172).

Examination of prevailing strategies suggests that, although there is a growing focus on developing GC attributes through internationalizing the curriculum, no universal consensus exists regarding their operationalization. This finding provided us with the impetus to explore how our university, and in particular our department, valued and encouraged the development of GC attributes amongst our students, through our teaching practices.

OUR APPROACH

Our aim was to uncover how faculty embed GC attributes to develop global citizenship attributes in students undertaking a management program. We saw an opportunity to explore whether gaps exist between how the institutional rhetoric on GC is interpreted, and how these interpretations are implemented as teaching practice in design and delivery of management curriculum - or alternatively between the rhetoric of the university, and the reality of the classroom practice.

Our project was conducted in the following stages:

Stage 1 – Collaborative literature review to select a range of responses to effectively implementing IoC;

Stage 2 – Developing our own shared definition of IoC and its relationship to GC as a framework for designing our data collection instrument;

Stage 3 – Survey Administration;

Stage 4 – Data Analysis and findings;

Stage 5 – Discussion and write up.

Stage 1

The four authors of this chapter conducted a collaborative literature review. Sharing the outcomes of our individual research was an integral part of mapping the process that followed subsequently. This discussion forum informed the research design and was foundational for evolving our shared understanding, and the relationship between IoC and GC. As a result of the review, we identified a range of strategies that represent current IoC initiatives at universities around the world. Consistent themes also emerged throughout our review, including the inevitability of globalisation, the critical importance of ethics and sustainability, as well as the role of internationalization of the curriculum in enhancing student employability. A selective representation of this stage is presented in the literature review section of this chapter which provided a framework for the next stages.

Stage 2

Based on the outcomes of the literature review, the research team agreed on the following shared definition of the concept of IOC - *'IoC requires an acknowledgement and understanding of how different cultural and societal values may underpin and fundamentally contribute within (and to) an educational context.'*

We agreed that IoC requires acknowledgement and understanding of how different cultural and societal values may underpin and fundamentally contribute within (and to) an educational context; and, saw this as being 'foundational to adopting a counter hegemonic approach to learning, based on critical analysis of Western ways of Knowing (epistemologies)' (see Rajendran et al., 2014). Our group deliberated further to agree on a useful working definition of Global Citizenship. To this end we selected the quintessential OXFAM (2006) definition stating a global citizen is an individual who:

GCA1. Is aware of the wider world and has a sense of their own role as a world citizen;

GCA2. Respects and values diversity;

GCA3. Has an understanding of how the world works economically, politically, socially, culturally, technologically, and environmentally;

GCA4. Is outraged by social injustice;

GCA5. Participates in and contributes to the community at a range of levels from local to global;

GCA6. Is willing to act to make the world a more sustainable place

GCA7. Takes responsibility for their actions.

The impetus for using this OXFAM framework of GC attributes was that Zahabioun et al. (2013) and Shiel (2007), who discuss its utility for determining GC attributes within diverse international contexts. Zahabioun et al. (2013) focuses on the moral importance of GC, explaining that it is inextricably linked to ethics, and to the understanding that the world and humankind are interdependent. Similarly, Shiel (2007) discusses the OXFAM attributes within the context of 'respecting diversity' and 'developing a global perspective' to empower students to develop as critical beings (p. 154). We noted that both of these researchers embraced definitions of GC that were process based, thus aligning clearly with the definitions we had arrived at within our research group. Thus we applied the OXFAM framework for initiating dialogue with faculty, specifically responsible for designing and implementing curriculum for the Management discipline at our University.

Stage 3

Together the research team designed and administered a survey to initially establish how faculty in the management group firstly rated the importance of the OXFAM Global Citizenship attributes, and then to rate the extent to which these attributes were operationalized through their teaching practice. Using a Rating Scale participants were asked to indicate how important they believed each of the GC attributes was, (1= Extremely Important, 2= Very Important, 3=Somewhat Important, 4=Slightly Important, 5=Not Important). Next, they were asked to rank how much they believed they actually encouraged or developed these attributes in students through their teaching 1=Always, 2=Nearly Always, 3=Sometimes, 4= Rarely, 5= Never). Given the small sample size, and the high degree of consensus of ranking around these categories, a later decision was made to collapse the 5 point Rating scale into three categories for data analysis. This facilitated clearer representation of the findings. As we administered this survey in a face-to-face context it did not preclude a few passing comments or reflections from the participants. These were duly noted.

Stage 4

A specific understanding of how faculty ranked the importance of the OXFAM GC attributes and how they thought that they encouraged or developed the GC attributes in students is represented in Table 1.

For Question 1, participants were asked to rate each of the GC attributes, from 'Extremely Important' to 'Unimportant'. The initial results suggest overall agreement amongst all participants that each of the GC attributes was important. However, two participants (Participants 5 and 8) identified some attributes as only 'Slightly Important', or even 'Unimportant'. Interestingly, both of these participants referred to Statement 4, 'The student is outraged by social injustice' with Participant 5 claiming that this attribute was only 'Slightly Important', and Participant 8 ranking it as 'Unimportant'. Given that Participant 5 was ranking GC attributes in relation to an introductory management unit, we speculated that including issues of social injustice may have been too conceptually challenging to include at a first-year level. Alternatively, a social justice agenda may have been felt beyond the brief of first year curriculum already constrained by the demands of introducing students to basic management concepts. The same participant also classified Statement 5, as 'Slightly Important'. This could be interpreted as a pragmatic concern due to typically large first-year enrollments and the problem of operationalising the GC attribute that 'The student participates in and contributes to the community at a range of levels from local to global'.

For Question 2, participants were asked to rank the degree to which they felt they developed the GC attributes through their teaching practice. Overall, the results for Question 2 were in line with Question 1, with participants stating that they 'Always', 'Nearly Always', or 'Sometimes' encourage students to develop each of these attributes. Interestingly, the only participants to answer with either 'Rarely' or 'Never' were participants 5 and 8, the same individuals discussed in relation to Question 1. Furthermore, their non-committal responses were consistent with their answers to Question 1, and made in relation to Statement 4, 'The student is outraged by social injustice'.

When the results of Q1 were compared with participants' rankings in Q2 of how they embedded the GC attributes via their teaching practice, while overall the rankings for each attribute in Q1 and Q2 followed quite similar response patterns for Q2, there was once again variation in response to GC attribute 3. Although all participants deemed this GC attribute to be 'Extremely Important' in Q1, only 70% ranked it as something they felt able to develop in their students through their teaching.

Some unexpected comments emerged from faculty in the course of administering the survey, as they undertook the ranking exercise. From these, it was evident to those administering the survey that while Q1 presented faculty with few challenges, the ranking exercise for Q2 presented a much greater struggle for faculty to find common ground for articulating how the GC attributes could be and were embedded into their teaching practice.

Table 1. Comparison of participants' perceived importance of the Oxfam GC Attributes and their operationalization in teaching.

Perceived Importance of the OXFAM GC Attributes			OXFAM Global Citizenship Attributes (GCAs)	Operationalization of GC Attributes Through Teaching		
1-2 Extremely Important Or Very Important	3-4 Somewhat Important Or Slightly Important	5 Not Important		1-2 Always Or Nearly Always	3-4 Sometimes Or Rarely	5 Never
90% (n=9)	10% (n=1)	0% (n=0)	**GCA 1** Is aware of the wider world and has a sense of their own role as a world citizen	90% (n=9)	10% (n=1)	0% (n=0)
90% (n=9)	10% (n=1)	0% (n=0)	**GCA 2:** Respects and values diversity	80% (n=8)	20% (n=2)	0% (n=0)
100% (n=10)	0% (n=0)	0% (n=0)	**GCA 3:** Has an understanding of how the world works economically, politically, socially, culturally, technologically and environmentally	80% (n=8)	20% (n=2)	0% (n=0)
60% (n=6)	30% (n=3)	10% (n=1)	**GCA 4:** Is outraged by social injustice	60% (n=6)	30% (n=3)	10% (n=1)
60% (n=6)	40% (n=4)	0% (n=0)	**GCA 5:** Participates in and contributes to the community at a range of levels from local to global	50% (n=5)	50% (n=5)	0% (n=0)
90% (n=9)	10% (n=1)	0% (n=0)	**GCA 6:** Is willing to act to make the world a more sustainable place	60% (n=6)	40% (n=4)	0% (n=0)
90% (n=9)	10% (n=1)	0% (n=0)	**GCA 7:** Takes responsibility for their actions	70% (n=7)	30% (n=3)	0% (n=0)

Our overall finding was a lack of alignment between valuing an attribute highly (as evidenced in Q1), and the capacity for articulating how the values could be effectively realised (see Q2) through intercultural pedagogical processes to operationalise IoC.

DISCUSSION

Despite high levels of commitment exhibited to the values of GC (see Q1), from the rankings given for Q2, varying degrees of awareness amongst our faculty were evident about embedding the OXFAM GC attributes into curriculum by using specific intercultural pedagogical approaches. Importantly, our findings suggest that, although faculty positively endorsed the OXFAM GC attributes, and willingly took part in the ranking exercises, their comments suggested it was a challenge for them to engage in discourse around pedagogical approaches to make GC attributes operational in curriculum they design. Thus, we concur with Clifford and Montgomery (2014), who found that although faculty are a vital part of the change process, they lacked confidence in expressing "the knowledge and skills [required by] teaching staff to create and deliver, a curriculum for global citizenship" (p. 43).

Although faculty engaged willingly in the ranking exercise, as they participated their passing comments indicated uncertainties about sharing their understandings of intercultural pedagogical processes. Ready engagement in shared conversations around global citizenship attributes was indicative that faculty had not always had opportunities to develop intercultural pedagogical tools and skills. Despite expressing a keen commitment to the overall institutional vision for our university on IoC, and although participants genuinely endorsed the GC attributes of the OXFAM framework, their capacity for conceptualising IoC as an intercultural pedagogical process was more limited. Roman (2003) characterises this type of content oriented endorsement of IoC as the 'add and stir approach' rather than a transformative pedagogy. Indeed, Clifford and Montgomery (2014) raise the very pertinent question of whether faculty have the ability "to move beyond embedded Western, colonial knowledge and envision new curricula" (p. 43).

In addition, faculty face significant workload challenges, clearly a resource based constraint. Anecdotally, comments made by faculty suggested it was difficult to find time to incorporate various aspects of IoC and GC into the curriculum. Indeed, faculty are often time-poor (Pharo et al., 2012) and development of practical intercultural learning experiences and global case studies to inform sound intercultural pedagogical approaches can be time-consuming. Whilst some universities have support services to assist faculty with the development of programs and assessments, others are restricted by budget. This makes it difficult to incorporate GC attributes as the basis for innovative curriculum, and often requires high levels of individual commitment. Furthermore, not all universities may have the financial capacity to offer students international internships or intercultural immersion via study tours. If universities are to live up to the espoused rhetoric of internationalization, then, it is apparent that faculty need to be supported appropriately.

The outcomes of a curriculum design intervention used by Schuerholz-Lehr (2007) directly parallel our findings in that faculty struggle "with concepts such as internationalization, intercultural sensitivity, international education, global awareness, and the nefariously overused concept of Global Citizenship" (p. 181–182). Another study using a cross-disciplinary approach recommended that faculty "need a sense of psychological ownership to self-initiate changes, which are evolutionary and additive rather than subtractive" which clearly aligns with our findings (see Crossling et al. 2008, p. 113–114). Although many respondents identified ways in which they had, or may, internationalise their curricula, their quest to move beyond institutional rhetoric on GC to a more transformative curriculum in order to transcend the 'add and stir' approach, discussed above, was rather challenging.

RECOMMENDATIONS

This final section of this chapter is informed by our findings, the literature, and our discussions resulting from exploring intercultural pedagogies used within our management school. The literature review revealed the catalytic nature of the globalisation agenda and its role in driving choices made in educational institutions about student markets, degree programs to be offered, curriculum content and graduate outcomes.

Our recommendations are designed with the University, faculty, the individual scholar-practitioner, and student learner in mind. Firstly then, at the *University level* resource constraints as well as the responsibility and challenge of balancing competing interests is ever-present. Like Kroesen et al. (2012), we suggest the imperative for each institution to deal with the challenge of IoC to better strengthen inter-cultural competencies in our students, by asking the question – "Do we have an appropriate intercultural pedagogical framework for our students to become world citizens" (p. 80)?

We recommend that institutional internationalization goals are carefully articulated to ensure they reflect global citizenship / student learning objectives, such as those specified in the OXFAM attributes. In addition, some key questions must be posed, including – does the institutional vision clearly specify pedagogical bench marks that will enable evaluation against current best practice findings of international research scholars? Are there adequate resources, time allowances (workload), credit given for faculty in different disciplines to develop an intercultural pedagogy that supports students' development of GC attributes? If appropriate metrics are in place, are they equally viable for evaluating teaching practice across all disciplines?

Secondly, within the business school at our university, we recognise that one method to develop global citizens is to offer exchanges and study tours for cultural immersion. This remains a practice common for students, but not one broadly extended to academic staff (Svensson & Wihlborg, 2010). Although such pedagogies engender expansion of cultural consciousness, and undoubtedly build the 'world-mindedness' characteristics of individual staff and students, resource constraints ensure that only a few staff and very small cohorts of students are likely to benefit from such experiences. We suggest however that inquiries such as our own, at an intra-school level, help capitalise on 'world-mindedness' as a teaching resource. Extended to the inter-school level, such discourse has the potential to engage faculty with the challenges of moving beyond the paradigm of 'add on and stir' approaches. Authentic and realistic understanding and promotion of the GC attributes at the school-level is vital to student outcomes in teaching management at our business school.

At the *scholar-practitioner level,* through our inquiry we discovered that comprehension of IoC and GC is likely informed as much by individual identity and lived experiences of faculty, as it is by the rhetoric of the University. As a resource, the role of 'world-mindedness' may often be ignored or undervalued by the Academy. That said, we recommend that more effort be given to evaluating, and articulating, how our teaching practice relating to IoC and GC may be influenced by what we do 'beyond' the classic description of our professional roles. Extra-curricular activities such as engaging in lively debates amongst authors on the world stage, personal travel experiences, and reading widely and beyond one's discipline to develop an appreciation of the existence of multiple viewpoints, may contribute to faculty's ability to engage more meaningfully in the process of IoC. Indeed, authentic participation in our increasingly rich *melting-pot* classrooms, and the wider community, is a valuable and readily available source of mutual learning for both teacher and students. Such life experiences, of academics and students, make an important contribution to developing transformative curricula. Schuerholz-Lehr (2007) offers a hypothesis which we willingly subscribe to: "the ability of higher education instructors to teach for intercultural competence and world-mindedness within their professional landscape is positively related with the extent to which they have acquired a world minded-identity both on and *off* the professional landscape" (p. 188).

Finally, as international education today represents a complex and contested terrain, we strongly emphasise the need to develop an approach to curriculum design, whereby faculty are invited to look beyond the constraints of their disciplinary domains. IoC must start at the grass-roots level and extend as a *thread* across programs, subjects, and to teaching plans; most importantly it will benefit from trans-disciplinary engagement.

ALIGNING REFLECTION AND PRACTICE

We found our colleagues within the Business School were genuinely interested in IoC and GC, but were confounded by how to internationalize their curriculum so as to support students' development of GC attributes in the teaching-learning space. This resulted in IoC and GC becoming 'background work'. We recognised that interfacing reflection with practice requires intervention at many levels. This depends on clearly articulating the appropriate intercultural pedagogies to scaffold institutional rhetoric, if it is to provide a robust foundation for global citizenship objectives. Activities should capitalise on the diversity of experiences of faculty and students in a holistic way, drawing on the 'world-mindedness' of both. If this *thread* is not evident, then the link between GC and IoC is not being attended to and articulated in teaching. *How to* operationalize IoC and GC goals is likely to remain as an on-going challenge for scholar-practitioners, drawing on their 'world-mindedness' to enrich curriculum.

A useful starting point is the establishment of a 'community of practice' whose primary purpose is for the membership to share and learn from others about IoC and GC. Deciding upon a workable and accepted definition of IoC and GC will provide a strong foundation for discussion at the faculty level. A further proactive step would be a formal review of programs of study to ensure that they reflect content and assessment aimed at achieving Global Citizens.

We take pride in sharing our experience and the outcomes of this pilot project. We believe the OXFAM GC attributes are valuable as an original vehicle for instigating meaningful and intriguing conversations on IoC within groups, and among faculty. As this exploratory research has surfaced concerns regarding the operationalization of GC attributes within our Management curriculum, it has also provided impetus for further reflection on how we can work to close the gap between our institutional rhetoric and the reality of IoC to ensure our students are truly global citizens. From here the conversation begins…

CONCLUSION

A review of the literature has demonstrated the need for global recognition of the importance of an internationalized curricula and which contributes to the development of students GC attributes (Aneas & Montané, 2009; Brigham, 2011; Kelleher & Klein, 2005; Shiel, 2007; Thanosawan & Laws, 2013; Zahabioun et al., 2013). In particular, students need to understand the challenges of globalisation as well as the centrality of ethics and sustainability within the management context. From a purely pragmatic standpoint, few would argue with the proposition that a student with well-developed GC attributes gain employment more readily in managerial roles, in global organisations.

However, both the literature and the outcomes of our exploration suggest that several challenges impede realisation of such ideals. In particular, we agree with the findings of Clifford and Montgomery (2014) and Thanosawan and Laws (2013), and recognise the need for higher education administrators and teaching fraternity to broaden their thinking, and pedagogical commitments if they wish to assist students to develop GC characteristics. While our data revealed the importance of IoC and GC to teaching staff in the Management discipline, it also suggested that the curriculum is still constructed within the constraints of a dominant western paradigm. Thus, the opportunity to engage with and benefit from national and cultural diversity is not fully capitalised upon to systematically build inclusivity. We agree with authors such as Haigh (2014) and Ninnes and Hellstén (2005), who point out that IoC is a key site for the exchanges and conflicts induced by globalisation, thereby accentuating the potential for Higher Education Institutes to compromise the social ideals of GC for the sake of economic or political advantage. Proponents of emergent models of internationalization address these complex issues, by arguing that scaffolding IoC through transformative education agendas, and deepening reflective practice (see, for example, Brigham, 2011; Haigh, 2014), will implicitly mitigate such risk. In this way, inclusivity may become a reality, as well as a means for addressing the power differentials of the colonial and post-colonial world.

ACKNOWLEDGEMENTS

We gratefully acknowledge the seed funding provided by HERSDA for this study, and we would like to thank Dr. Valerie Clifford for her inspirational mentorship.

REFERENCES

Andrzejewski, J., & Alessio, J. (1999). Education for global citizenship and social responsibility. *Progressive Perspectives 1998–99 Monograph Series*, *1*, 2. Retrieved May 15, 2014 from http://www.uvm.edu/~desey/monographs

Aneas, A., & Montané, A. (2009). Let's go work together: Introducing intercultural competencies at the Universitat de Barcelona. *International Journal of Learning*, *16*(10), 355–367.

Brigham, M. (2011). Creating a global citizen and assessing outcomes. *Journal of Global Citizenship & Equity Education*, *1*(1), 15–43.

Clifford, V. (2014). Challenging conceptions of western education and promoting graduates as global citizens. *Higher Education Quarterly*, *68*(1), 28–45.

Clifford, V., & Montgomery, C. (2014) Challenging conceptions of western higher education and promoting graduates as global citizens. *Higher Education Quarterly*, *68*(1), 28–45.

Crosling, G., Edwards, R., & Schroder, B. (2008). Internationalizing the curriculum: The implementation experience in a Faculty of Business and Economics. *Journal of Higher education Policy and Management*, *30*(2), 107–121.

Earley, P. C., & Ang, S. (2003). *Cultural intelligence: Individual interactions across cultures*. Stanford, CA: Stanford University Press.

Eisenberg, J., Hyun-Jung, L., Bruck, F., Brenner, B., Claes, M-T., Mironski, J., & Bell, R. (2013). Can business schools make students culturally competent? Effects of cross-cultural management courses on cultural intelligence. *Academy of Management Learning & Education*, *12*(4), 603–621.

Haigh, M. (2014). Internationalisation, planetary citizenship and higher education Inc. *Compare*, *38*(4), 427–440.

Haigh, M. (2008). From Internationalisation to education for global citizenship: A multi-layered history. *Higher Education Quarterly*, *68*(1), 6–27.

Hicks, D. (2003). *Global education: What does it mean? The challenge of the global dimension in education*. London, England: Institute of Education.

Kelleher, A., & Klein, L. (2005). *Global perspectives: A handbook for understanding global issues* (2nd ed.). Upper Saddle River, NJ: Prentice Hall.

Kim, K., Kirkman, B. L., & Chen, G. (2008). *Cultural intelligence and international assignment effectiveness*. Armonk, NY: M. E. Sharpe.

Kroesen, O., Klaassen, R., & Enserink, B. (2012). The flowers of global citizenship. *Widening Participation and Lifelong Learning*, *13*(3), 74–78.

Leask, B. (2009). Using formal and informal curricula to improve interactions between Home and International Students. *Journal of Studies and International Education*, *13*(2), 205–221.

Leask, B. (2012). *Internationalisation of the curriculum in action: A guide*. Sydney: University of South Australia.

Ninnes, P., & Hellstén., M. (2005). Introduction: Critical engagements in the internationalization of higher education. In P. Ninnes & M. Meeri Hellstén (Eds.), *Internationalizing higher education critical explorations of pedagogy and policy* (pp. 1–8). Dordrecht, NL: Springer.

OECD. (1994). *Education in a new international setting: Curriculum development for internationalisation – Guidelines for country case study.* Paris: OECD (CERI).

Oxfam Development Education Program. (2006). *Education for global citizenship: A guide for schools.* Retrieved July 10, 2013 from http://www.oxfam.org.uk/education/gc/files/education_for_global_citizenship_a_guide_for_schools.pdf

Pharo, E. J., Davison, A., Warr, K., Nursey-Bray, M., Beswick, K., Wapstra, E., & Jones, C. (2012). Can teacher collaboration overcome barriers to interdisciplinary learning in a disciplinary university? A case study using climate change. *Teaching in Higher Education, 17*(5), 497–507. doi:10.1080/13562 517.2012.658560

Rajendran, D., Bryant, M., Buckley, P., & Jopp. R. (2014). Why internationalisation of the curriculum matters for management programs. *HERDSA News, 36*(1), 10–12.

Roman, L. (2003). Education and the contested meanings of 'Global Citizenship.' *Journal of Educational Change, 4,* 269–293. Kluwer Academic Publishers, Netherlands.

Schuerholz-Lehr, S. (2007). Teaching for global literacy in higher education: How prepared are the educators? *Journal of International Education, 11*(2), 180–204.

Shiel, C. (2007). Developing global citizens: The way forward? *International Journal of Learning, 14*(4), 153–167.

Shiel, C. (2011). *Global perspectives: ESD by another name.* Paper presented at the Green Academy, Leeds, UK.

Shiel, C. (2013). Developing global perspectives: Global citizenship and sustainable development within higher education (Doctor of Philosophy Publication), Bournemouth University.

Simms, M. (2006). The citizen factor: Engaging the language of citizenship in a global classroom. *Journal of Hispanic Higher Education, 5,* 171–183.

Svensson, L., & Wihlborg, M. (2010). Internationalising the content of higher education: The need for a curriculum perspective. *Higher Education, 60,* 595–613.

Swinburne University of Technology. (2013). Retrieved October 15, 2013 from http://www.swinburne.edu.au/policies/academic/course_approvals_policy_hed.pdf.

Thanosawan, P., & Laws, K. (2013). Global citizenship: Differing perceptions within two Thai higher education institutions. *Journal of Higher Education Policy and Management, 35*(3), 293.

Zahabioun, S., Yousefy, A., Yarmohammadian, M. H., & Keshtiaray, N. (2013). Global citizenship education and its implications for curriculum goals at the age of globalization. *International Education Studies, 6*(1), 195.

Diana Rajendran
Faculty of Business and Enterprise
Swinburne University of Technology

Janet Bryant
Faculty of Business and Enterprise
Swinburne University of Technology

Patricia Buckley
Faculty of Business and Enterprise
Swinburne University of Technology

Ryan Jopp
Faculty of Business and Enterprise
Swinburne University of Technology

EWA CHMIELECKA AND IZABELA BUCHOWICZ

8. SOCIAL COMPETENCIES IN THE EUROPEAN AND POLISH QUALIFICATIONS FRAMEWORK

A Tool for Designing Intercultural Environments

INTRODUCTION

The legacy of the communist system in Polish society manifests itself in a number of aspects. One of them is a lack of suitable preparation or readiness to participate in the functioning and development of a democratic society. This regards institutional and local dimensions of a democratic society, its functioning at a national level, as well as a wider context, such as the emerging European Union citizenship and participating in global events. This legacy can be observed in virtually all aspects of social life, including involvement in activities within a multicultural environment. The responsibility of higher education for preparing graduates to act as leaders of social change, in particular, to develop a democratic society meeting the above mentioned criteria - ranging from institutional communities through civic participation at the levels of local, national, and European communities, to global citizenship, seems to be undeniable. However, it is a real challenge to adequately shape the educational process so that this task can be effectively accomplished. The responsibility of shaping global citizens should be met by all educational programs offered by Higher Education Institutions (HEIs), including the development and validation of learning outcomes, contents, and educational methods involved.

International Provisions Obliging HEIs to Develop Students' Social Competencies

National and international regulations, obliging Polish HEIs to conduct activities to develop students' social competencies, are worth mentioning here. The Bologna Process documents: from the Bologna Declaration to subsequent communiqués of the ministers responsible for higher education[1] are a primary source of international regulation. The documents formulate recommendations regarding the development of the European Higher Education Area (see references). The tasks to be accomplished by HEIs, specified there, could be briefly presented as follows:

- preparing graduates to function in the labour market;
- developing and maintaining a broad scope of advanced knowledge indispensable in the process of forming an economy and knowledge society;

- students' personal development;
- readiness to act as an active member of a developed democratic society.

As we can see, in the areas specified above, a number of requirements have been formulated, which are directly related to forming pro-social attitudes. On numerous occasions they were specifically addressed in other Bologna Process documents. For instance, in Bergen Communiqué (May 2005) we can find requirements regarding:

- the importance of developing an attitude of respect and understanding of intercultural and supra-cultural values;
- the reinforcement of the principle of public responsibility of higher education with respect to building a contemporary European society;
- preparing students to function as active citizens.

The recommendations mentioned above were specifically discussed in two other European documents implementing so called "national frameworks"[2] in higher education and in the whole educational system. In one crucial document regarding national frameworks, namely "A Framework for Qualifications of the European Higher Education Area", we can find recommendations as follows:

- European and national structures for graduate qualifications are supposed to enhance social unity in Europe and emphasize the social dimension of graduates' qualifications;
- Education plays a key role as regards the development of the culture of functioning in democracy; higher education, on top of that, should enhance attitudes and adapt values specific to democracy, in particular, through developing critical thinking in relation to democracy (these demands are also explicitly expressed in the Prague and Berlin Communiqués of the Bologna Process);
- Learning outcomes descriptors should comprise three components: (i) knowing and understanding, (ii) knowing how to act and (iii) knowing how to be. The latter component postulates transfer of values as an inherent part of cognition and coexistence with others in a social environment, in Polish it is expressed by the notion of "postawa" ("attitude").

Qualifications Frameworks can be generally defined as descriptions of qualifications acquired in a particular national higher education system, which is comprehendible both nationally and internationally. The notion of "qualification" is defined as a title, acknowledged as equal to a corresponding diploma, certificate, or other document issued following the completion of a particular stage of education. A similar document, which is issued by an authorized institution (HEI) certifies the accomplishment of learning outcomes specified for that particular stage of education. In April 2008 the European Parliament passed a recommendation requiring all EU member countries to equip their systems of education and training with National Qualifications Frameworks in compliance with the European Qualifications Framework for Lifelong Learning (EQF LLL,

2008). This document provides that the European Qualifications Framework is compatible with the framework for the:

> European Higher Education Area developed in compliance with the Bologna Process. In particular, the descriptors in the European Qualifications Framework at levels 5-8 refer to the descriptors agreed within the framework of the Bologna process. The only feature differentiating the descriptors in the European Qualifications Framework from the Bologna ones is the fact that they also refer to vocational education and training, as well as to working context – at all the levels – including the highest ones (13).

In EQF LLL learning outcomes are defined in three categories of descriptors: 1) Knowledge, which in the EQF context may be of theoretical or factual nature, being the representation of information assimilated during the learning process; it is a set of descriptions of facts, principles, theories, and practices relating to a field of learning or professional activity; 2) Skills, which according to EQF, may be mental/cognitive (logical, intuitive, and creative thinking) and practical (involving manual dexterity and the use of methods, materials, tools and instruments), imply the ability to use knowledge and *know-how* in order to carry out tasks and solve problems; 3) Social competences, which in EQF are defined in terms of responsibility and autonomy, imply a proven ability to use knowledge, skills, and personal, social, and/or methodological abilities in work or study situations and in professional and personal development.

The implementation of qualifications frameworks in educational systems of EU member states led to the necessity of incorporating the component of "social competence" in the process of developing and conducting educational programs aimed at attaining full qualifications in those countries.

Qualifications Frameworks and Developing Social Competence in Polish Higher Education

Although the need for developing pro-social attitudes have been realized by Polish HEIs since 1990, bringing this process to life was rather difficult. Firstly, the attitude of the academic community towards shaping students' attitudes was affected by concerns stemming from the communist past, when similar activities were perceived as ideological indoctrination. Polish HEIs after 1990 had neither good practices nor new methods regarding the implementation of this aspect of education. Secondly, the main challenge that the HEIs faced at that time was updating teaching contents and methods and developing knowledge and skills in particular fields, attitude formation was rather marginalized at that time. Thirdly, the quantitative explosion in higher education (approximately 5-fold increase in the number of students over the years 1990 – 2000) caused academic teachers' work overload thus forcing them to minimize their involvement in the spheres exceeding knowledge and skills transfer (citation).

These factors, among others, affected the effectiveness of developing pro-social attitudes. HEIs did not launch programs aimed at meeting this objective; they tended to satisfy only the basic provisions of legal requirements. Under the Directives of the Ministry of Science and Higher Education accompanying the "Act on Higher Education" of 1990 and 2005, it was required that elements of pro-social education be incorporated into curricula. Hence, HEIs typically extended their curricula by incorporating supplementary courses in philosophy, sociology, and political sciences, which were meant to meet the specified requirements.

Regrettably, in Poland there was no complex research conducted on those aspects of higher education, therefore presenting a scientifically reliable report on Polish HEIs' efforts to meet the requirement is virtually impossible. Monitoring the implementation of the Bologna Process in individual countries,[3] including Poland, focused on formal aspects (mobility, ECTS implementation, etc.). In those reports Poland was given positive assessments; yet, they did not reflect students' readiness to participate in social life. Based on the experience of the authors of the present paper, gained through the process of participating in the activities of a Bologna Experts team,[4] as well as the accreditation carried out by the Polish Accreditation Committee, we can state that pro-social education, in particular developing the readiness to function in a multicultural environment, was a quite neglected aspect of education in most HEIs. Locally conducted research seems to prove this statement.

In 2006, a survey study on students' opinions regarding the quality of teaching was completed in the Warsaw School of Economics (WSE) and Poznań University of Economics (PUE)[5]. The objective was to develop the elements of the method that would measure the quality of teaching in those HEIs, with the initial premise stating that those HEIs show a market-oriented approach; also, their quality of teaching is primarily determined by meeting students' expectations. Over one stage of the study, an analysis was conducted of four basic models of education, adopted from psychological-pedagogical sciences. The networks of issues based on those models were compared with students' opinions regarding the satisfaction of their educational expectations ("HEI's ability to…"). This analysis provided particularly interesting results by demonstrating the connections between the results and the hierarchy of importance attributed by students to aggregated educational dimensions. The analysis of the hierarchy of importance of dimensional characteristic features showed that the highest importance was attributed by students to their decision-making ability, as well as to clearly measurable practical skills and abilities. These aspects of education contributed to their feeling of having suitable preparation to meet labour market requirements in the roles of an economist or a manager, to control their decisions; they enabled them to evaluate the effectiveness of their activities. The following results were received:

- class "A" of the most important dimensions (weighs' total 70%) was attributed to a HEI's ability to professionally transfer the contents, language teaching,

communication, and negotiating techniques, educating for a dynamic labour market, coordinating additional students' activities with the core curriculum;
- class "B" of moderately important dimensions (25%) was attributed to a HEI's ability to use knowledge sourcing from economic reality, creating conditions for independent studies, offering mobility – a possibility to study abroad;
- class "C" comprising dimensions of minor importance (5%) involved a HEI's ability to create a friendly environment for students' organizations, stimulate their independence, offer access to scientific data, as well as to "educate in basic knowledge and skills in economics", also, to make studying accessible to disabled people and to foreigners.

The conflict between the opinions received in the study with the educational models, conveys a rather unfavorable message to HEIs in terms of their educational objectives and the need for social involvement demonstrated by graduates. The totals of parameters (weighs) of quality equation (in connection with Joyce's models) can be presented as follows: Social model ("civic cooperation"): 0.03; Personal model ("productive independence"): 0.42; Cognitive model ("critical thinking"): 0.29; And behavioral system model ("skills repertoire"): 0.27.

When attempting to formulate the above data in plain language and address the question of the most appreciated education by the students of leading HEIs in Poland, we could provisionally state that the most valued elements are not typically provided by universities; students appreciate personal traits such as a decision-making ability (which a HEI may obviously either inhibit or stimulate). At the same time, the role of knowledge (critical thinking in relation to economic reality) in the decision-making process is assessed as moderate; similarly, useful information underlying the practical skills repertoire is of moderate importance. Their pro-social attitudes seem to be rudimentary.

A unique opportunity for a shift to occur in developing pro-social attitudes in students was offered by the implementation in Poland of the National Qualifications Framework for higher education. In Poland the NQF stimulated a large scale reform in higher education. The formal NQF implementation in higher education commenced upon the adoption on March 18th 2011 of the amended *Act on Higher Education,* and subsequent directives regarding NQF. Thus, the legal framework was created specifying the form of NQF for higher education in Poland. Over the academic year of 2011/2012 in HEIs work was undertaken on designing educational programs complying with new regulations. In the academic year of 2012/2013 HEIs first conducted the educational programs designed in accordance with the NQF for higher education. Subsequent to the formal implementation of NQF for higher education, the Polish Accreditation Committee introduced corresponding amendments in the internal regulations, regarding the principles and procedures of accreditation and consistent with NQF – they guarantee the proper implementation of the related directives.

The most important consequence of the NQF implementation in the educational system is the necessity to express the description of all educational programs in terms of learning outcomes, as well as in terms of their validation. Learning outcomes are to be formulated in three categories: knowledge, skills, and social competence developed as a result of learning process; in other words, what a graduate knows, what he/she can do and, what he/she is ready to do upon the completion of a particular stage of their education. It is necessary to define the learning outcomes in a manner enabling the validation of their attainment. The validated sets of learning outcomes are defined as graduate's competencies.

The expected learning outcomes specified by a HEI (a unit conducting studies) in terms of knowledge, skills, and social competencies constitute the core element of the educational programme description, i.e. the information for stakeholders; at the same time, they constitute a formal obligation, whose fulfillment shall be subject to analysis during the programme accreditation process. The importance of learning outcomes is reflected in the regulation requiring their written approval at a HEI's level (by means of Senate's or equal body's resolution), whereas the decisions related to any other components of a given educational programme, in particular, the list of subjects constituting the programme of studies, are made at the level of a faculty or other unit conducting studies.

In view of this, what adjustments were Polish HEIs expected to introduce, as regards developing social competences in students? The key descriptive categories and aspects of fundamental significance for the comprehensive description of social competence include:

- Identity – specified in sub-categories of Participation
  - Sense of responsibility
  - Conduct

- Cooperation – specified in sub-categories of Team work
  - Conditions under which one acts
  - Leadership

- Responsibility – specified in sub-categories of Consequences of one's own actions
  - Consequences of the team's actions
  - Evaluation

Universal level descriptors of the Polish Qualifications Framework state that a graduate demonstrates their readiness as follows: At level 6 (corresponding to BA): to cultivate and disseminate models of good practice in the workplace and beyond; make decisions independently; critically evaluate one's own actions, those of the team one directs, and the organizations in which one participates; assume responsibility for the results of those actions; At level 7 (corresponding to MA): to establish and develop models of good practice in the environments of work and life; initiate actions, critically assess oneself as well as the teams and organizations in which one participates; lead a group and take responsibility for it And at level 8 (corresponding to PhD); to conduct independent research which contributes to existing scientific and creative achievements; assume professional and public challenges that take into consideration their ethical dimension, responsibility for their results, and develop models of good practice in such situations.

The above quoted provisions of the Polish Qualifications Framework do not directly refer to intercultural attitudes, however, they lay a sound foundation for developing intercultural environments in HEIs. They offer HEIs full autonomy in the process of unfolding generic descriptors into contents reflecting their own pedagogical ideas and initiatives. What is the attitude of Polish HEIs towards this task? A benchmark study on the implementation of NQF in Polish HEIs conducted in 2013 by the Polish Rectors Foundation[6] showed that "social competencies" are much more challenging for HEIs than "knowledge" or "skills" in terms of their targeted educational activity. No other research on the development of pro-social attitude in students has been done so far. To indicate that insufficient attention is paid to similar activity, or it is often completely neglected, we can refer to the directive of the Minister of Science and Higher Education on the provisions of conducting educational programs, accompanying the amended Act on Higher Education of July 2014, which stipulates that 5 European Credit Transfer and Accumulation System (ECTS)[7] credits in the program of study are to be devoted to a certain educational activity aimed at forming pro-social attitudes in students. Clearly, HEIs failed to conduct a similar pedagogical activity at their initiative. Let us now take a look at a few examples of classes, conducted with the aim of attaining this objective.

Warsaw School of Economics (WSE) – An Example of Classes

WSE observes the rules introduced by the qualifications frameworks and makes an effort to face the challenge of social (including intercultural) skills development in its students by means of forming a friendly environment, which enhances this process. The examples of classes provided below refer to the subjects that in the studies curriculum, are classified as primarily building those competencies in students. However, this objective is met in a specific sense. The students of WSE form a relatively homogeneous environment, the majority of them are Poles. The number of foreign students typically does not exceed 2–3% of the whole group composition, with foreign students coming mainly from Central Europe. The proportion is different in doctoral studies conducted in English, where foreigners amount to nearly 50% of the group and they come from all over the world. The proportion between men and women is close to 50:50; the social background, due to high admission requirements (high score in matura final upper-secondary school examination, high admission requirements for doctoral studies), is insignificant in terms of adaptability to WSE and overcoming its intellectual challenges. Also, religious or other views do not emerge during students' activities. Due to the fact that the examples described refer to full-time studies, where a fee is not charged, the students' material status does not manifest itself in any significant way. However, a distinctive feature of

WSE students in comparison to other student populations in Poland is their highly pragmatic approach to education, as well as their drive for professional success. WSE is recognized as a HEI which can almost guarantee a successful career; therefore, it attracts young people who value their intellectual development lower than their market success. Most PhD degrees obtained in this HEI do not serve as an introduction to a scientific career; they supplement qualifications required by top level managers in their career development in such sectors as finance, banking, economy, and social policy.

The characteristics of students presented above indicate that issues regarding "intercultural environment" may emerge in different spheres than in societies with ethnic, religious, or social background divergence. Cultural clash observed in the examples described below occurs at an axiological level, illustrating the conflict between two different systems of values. The pragmatic, business-oriented approach, targeted at the effectiveness of action and benefits as they are defined in economics and management, is challenged by the values constituting "social competences" described above, including conduct complying with autotelic values (ethical and other), which refer to a non-instrumental approach to one's activity. All of these considerations lead to an internal conflict which has to be overcome by students. First, students need to find a motivation to reflect on their own decisions and then to develop their own internal way of overcoming the conflict between two cultures; the business-oriented spheres acting mainly to achieve instrumental values versus the sphere of convictions regarding autonomous (non-instrumental) cognitive, moral, and social values, which cannot be ignored in any kind of activity. Is it possible to define this conflict as "intercultural"? It emerges at all the levels mentioned above, ranging from institutional through local, national to global. This conflict also manifests itself in various ways in different environments, however, its nature remains the same. We can risk the statement that it is a HEI's role to create an environment which may provide suitable conditions for the clash of those two cultures, the resolution of the conflicts arising, and subsequent development of intercultural competencies in its students.

The creation of a safe environment for this type of cultural clash to be experienced and explored by students can be highlighted using the classes on Ethics in Business conducted in Polish for students of first cycle studies (BA).[8] Developing the programme of the classes was based on the WSE guidelines on social competences of graduates from BA and MA studies. They are expected to demonstrate, among other skills: Responsibility for their own and other people's work, as well as the implementation and development of profession-related ethical rules; Leadership and awareness of their professional role to be performed; and awareness of their social role to be performed, realizing their own and other parties' responsibility for socially significant events. They are also expected to develop their particular sensitivity to pro-social and constructive conduct in new circumstances, involving unpredictable problems and tasks arising, and spotting unethical behaviors and undertaking activities to prevent them.

The competencies defined above served as the basis for the formulation of the general characteristic of the objectives of the classes in "Ethics in business", as well as the expected learning outcomes. The classes present the issues from a purely humanistic perspective (they are not operationally identified with "Business ethics"), thus contributing to forming ethical attitudes in prospective business people, rather than to developing their professional skills. They also familiarize students with inevitable conflicts of values and interests inherent in business activity, as well as bearing responsibility for the decisions made, at personal, company, economic, and global levels.

Learning outcomes expected for the classes were mainly in two areas, knowledge and skills and social competencies and attitudes. The table below provides examples of the types of skills engendered by the class.

Table 1. Expected learning outcomes from Ethics in Business.

Knowledge and Skills	Social Competences / Attitudes
Defining and understanding basic notions in ethics and business ethics, as well as understanding their role in justifying personal choices and forming attitudes	Active attitude towards ethical problems in business
Understanding professional and social responsibilities of a HEI's graduate	Motivation to accept the role of a leader in professional and social spheres, understanding the related ethical responsibilities
Identifying basic indicators of humanity, distinguishing it from other roles performed by a man	Openness to multiple solutions in a moral conflict, tolerance towards non-standard and non-stereotypic resolutions
Distinguishing the sphere of pure values from the sphere of interest/benefit – interpreting their interrelation and its application in the process of evaluating business activity and related responsibility	Awareness of the inherit character of personal responsibility for the decisions made
Identifying and understanding basic moral conflicts in business activity; indicating the methods, their inherent nature and drawbacks in the methods of their resolution	Perceiving the limited character of the tools applied in business to guarantee its ethical character
Recognizing the main pathologies occurring in business	Sensitivity to any case of compromising the ethical sphere, accompanying business activity
Interpreting solutions undertaken by business people facing a moral conflict	

The classes are conducted with the use of the conversation method in groups consisting of approximately 20 students. Due to the fact that the classes are offered to students who by and large have not gained any professional experience, the most frequently used method is developing solutions to case studies, combined with the presentation of those solutions to the whole group, attempting to justify the choices made and the concluding discussion. The students often find most interesting the cases of conflicting spheres of instrumental business values and ethical values, in particular, cases where each decision leads to negative consequences, despite their sound justification either by economic benefits or other values such as honesty.[9] A clash takes place between two cultures rooted in two different systems of values and adopting one of them is inherent in the activities of a person working in the economic sphere, which students had not previously been aware of. There is also space here for genuine dialogue between students related to their varying systems of values. The discussions are often very difficult, as they refer to personal values and attitudes, on certain occasions requiring declarations of a clearly ethical nature. Presumably, the most valuable students' reflection resulting from the classes is their awareness of the lack of one unambiguous solution to the conflict of values, despite their source or character. Students also learn that the ethical sphere does not offer conclusive justifications for decisions and does not exclude debate or justified compromise. Realizing this enhances openness to other sets of values, different from those adopted by an individual; it also helps to understand that each of those sets may imply a different decision and way of conduct. This in turn reinforces the feeling of identification and responsibility for the choice made and the understanding that this responsibility is attributed to a particular individual and its gravity cannot be diminished by the instruments of skillful and effective management. It also helps to understand that the justification promoted by management-related disciplines, which is based on economic effectiveness, also in its broad meaning, does not offer a justification of absolute cognitive strength, definitely concluding the problem since it is just one of many worldview options. It helps to overcome managerism – a doctrine claiming that effective management can solve any problem. Regrettably, this view is commonly shared by WSE students (being, in general, closely related to managerial education). It is, however, contradictory to dialogue and social competence which are present in students' discussions and case studies offered during classes.

It is worth considering, at this point, whether the classes conducted in the way described above allow for reaching the expected learning outcomes; is there a possibility to effectively validate them? It is a complex question, since we do not deal with validating knowledge or "legitimate views" on ethical issues in business. Our objective here is to ascertain whether the students attending the course are motivated to reflect on the ethical aspect of their professional activity and that of a wider social environment. The question arises whether they are able to look at a moral conflict from a number of perspectives, consider the reasons for possible decisions and as a consequence assume the responsibility for those decisions. The topics of the essays assigned at the end of the course require the students to consider many options of possible decisions made to resolve a conflict. In view of this, we can make a legitimate statement that students are aware of the nature of a conflict involving business and ethics in individual, institutional, and local dimensions, not to mention global economy. However, it is impossible to conclusively state whether students develop the habit to reflect, or are motivated to do so.

CONCLUSION

Developing students' social competencies in an intercultural environment seems to be a significant factor contributing to the growth of social capital, indispensable for the development of a democratic and well-functioning society, which also remains active in the global context. The entrance of Polish higher education into the European Higher Education Area, as well as joining the global system at this level of education along with the growing mobility of HEIs' students and graduates reveals the need for overcoming intercultural challenges, despite the fact that in Poland today their form is slightly different than in other countries. Polish HEIs, when undertaking this effort, are supported by the provisions of the European and Polish Qualifications Frameworks. However, in most cases they rely, in this respect, on teachers' experience and their own initiative, in rare instances being based on the findings of modern pedagogy. It seems that developing and disseminating the idea of intercultural pedagogies would be highly appreciated in this activity.

NOTES

[1] Following each conference the ministers issue a Communiqué specifying the objectives for the next few years. Up to date similar communiqués have been issued at the conferences in Prague (2001), Berlin (2003), Bergen (2005), London (2007), Leuven/Louvain-la-Neuve (2009), Budapest and Vienna (2010) and Bucharest (2012).

[2] These were "A Framework for Qualifcations of the European Higher Education Area" accompanying the Bergen Communiqué, May 2005 r. and "Recommendation of the European Parliament and Council for Qualification Framework for LLL", Brussels, April 2008

[3] The crucial reports include Trends (*Trends in European Higher Education*), developed under the auspices of the European University Association (EUA), *Bologna Process Stocktaking* reports prepared by BFUG, illustrating, among others, the status of the implementation of the Bologna Process requirements in individual member countries and Bologna with Students' Eyes carried out under the auspices of the European Students' Union (ESU). The main source of information is the Process portal www.ond.vlaanderen.be/hogeronderwijs/bologna.

[4] Ewa Chmielecka, acting as a Bologna Expert over 2004–2014 every year participated in dozens of meetings in various academic centers discussing and supporting academic communities over the process of implementing the Bologna process tools.

[5] The study was conducted over 2002–2006 by a team supervised by Professor Stefan Doroszewicz from WSE.

[6] Andrzej Kraśniewski, Maria Próchnicka, Benchmarking procesu wdrażania Krajowych Ram Kwalifikacji w polskich uczelniach, FRP, 2013

[7] 1 ECTS point refers to 25–30 hours of student workload. One academic year contains 60 ECTS points. Approximately 5 ECTS = 3 credit US College Credit Hours.

[8] Conducted since 2006 by Professor Ewa Chmielecka.
[9] One of the most attractive and discussed cases is the instance of an entrepreneur wishing to win in the bidding procedure in a big public tender in a local administrative unit; he is also aware that in order to win it, he is expected to give a bribe (regrettably, quite a common situation in Poland).

REFERENCES

Bologna Working Group. (2005). *A framework for qualifications of the european higher education area. Bologna working group report on qualifications frameworks.* Copenhagen, Denmark: Danish Ministry Of Science, Technology and Innovation.

Chmielecka, E. (Ed.). (2010). *Autonomia programowa uczelni. Ramy kwalifikacji dla szkolnictwa wyższego.* Warsaw: MNiSzW.

Chmielecka, E., Kraśniewski, A., & Marciniak, Z. (2013). Krajowe ramy kwalifikacji w szkolnictwie wyższym. In M. Fedorowicz & M. Sitek (Eds.), *Liczą się efekty. Raport o stanie edukacji 2012* (pp. 165–197). Warsaw: IBE – Educational Research Institute.

Chmielecka, E., Kraśniewski, A., Marciniak, Z., & Saryusz-Wolski, T. (2013). Self-certification report of the national qualifications framework for higher education. In Z. Marciniak (Ed.), *Raport samopotwierdzenia krajowych Ram Kwalifikacji dla Szkolnictwa Wyższego.* Warsaw, Poland: IBE – Educational Research Institute.

Communiqués of the Conferences of European Ministers Responsible for Higher Education: Prague (2001), Berlin (2003), Bergen (2005), London (2007), Leuven/Louvain-la-Neuve (2009), Budapest and Vienna (2010), Bucharest (2012)

European Union. (2008). *Recommendation of the European Parliament and Council for Qualification Framework for LLL.* Brussels, Belgium.

Kraśniewski, A. (2009). *Proces Boloński. To już 10 lat. Warsaw*, Poland: FRSE – Fundacja Rozwoju Systemu Edukacji.

Sławiński, S., & Dębowski, H. (Eds.). (2013). *Referencing the polish qualifications framework to the European qualification framework for lifelong learning.* Warsaw, Poland: IBE – Educational Research Institute.

Ewa Chmielecka
Educational and Scientific Policy Unit
Warsaw School of Economics, Poland

Izabela Buchowicz
Educational and Scientific Policy Unit
Warsaw School of Economics, Poland

SECTION 3

CRITICAL REFLECTIONS FROM ACROSS THE CURRICULUM

MARY BENBENEK

9. INTERNATIONALIZING TEACHING AND LEARNING IN A GRADUATE DOCTOR OF NURSING PROGRAM CURRICULUM

INTRODUCTION

The population of the United States (U.S.) was estimated at 318,892,103 in 2014 (Central Intelligence Agency, 2014). U.S. Census data in 2012 revealed there were 40 different languages spoken in U.S. homes and 79 ethnicities were reported. For the first time, in 2010, individuals were also allowed to list more than one race when completing census information. This demonstrates an increasingly diverse society in the U.S. and mandates the need to better educate students regarding the richness and potential that multiculturalism brings to today's world. Census data also showed a shift in age demographics toward older age groups with the largest populations reported in young adult and middle age groups rather than in pediatric age groups (see Table 1).

Table 1. Age demographics 2012 U.S. Census.

Age	Percent
0 – 14 years	19.4%
15-24 years	13.7%
25 – 54 years	39.9%
55 – 64 years	12.6%
65 years and older	13.9%

Central Intelligence Agency, The World Fact Book, 2014

With an increasingly diverse population comes diversity in health care beliefs and approaches to health and illness. For many immigrants to the U.S., the concept of "well care" or health maintenance may be a new notion. Individuals may be more accustomed to seeking medical care only when they are ill and not fully understand the concepts of well care, health promotion, and disease prevention. Other factors such as structural and non-structural barriers (e.g., lack of transportation, being uninsured) to seeking health maintenance and health care are also reported among new immigrants (Garces, Scarinci, & Harrison, 2006), but may not be appreciated by health care providers in the U.S. Similarly, individuals from diverse cultures may be more likely to engage in traditional health care practices prior to seeking care from western health care providers (Garces et al., 2006). It is not uncommon for western health care providers to interact with patients who practice cupping, coining, acupuncture, and herbal therapies. In a study of Chinese immigrants living in San Francisco, for example, almost 100% of those surveyed reported using Traditional Chinese Medicine (TCM) in the past year, but only 5% reported their western health care providers had asked about it (Wu, Burke & LeBaron, 2007). It behooves western health care providers, therefore, to be aware of these traditional healing practices and to acknowledge their importance when collaboratively formulating plans of care with patients, families, and communities.

Health disparities have been reported in numerous areas partially arising due to care giver assumptions, attitudes, and miscommunication. Disparities in pain care among African American and Hispanic patients, for example, were highlighted by Green, Anderson, Baker, Campbell, Decker, Fillingim, Kaloukalani et al. (2009). The authors suggested that disparities in pain management among ethnic and racial minorities are multifactorial, but at least partially rooted in patient-health care provider communication and attitudes. Similarly, the IOM Report on Health Care Disparities (2002) identified that in addition to health care system policies and practices, the health care encounter itself may be the source of disparities. Specifically, provider bias, provider uncertainly when interacting with minorities, and beliefs or stereotypes held by providers have been suggested as sources of disparities in health care.

The profession of nursing has long embraced a patient-centered holistic framework in its approach to patient care. The patient is considered a partner in care planning. It is recognized that the social, environmental, cultural, and psychological context in which a patient lives must be considered when planning and addressing the unique health care needs of the patient and family. Awareness of patient values and health beliefs is essential to foster successful health promotion and disease intervention. With an increasingly global and diverse patient base in the United States (U.S.), it is a natural extension for programs of nursing higher education to more formally and purposefully internationalize their curricula.

The concept of internationalizing curricula can be construed in many different ways. While for some, internationalizing teaching and learning is interpreted as developing study abroad experiences or linking with international partnerships or universities, the approach outlined in this chapter focuses on an initiative to internationalize programs educating advanced practice nurses by integrating principles of cultural humility and multiculturalism into course work across the curricula. Nursing graduate faculty in the School of Nursing at the University of Minnesota developed activities and obtained Health Resources and Services Administration (HRSA) funding to design student learning experiences aimed at developing advanced practice nurses who are better able to address the unique and diverse needs of individual patients. Information in this chapter will explore the concepts of cultural humility, culturally congruent care, and multiculturalism and contrast them with cultural competency. Methods for adapting curriculum to foster heightened cultural sensitivity and the development of culturally congruent interactive skills among students enrolled in the programs will be described. While the examples reported in this chapter relate to a nursing curriculum, these methods could be adapted to other educational programs.

Historical Context of Cultural Care Provision in Nursing

In health care professions, there is a need to educate care providers to meet the health care needs of patients from diverse cultures and backgrounds. Subsequently, there has been a sustained effort to develop competencies in providing culturally congruent care in medicine, nursing, and other health professions (American Association of Colleges of Nursing, 2009; American Association of Medical Colleges, 2005). The American Association of Colleges of Nursing (AACN) published cultural competencies for nursing graduate students in 2009 (see Table 2).

Table 2. American Association of Colleges of Nursing Cultural Competencies of Graduate Nursing Students.

Competency
• Prioritize the social and cultural factors that affect health in designing and delivering care across multiple contexts. • Construct socially and empirically derived cultural knowledge of people and populations to guide practice and research. • Assume leadership in developing, implementing, and evaluating culturally competent nursing and other healthcare services. • Transform systems to address social justice and health disparities. • Provide leadership to educators and members of the healthcare or research team in learning, applying, and evaluating continuous cultural competence development. • Conduct culturally competent scholarship that can be used in practice.

Adapted from the American Association of Colleges of Nursing, 2009.

Prior to these official competencies, nurse Madeleine Leininger was instrumental in initially developing language to articulate the significance of culture and care to nursing practice. Madeline Leininger developed the concept of "culturally congruent nursing care" and identified it as the goal of transcultural nursing. Providing culturally congruent care requires the nurse to work with patients, families, communities, and institutions to identify, implement, plan and evaluate nursing care plans. Nursing actions and decisions are designed based on new knowledge and culturally-based ways to provide meaningful and satisfying holistic care (Leininger, 1991). She highlighted the importance of focusing on values, beliefs, and practices of individuals and groups to provide culturally-specific care to promote health and to address adverse health concerns. Her work in this area began in the 1950s. In 1995 she formulated a formal definition of transcultural nursing:

> A substantive area of study and practice focused on comparative cultural care (caring) values, beliefs, and practices of individual or groups of similar or different cultures with the goal of providing culture-specific and universal nursing care practice in promoting health or well-being or to help people to face unfavorable human conditions, illness, or death in culturally meaningful ways. (Leininger & McFarland, 2002)

While Leininger provided the foundation for developing a commitment to providing culturally congruent care, she focused primarily on developing awareness of and respect for diverse health beliefs and practices among care providers. While she had an "other focus", she did not give attention to the concept of self-evaluation in providing culturally congruent care. As a graduate clinical faculty member, part of a team in the School of Nursing, our goal was to enhance and develop students' foundation for providing culturally congruent care by internationalizing the curriculum. Part of our goal was to integrate the concept of cultural humility into the existing foundation students had gained in previous undergraduate nursing studies. Cultural humility speaks to the role of self-evaluation in providing culturally congruent care, and was conceptualized by Hook, Davis, Owen, Worthington and Utsey (2013) as the "ability to maintain an interpersonal stance that is other-oriented (or open to the other) in relation to aspects of cultural identity that are most important to the [person]" (p. 2). In essence, cultural humility implies a **lifelong commitment to self-evaluation and self-critique**" (Tervalon & Murray-Garcia, 1998, p. 123). Health care professionals must acknowledge their own biases when interacting with patients whose culture, belief systems, religion, socioeconomic status, values, gender, race, or sexual orientation may be different from their own. It strives to move individuals beyond obtaining cultural knowledge and toward the development of respectful and dynamic partnerships with patients, families, and communities. While cultural humility theorists acknowledge that it is important to have some understanding of health care practices among members of a community, they caution against developing stereotypes about the behaviors of individual members within that community. Cultural humility is an important concept in moving toward the goal of providing culturally congruent care. The concept of cultural humility was introduced to nursing faculty involved in internationalizing the curriculum in the School of Nursing at the University of Minnesota by Dr. Linda Lindeke, who was Director of Graduate Education in the School of Nursing at the time.

Cultural competence is a term widely used in health care to define an expected level of practice by health care providers. Cultural competence implies steady movement through stages of growth toward optimal mastery of working effectively in cross-cultural situations, as depicted by a ladder model (National Center for Cultural Competence, 2005). Our nursing faculty concurred that movement toward mastery was ongoing and questioned whether there was truly an "endpoint" of cultural competence. The concept of cultural competence did not acknowledge the ongoing process of learning that is inherent in provider-patient interaction.

There was consensus that the concept of cultural humility was better aligned with the tenets of nursing practice and fosters the students' ability to reflect on their own biases and behaviors as well as to consider the perspective of the patients, families, and communities with which they work.

Additionally, discussion evolved around integrating the concept of cultural humility with the broader concept of multiculturalism. Multiculturalism can be defined as the preservation of different cultures or identities within a society. While it is important for students to reflect on their own belief systems when providing culturally congruent care, it is equally important for students to learn about the unique attributes of other cultures. Faculty in the School of Nursing elected, therefore, to focus not only on developing student learning activities that would prompt student self-awareness of intentional and unintentional bias, a cornerstone of cultural humility, but to design student learning activities that also embraced the concept of multiculturalism. Some of the learning activities developed were implemented across graduate nurse specialties based on grants received, while other activities, some of which will be explored in this chapter, were undertaken by individual faculty in the family nurse practitioner area of study.

APPROACHES TO MULTICULTURAL CURRICULAR TRANSFORMATION

The student population for whom the curricular redesign took place is comprised of advanced practice nursing (APRN) students engaged in a doctoral program to become nurse midwives or nurse practitioners in the fields of family practice, adult-gerontology, pediatrics, women's health, or mental health. These students are post-baccalaureate students with variable nursing experience who are pursuing a doctor of nursing practice (DNP) degree in their area of study. Individual program size varies from 10 students across three years to 44 students across 3 years. There are roughly 150 students total in the DNP program across all APRN specialties. Students are initially admitted in the fall semester to begin either a three-year full time or a four-year part time program of study. Faculty members involved in activities to internationalize the curriculum came from the specialty program areas of Family Practice, Pediatrics, Mental Health, Women's Health, and Midwifery as well as Administration. There were six to eight faculty members from various specialty areas who regularly participated in initiatives. Participation was dependent on grant involvement, but members were encouraged to integrate lessons learned into other areas of the curricula as well. The family practice faculty representative was the only consistent member in all groups. To design curricular changes, faculty met at regularly scheduled times over a span of five years. Initially APRN core courses (those courses taken by all nurse practitioner and midwifery students) were reviewed for existing content and activities relative to multi-cultural content and experiences. Ideas were brainstormed to identify areas for development and to plan potential learning and clinical activities. There are other core DNP courses beyond the APRN core courses that all students take throughout their education, that were not addressed.

135

The policy courses, for example, were known to already contain information about social justice and sociopolitical policies that affect health outcomes. A standard pedagogical approach to align student learning objectives for educational activities with national objectives relative to developing culturally-congruent nursing care as defined by the American Colleges of Nursing, the American Association of Colleges of Nursing, and the National Organization of Nurse Practitioner Faculty were followed. Specifically, teaching and learning methods for the University of Minnesota post-baccalaureate to DNP program were designed to:

- Develop a socially and empirically derived understanding of complex causes of disparities;
- Implement culturally competent nursing care;
- Address social justice;
- Advocate for patients and policies that advance health care;
- Develop competency in collaboration with patients, key persons, agencies, and various stakeholders;
- Modify attitude and transform personally;
- Contribute to culturally competent scholarship
  (American Association of Colleges of Nursing (AACN), 2009).

To internationalize the curriculum, an effort was made to integrate principles of cultural humility and multiculturalism into core APRN courses for all specialty areas across the clinical curriculum. The faculty members engaged in design were involved in teaching many of the core courses and/or engaged in grant activities. Given the shared commitment to these initiatives, efforts to transform the curriculum were readily commenced by faculty. Reaching consensus on curriculum overhaul is best achieved through shared decision-making which was employed throughout the grant funded projects. The initiatives described in this chapter were undertaken through discussion, research, and consensus by teams of faculty who met regularly and had a strong commitment to the process. Specific aims of the HRSA grants guided discussion and planning as well as timelines. Some activities implemented in core courses emerged directly from grant aims, while others were developed as an offshoot to the grants. Setting defined timelines and delegating specific tasks to team members were crucial to the success of development and implementation of learning activities. While there were grant- specific group activities across specialties, other activities were undertaken by individual team faculty members within the contexts of the specialty courses taught by them. Many of the core APRN courses are taught by a group of two to three faculty members, but some at the specialty level are taught by individuals. It was up to individual faculty members from the team to introduce and address curriculum changes aimed at internationalizing the curriculum at the course level.

In the DNP program, there is not one, single, course targeted to teach students about multiculturalism and cultural humility. There was a conscious decision to integrate it throughout the program. Much as students will encounter multicultural issues in clinical practice, core APRN courses targeted for specific multicultural teaching and learning activities included Clinical Pharmacotherapeutics, Holistic Health Assessment, Assessment and Management of Health, and all areas of study clinical seminars. The specialty areas of family practice, mental health, and pediatrics made concerted efforts to enhance the development of cultural humility and multiculturalism into their three to six clinical seminar courses because these faculty members participated in one of the initial funded HRSA grants. Additionally, family practice, adult-gerontology, midwifery, and women's health also engaged in developing a joint activity aimed at facilitating students' ability to work effectively with culturally diverse patients. Students were engaged in activities aimed at developing a better understanding of the patient experience as well as improved understanding of personal cultural views and biases. Ultimately the goal was for students to gain skills to interact with and work effectively across differences in multicultural clinical situations. The purpose of the overall curriculum transformation was to integrate cultural humility and to enhance cultural awareness across the curriculum to prepare APRNs who are better able to deliver culturally congruent health care. A secondary goal was to foster increased multicultural awareness among faculty.

Pedagogical Tools/Curricula

The re-design approach utilized was multimodal. Learning activities were developed from grant funding as well as by individual faculty efforts. Activities included student reflection as well as clinical case studies, observed standardized clinical encounters (OSCEs), and interaction with various cultural representatives. Engaged faculty participated in funded grants aimed at developing student experiences to foster cultural humility and to develop culturally-congruent care (Edwardson, 2007; Juve, 2009). In the Edwardson grant, APRN faculty partnered with diverse clinical practice sites in the community to provide patient care. The intent was to engage faculty directly in providing patient care in diverse settings and to provide clinical learning sites for students where they might have an opportunity to interact and develop multicultural skills. The faculty chosen had previous clinical practices in similar settings.

Classroom Activities

Classroom activities in specialty (FNP, AGNP, WHNP, Nurse midwifery, Psych Mental Health NP) clinical seminar courses were designed by individual instructors. For example, a faculty member in the family nurse practitioner (FNP) area of study designed activities for clinical seminars based on activities included in Paul Gorsky's Multicultural Education Pavilion (Gorksi, 1995-2014). These activities were adapted to the nursing context and integrated principles learned in a university-wide initiative to enhance the international focus of teaching and learning. The concept of cultural humility was also integrated into these activities, requiring students to use reflection and to probe thoughts and feelings about culture during the activities. Some of these activities will be reviewed here.

There are eight FNP clinical seminars in the final two years of the program. One of the seminars focuses on leadership and includes activities that specifically support students' self discovery through cultural humility. FNP students participate in several scaffolded activities to foster their understanding about their own culture and to probe their beliefs about cultures different from their own. To introduce the topic of culture, students are asked to describe their own culture. It is not uncommon for majority students to propose that they have no specific culture. To address that, one of the first learning activities designed for students was to partner with another student and recount a story stemming from their childhood. No specific direction was given about content and was left entirely to the discretion of each individual student. Students were given roughly 20 minutes to swap stories. At the end of the story swap, each student was asked to recount what they learned about their peer's culture. For example, students often contrasted a rural upbringing with an urban upbringing, citing differences in childhood activities, rules, even food choices. Another common difference noted was the types of holidays celebrated and the ways holidays were celebrated which might relate to food, religion, family, or community traditions. Students quickly recognized their unfolding cultures as they talked about their backgrounds. Despite the fact that many of these students had been together in previous courses, they were amazed to discover what they did not know about their peers just by allowing the peer to tell his or her story. This provides a jumping off point for a discussion of culture.

Students were next asked to brainstorm about what culture means. The clinical courses are typically small, having only 6–10 students, so conducting a discussion is easier to facilitate, but this activity could be conducted in a larger class using small groups. The instructor typically asks an open ended question such as "What is culture?" A vigorous discussion typically ensues about what concepts are inherent in culture and how culture is defined. Students are asked to explain why they think a particular concept is part of culture and to consider how that might affect a person's health. Conversations typically begin around more concrete, safe constructs such as language, dress, and food. Richer discussion eventually follows with emerging concepts relative to world view, family wisdom, child-rearing practices to name a few. Through this exercise the class can build its own conceptual diagram of culture in the classroom which includes their definitions of culture. This picture is then contrasted with a formal definition of culture from the Merriam Webster Online Dictionary, "the beliefs, customs, arts, etc., of a particular society, group, place, or time". The diagram and definition can be used by students to reflect on the childhood story they shared to gain insight into and to identify key aspects about their own culture and belief systems. This provides them an opportunity to self-reflect on what culture means to them and to identify some of the beliefs that help shape their own world view.

Next steps include translating their conceptual diagram of culture to the clinical world. They are asked to think about how all these aspects of culture might affect health, health care access, health disparities, health outcomes, and patient –provider interactions. They are asked to think about western medicine practices that might align with or be at odds with an individual patient's cultural background. Students have been in clinical settings by this point in their program and can readily cite examples they encountered or observed where culture or social situation did affect some aspect of health or health care delivery in each unique clinical encounter. For example, a student might provide an example of a lack of understanding of the concept of "well care" for immigrants from some countries and how his or her preceptor addressed that in clinic. One rural FNP student commented on a strong sense of self-reliance she encountered in some interactions with older rural patients. She commented that some patients declined assistance and did not routinely seek care until they were quite ill, because it was part of their culture to be self-sufficient and "work it out." A case in point was an 80 year-old woman whose heat went out during the winter, but she did not want to trouble anyone, so she set about hauling in wood and keeping her wood burning stove going until a son visited her. At that point, she had developed frost bite on her fingers. Similarly, a student working in an urban inner city clinic cited an elderly Hmong patient who typically tried traditional medicine to treat high blood pressure before coming into the western medicine clinic and only sporadically took prescribed medications, because it was not congruent with his health beliefs. In addition to differences in health beliefs and practices, there are existing health disparities in our society due to lack of access, being uninsured, underinsured, or undocumented that students must be aware of when managing care. For example, choosing an affordable appropriate medication to treat a condition is essential for patients with limited resources and lack of health insurance. Because both social and cultural factors can be determinants of health, developing awareness, appreciation and consideration of sociocultural enablers and barriers to health is key to this exercise.

Other activities are drawn from Paul Gorski on his Multicultural Education Pavilion website (Gorski, 1995–2014). On the website, Gorski offers numerous examples of activities that could be utilized to foster growth and awareness of cultural issues. These included exercises to define terminology, icebreakers to begin the discussion about multiculturalism, and case studies to explore the broad concept of multiculturalism. There are several options for quizzes students can take to raise their awareness about cultural, social, and political issues. The quizzes challenged students to confront their own bias concerning social, political, and policy issues. Students could answer collectively or individually and were not required to share their responses. For this activity, clickers can be used to collect, tally, and report responses. Once the response was made, the actual correct answer was reviewed. Many of the items reflect on disparities in judicial, health, and social systems such as rates of infant mortality among different ethnicities in the US, incarceration rates by drug and ethnicity, educational outcomes by ethnicity and school, legacy policies for college admission. The intent behind the exercise in the class was for students to reflect on, question, and analyze current policies and beliefs both personally and nationally related to racial inequality, health, and economic disparities. This activity stimulates a class room discussion about issues and discrepancies that arise between their own beliefs and reality and to gain a sense of the barriers to health patients they see might encounter. As DNP students, they are challenged to think beyond the individual patient and to consider both social and cultural systems that shape health and to offer proposals for systems improvement. This exercise aligns well with that task.

Additionally, throughout students' clinical practicum experiences they are encouraged to journal. They are encouraged to write down observations, feelings, notes, triumphs, and challenges encountered in the clinical setting and with patient encounters. These observations may be knowledge based but also provide a means for them to reflect on their own growth and to uncover hidden biases, changes in belief systems, and to develop new approaches to patients and clinical problems. The purpose of reflection as a learning to tool is to assist students to reorganize perceptions, form new relationships, and influence future thoughts and actions in order to learn from the experience (Sugerman, Doherty, Garvey, & Glass, 2000). Each clinical seminar, they are also given an opportunity in round robin to offer something unique they learned that particular week, whether related to clinical skill development or personal growth. Students gain a stronger sense of self and can more readily confront beliefs they may hold in interacting with diverse patients and patient problems.

Case Studies as Tools to Foster Culturally Congruent Care

As noted earlier, increasingly, medical professionals will be serving individuals who have different views, beliefs, and experiences with medical care than themselves. It is of vital importance that professionals, therefore, have the ability to work in a culturally congruent manner. One of the main educational tools that has proven to be successful in developing students' clinical competencies as well as enhancing multicultural awareness and sensitivity is the development and use of multicultural case studies. The use of multicultural case studies was woven into the clinical practicums as well as into several core APRN courses including Clinical Pharmacotherapeutics, Holistic Health Assessment, and Assessment and Management of Health I and II.

Several grants obtained by faculty in the School of Nursing funded initiatives to develop culturally sensitive case studies and to promote culturally congruent care provision among students (Edwards, 2007; Juve, 2011). The Quest grant (Juve, 2011) provided for focus groups with community members from various immigrant communities in the metropolitan area to confer with faculty on the development of cases that were culturally sensitive and accurate. Community members were also engaged to assist the school in developing interest among members of their communities to become standardized patients for Observed Structured Clinical Encounters (OSCEs). Ultimately, these cases would be utilized in the final test out exams at the end of the students' programs. OSCEs provide meaningful formative evaluations of students' communication and clinical decision-making skills throughout the curriculum. In these encounters, standardized patients who have been trained by interprofessional educational resource staff play the part of patients seeking care for a particular health concern. Students are asked to interview, examine, and treat the patient as though in a real clinical encounter. They are ultimately evaluated based on their clinical decision-making with core concepts identified for all aspects of the encounter, including communication. Expanding these scenarios to include patients from backgrounds different from the mainstream is a unique way to provide students with multicultural clinical experiences. These could be adapted for other professional scenarios as well. By working through multicultural cases in the classroom setting and via OSCEs, students are given the opportunity to build skills in cross-cultural communication, to gain awareness and sensitivity surrounding cultural issues, and to reflect on and confront their own beliefs and biases beyond the traditional clinical setting.

Material for the development of these cases was informed through clinical literature and research as well as clinical experience and community and expert input. Because these cases are used as summative evaluation tools, the specific details of these cases cannot be discussed here. However, case scenarios were developed specifically for the activity by one to two faculty members to represent common clinical encounters for each specialty. There was some overlap in cases among specialty areas, but only one case was performed by APRN students in all specialties that participated in the grant. Essential components for each case were decided by clinical faculty case writers and then reviewed with the larger group for final editing. Efforts were made to diversify cases by considering ethnicity, age and developmental stage, race, sexual orientation, geographic location (rural and urban), socioeconomic status, disability and functional status, gender, health and language literacy, religious beliefs, methods of communication, and health conditions (acute, chronic, preventive) and by incorporating input from the community focus groups held prior to case development.

Another tool used was the *Worlds Apart* videos (Granger-Monson, Hazlett, Green, Betancourt, Camillo et al., 2003) which highlight four scenarios on encounters with individuals from cultures other than the majority culture in the U.S. The first case highlights the case of an older Afghan man who has cancer and refuses chemotherapy. The second case is that of an adult African American male awaiting kidney transplant. He vocalizes frustration and verbalizes that he doesn't think black men are high on the list for transplant. The third case explores the struggle between traditional beliefs and western approaches to medicine for a young Laotian girl with a congenital heart defect for whom surgery is recommended. The final case is that of a middle-aged Hispanic woman with multiple health issues who becomes depressed after being evicted from her apartment. All of these scenarios prompt deep discussion among students around the roles that health beliefs, traditions, and perceptions play in the clinical encounter between patient and provider. Students are asked to reflect on the impact of misunderstanding and poor communication on patient outcomes and the patient-provider relationship. For example in the case highlighting the young Laotian girl with the heart defect, students are given the opportunity to witness the family's interaction with a pediatric nurse practitioner in primary care, a cardiologist, and a cardiac surgeon. Students also hear the perspective of the mother, grandmother, the child, the interpreter, and each health care provider in the scenario regarding their thoughts, reactions, frustrations, and fears. Students actively discuss what worked well in communication and what could be improved upon. They gain insight into perspectives of the child and family as well as the health care providers. They ponder the impact of health beliefs on clinical decision-making in the community and health care setting. This is a formative evaluation and students are not tested on the information, but participation is required and students earn points by contributing to discussion. In some cases, questions emerge that require students to research findings and post these on the course website. This might involve clinical health information or cultural information.

Other examples of health issues involving culture that prompt discussion and are included in clinical case studies developed for course work include: cultural issues that arise around immunizations such as distrust of the measles vaccine due to fears of autism in some communities, misunderstandings about the purpose of mammography, differences in beliefs about destiny that shape patient responses to illness and treatment, use of nontraditional therapies as first-line, misunderstandings about the use of medication to treat chronic illness, or the impact of dietary practices on some chronic conditions. Clinical cases are developed depending on the course objectives. If the case is developed for Clinical Pharmacotherapeutics, for example, the focus of the case will be on medication management, but may involve a patient from diverse ethnic background, varying literacy or cognitive level, socioeconomic status, or age. All of these factors will impact medication management and must be considered when prescribing. A clinical case surrounding immunizations might be developed for a pediatric- focused class.

In these scenarios students are asked to diagnose illness conditions and patient status and to design a patient-centered care plan to address identified health concerns, mental-emotional concerns, health maintenance or health promotion/ disease prevention issues for the individual patient. Students are asked to formulate a holistic, culturally-congruent individual care plan that considers patient factors as well as broader family, community, and system influences on health. They must provide evidence-based rationale for each step of their plan. They are provided with tools to foster therapeutic communication and motivational interviewing skills in several different classes. Some of the cases are worked up individually and some are completed in a group format online or in class with group expectations clearly delineated or by role play. For example, a student in an FNP clinical seminar might be asked to role play a patient with a breast mass who does not want a mammogram and who shares that she believes only women in her culture are put through this sometimes uncomfortable procedure. Another student must play the role of the provider with the student "patient" and explore how best to address the patient's fears. Peers in the classroom can provide feedback or input into the role play.

In group case studies, students are usually assigned into groups by the course instructor. Groups may include students from the same specialty or from different specialties. Students collectively make decisions about all aspects of the clinical case from determining history and physical exam components to diagnostic testing to diagnosis and development of the care plan. One student is typically designated a leader for the week and may assign tasks to other students in the group. Students debate and reflect on the data they collect and collaboratively reach decisions by consensus. This provides an opportunity for students to share their perspectives and rationale while they "solve" the clinical case. An effort is made to include diversity in case studies. For example, in one case, students are asked to evaluate a 2 year-old child of Spanish-speaking parents who presents with ear pain, upper respiratory symptoms, and fever. They are given basic history and physical exam findings and told that the patient travels back and forth to Mexico with his parents. Students must indicate what additional information they would want to know. It is expected they will assess for immunization status, medications, allergies, and risk for infectious disease exposure. They must accurately diagnose the patient and formulate a culturally sensitive patient and family-centered plan of care which considers social determinants of health such as insurance status (medication coverage), assesses for understanding of plan, and ability of child and family to follow up. Students also bring their unique lenses through which they view the case to the discussion. Their clinical decisions should reflect evidence-based care and represent culturally congruent actions. Any uncertainties or muddy areas of knowledge that arise during the process generate study questions that students will research and post responses to on the course website.

ASSESSMENT AND EVALUATION

Effective teaching must align learning objectives with teaching methods and with evaluation. Evaluation is perhaps the most difficult aspect of internationalizing the curriculum. Clear outcomes must be developed for student evaluation. For advanced practice nursing students, these outcomes are linked to national competencies for APRN practice (National Organization of Nurse Practitioner Faculty, 2013) and to DNP essentials as specified by the American Association of Colleges of Nursing (AACN, 2006). Again, a team approach to developing evaluation tools is recommended. Other associations have also developed evaluation tools. The American Association of Colleges of Medicine has developed an objective tool to evaluate cultural competencies in medical students (American Association of Colleges of Medicine, 2005). The National Center for Cultural Competence (Georgetown University) offers multiple self- assessment checklists for personnel providing health and social services to individuals and families.

According to the National Center for Cultural Competence Experiential Learning: Cultural and Linguistic Competence Checklist for MCH Training Programs (Goode, 2012), culturally competent institutions have the capacity to:

- Value diversity;
- Practice with cultural humility;
- Conduct self-assessment;
- Manage the dynamics of difference;
- Acquire and institutionalize cultural knowledge;
- Adapt to diversity and the cultural contexts of communities they serve (pp.3–4).

We integrated these principles into our curriculum through the activities and learning experiences we designed. These are the characteristics to strive for when developing teaching and learning activities that foster behaviors promoting cultural congruence and cultural humility. These characteristics, along with national competencies, were used to inform evaluative tools. Student clinical performance is evaluated using a clinical tool that includes assessment of communication skills developed by the faculty team to identify core concepts that reflect effective communication techniques as well as culturally-sensitive interactions and culturally-congruent actions and that align with core APRN competencies as established by national nursing organizations. These core concepts were then incorporated into student evaluation of clinical encounters and OSCEs. Students are expected to consider the patient within the context in which they live. They must use therapeutic communication skills to elicit the patient history, clarify information, and offer encouragement and empathy in a respectful but effective manner. Students are graded on communication by their instructors as well as by standardized patients (actor patients who have been trained to play a role in a specific clinical case and to look for specific skill sets among students). Specifically, SPs provide them with feedback on their interactive skills: the clarity of the information relayed, sensitivity to the unique needs of the patient, degree of empathy, organization, willingness to listen, and ability to summarize key points of the visit. Faculty members review student clinical performance and communication abilities as well as SP feedback to the student. Students are also given the opportunity to review their own taped encounters with standardized patients and to reflect on their performance including their ability to: diagnose accurately and develop an evidence-based plan of care for the health condition and/or concerns that is culturally congruent and engages the patient, communicate effectively, conduct a well organized encounter, identify lessons learned as well as areas in need of improvement. This provides triangulated data relative to student performance and gives a composite picture of student communication abilities. Students are also evaluated by community preceptors and faculty on their ability to interact effectively with a diverse patient population.

As noted, clinical case studies focused on clinical conditions among patients from diverse backgrounds are used widely throughout the curriculum. Students' plan of care must articulate an understanding of cultural, behavioral, and health beliefs that might influence their plan of care and patient health outcomes. These traits emphasize the ongoing nature of the journey toward integrating multiculturalism and cultural humility into behavior and curricula. Not only must the thread be continuous throughout the curriculum, but faculty must reinforce and challenge students to continually reflect on personal behaviors and experiences as they journey through the educational program and beyond in order to attain a true appreciation for diversity.

Case Study grading rubrics also incorporate elements that would reflect assimilation of cultural humility and sensitivity indicating an ability to deliver culturally congruent care as well as clinical decision-making skill. An attempt to standardize these grading rubrics across specialty area of studies is ongoing. Since many of the courses are taken by all students in the APRN programs, efforts continue to thread similar concepts promoting culturally-congruent care across courses. For example, all advanced practice nursing students take the Holistic Health Assessment course and they are introduced to principles of culturally-sensitive communication in this course. Interpreters and community members from diverse communities engage students in a panel discussion about culture, approach, and communication, and assist students to avoid creating stereotypes. Students are challenged to reflect on their biases and to look at each patient as an individual. Currently, students participate in a clinical experience with a diverse virtual patient in an online simulated patient encounter. They are able to interact with the virtual patient online in much the same way they would in a real clinical encounter. Students are graded on clinical skills, but also on their ability to demonstrate empathy and to provide patient-centered education.

FACULTY MULTICULTURAL LEARNING

A secondary goal of the initiatives was to enhance multicultural sensitivity and awareness among faculty. The Quest grant allowed for the development of an interprofessional experiential learning day with health care providers who utilize complementary therapies such as acupuncture, traditional Chinese medicine, massage, and chiropractor skills. This allows students and faculty to become more knowledgeable of nontraditional therapeutic approaches and to be able to recommend such treatments to patients desiring them. Students are given the opportunity to participate in the modalities and to consider how they might be used. Case study scenarios are discussed and a blended treatment plan is formulated by students of complementary therapies and APRN students for the patients in the case studies using traditional and complementary therapies. Nursing and complementary professional faculty participate in case study discussion.

The Edwards grant (2009) directed funding toward the creation of diverse case scenarios, but also developed faculty practices in settings serving diverse patient populations. These clinical settings became clinical sites for students enrolled in the school. Emphasis was also given to developing faculty and preceptor resources promoting culturally-congruent care. Faculty participated in creating vignettes highlighting culturally congruent care as part of this grant.

Additionally regular meetings occurred during which faculty shared their own thoughts about evolving experiences. For example, in reviewing the focus group information gained from talking with community participants, faculty concurred that this was a valuable experience and community participants also conveyed that they valued the opportunity to engage with nursing faculty to improve the way people from their cultures were portrayed in clinical case studies. As a provider who has worked with diverse cultures for many years, I gained greater appreciation for the experience of Somali, Latino, and Souteast Asian patients in the health care system. One of the goals of the exercise was to try to increase interest among community members to participate as standardized patients. Despite learning about the OSCE and role of the standardized patient, only two Spanish-speaking individuals agreed to participate. The other ethnic groups did not wish to participate at this time. It is a start however, to building community and enhancing understanding across cultures. The OSCE that utilized an interpreter was an enriching learning experience for students as per their reflections.

The School of Nursing also has an active Diversity Committee including faculty as well as student representation. Various events are held throughout the year to inform and embrace multicultural issues. Some of these events highlight campus speakers including faculty, staff, and students as well as outside guest speakers. A school of nursing book club regularly features books with a multicultural theme such as, *The Immortal Life of Henrietta Lacks.* Book club discussions are open to staff, faculty, and students.

Challenges Encountered

Few challenges were encountered in designing activities that integrated principles of cultural humility into the curriculum, because team faculty members voluntarily (and enthusiastically) embarked on the process with a clear purpose to internationalize at least some aspects of the curriculum in order to facilitate the provision of culturally congruent care by our students. The biggest challenges arose in determining how to facilitate and evaluate effective communication across cultures, how to evaluate culturally congruent care and cultural humility and how to guard against stereotyping. One of the risks that is inherent in learning about diverse cultures is the possibility of developing stereotypes about whole groups of people. Stressing the importance of individual patient-centered care in the clinical setting was important. Facilitating students to check their own biases and to monitor their thought processes in planning and coordinating care with individuals of diverse cultures is essential. Another big challenge in a clinical setting is time. Most ambulatory settings have set time allotted to visit with a patient. As novice advanced practice nurses, the ability to conduct an efficient visit in a culturally congruent manner is challenging as it requires a thoughtful approach, and the time necessary to achieve a therapeutic relationship. For many, this will be an ongoing skill to develop as they progress in their professional careers.

While graduate nursing students arrive with some nursing experience and presumably some interaction with diverse populations, moving into a diverse ambulatory setting where efficiency and flexibility is required, encountering a language barrier may be an added challenge. Each year, more and more of our students are fluent in one or more languages, but a large percentage of students come from traditional mainstream backgrounds with English as the primary language resulting in a language barrier in the clinical setting. Providing them with simulated cultural experiences prior to their clinical rotations can be very helpful.

Finally, statistics on nursing faculty members reveal that there is a persistent shortage of faculty members and faculty are aging. The average ages for doctorally-prepared nurse faculty holding the ranks of professor, associate professor, and assistant professor are 61.3, 57.7, and 51.2 years (AACN, 2014). Statistics are similar for masters-prepared nurse faculty. Additionally, diverse faculty role models are lacking. The nursing profession will need to continue efforts to recruit into the field and to develop the next generation of nursing faculty.

Lastly, it is important to reiterate that developing cultural humility and translating that into providing culturally congruent care has no static endpoint. In developing a curriculum aimed at producing students who will become providers of culturally congruent care, it is important to communicate that they are given the tools in school, but they must continue to learn and develop once practicing in their professional role.

Future Implications

As we move forward in an increasingly diverse world with global connections, academia must continue to strive toward building connections with individuals and communities to enhance educational preparation for our students. Moving beyond academic walls into the community is not only desired, but, I believe, necessary. There is richness in real interaction that informs the educational experience for our students and pushes them to broaden their knowledge and curiosity beyond what we can provide theoretically in the classroom. The key to building a strong cadre of students moving into the future is to expand their horizons. Internationalizing the curriculum through multicultural experiences and reflection is a way to achieve this. Gaining consensus among faculty members is paramount to the development of a cohesive multicultural curriculum. Integration of multicultural activities and the intentional development of activities that build on lessons learned across coursework fosters this goal. We have learned at my institution that while the process of internationalizing the curriculum is ongoing and ever changing and takes commitment and motivation by those involved, it also breathes new life into our programs and ignites our students' enthusiasm for spreading their wings and engaging with the world around them.

The experiences they gain in their educational programs have prompted our graduates to pursue professional opportunities upon graduation in the inner city, suburbia, rural areas, Native American reservations, the far reaches of the Alaskan wild, and many have also pursued connections abroad. They work with the very young, the elderly, the infirm, the developmentally challenged, the mentally ill, as well as with healthy individuals. They consider the broader context affecting health and assume active roles in government, professional associations, and institutions. The desire to bridge the gap that can exist between and across cultures due to socioeconomics, education, belief systems, gender, age, and culture is a potent motivator toward change and the attainment of common goals. Activities and experiences as recounted here can be adapted to fit many other professions. In our increasingly connected world, engineers, business administrators, educators, all of us, daily interact with individuals different from ourselves. Reaching out toward understanding each other is a goal to be pursued and, as educators, we have a responsibility to promote and develop ways of doing this.

REFERENCES

American Association of Colleges of Nursing. (2006). *The essentials of doctoral education for advanced nursing practice*. Retrieved from http://www.aacn.nche.edu/publications/position/DNPEssentials.pdf

American Association of Colleges of Nursing. (2009). *Establishing a culturally competent master's and doctorally prepared nursing workforce*. Retrieved from http://www.aacn.nche.edu/education-resources/CulturalComp.pdf

American Association of Colleges of Nursing. (2009). *Tool kit for cultural competence in master's and doctoral nursing education*. Retrieved from http://www.aacn.nche.edu/education-resources/Cultural_Competency_Toolkit_Grad.pdf

American Association of Colleges of Nursing. (2014). *Fact sheet on nursing faculty shortage*. Retrieved from http://www.aacn.nche.edu/media-relations/fact-sheets/nursing-faculty-shortage

American Association of Medical Colleges. (2005). *Cultural competence education*. Retrieved from https://www.aamc.org/download/54338/data/culturalcomped.pdf

American Association of Medical Colleges. (2005). *Tool for assessing cultural competence training*. Retrieved from https://www.aamc.org/download/54344/data/tacct_pdf.pdf

Bacote, J. (2002). The process of cultural competence in the delivery of healthcare services: A model of care. *Journal of Transcultural Nursing, 13*, 181–184.

Betancourt, J. (2003). Cross-cultural medical education: Conceptual approaches and frameworks for evaluation. *Academic Medicine, 78*(6), 560–569.

Central Intelligence Agency. (2014). *The World Factbook*. Retrieved from: https://www.cia.gov/library/publications/the-world-factbook/geos/us.html

Cross, T., Bazron, B., Dennis, K., & Isaacs, M. (1989). *Towards a culturally competent system of care* (Vol. I). Washington, DC: Georgetown University Child Development Center, CASSP Technical Assistance Center.

Edwardson, S. (2009–2012). *Addressing health disparities through DNP preparation*. Funded grant, Health Resources and Services Administration.

Garces, I., Scarinci, I., & Harrison, L. (2006). An examination of sociocultural factors associated with health and health seeking among Latina immigrants. *Journal of Immigrant Health, 8*(4), 377–385. doi:10.1007/s.10903-006-9008-8

Georgetown University Center for Child and Human Development. (2014). *National center for cultural competence*. Retrieved from http://nccc.georgetown.edu/

Goode, T., & Bronheim, S. (2012). *Experiential learning: Cultural and linguistic competence checklist for MCH training programs Georgetown University Center for Child and Human Development.* Retrieved from http://nccc.georgetown.edu/documents/nccc_Learning_checklist_P4.pdf

Gorski, P. (1995–2014). *Multicultural education Pavilion.* Retrieved from http://www.edchange.org/multicultural/

Green, C., Anderson, K., Baker, T., Campbell, L., Decker, S., Fillingim, R., ... Vallerand, A.H. (2003). The unequal burden of pain: Confronting racial and ethnic disparities in pain. *Pain Medicine, 4*(3), 277–294. doi:10.1046/j.1526-4637.2003.03034.x

Hook, J. N., Davis, D. E., Owen, J., Worthington Jr., E. L., & Utsey, S. O. (2013). Cultural humility: Measuring openness to culturally diverse clients. *Journal of Counseling Psychology, 6*(3), 353–366. doi:10.1037/a0032595

Juve, C. (2011–2014). *Promoting excellence in APRN education: A regional approach to quality, safety, and diversity.* Funded grant, Health Resources and Services Administration.

Leask, B. (2004). Bridging the gap: Internationalizing university curricula. *Journal of Studies in International Education, 8*(1), 5–31. doi:10.1177/1028315303260832

Leininger, M. (1988). Leininger's theory of nursing: Cultural care diversity and universality. *Nursing Science Quarterly, 1*(4), 152–160. doi:10.1177/089431848800100408

Leininger, M. (1990). The significance of cultural concepts in nursing. *Journal of Transcultural Nursing, 2*(1), 52–59. doi:10.1177/104365969000200108

Leininger, M. (1991). Becoming aware of types of health practitioners and cultural imposition. *Journal of Transcultural Nursing, 2*(2), 32–39. doi:10.1177/104365969100200205

Leininger, M. (2002). Culture care theory: A major contribution to advance transcultural nursing knowledge and practices. *Journal of Transcultural Nursing, 13*(3), 189–192. doi:10.1177/10459602013003005

Leininger, M., & McFarland, M. (2002). *Transcultural nursing: Concepts, theories, research, and practices* (3rd ed.). New York, NY: McGraw-Hill

Lindeke, L., & Benbenek, M. (2012). *Embracing a global framework: Integrating the new AACN cultural competency standards into nurse practitioner education.* National Organization of Nurse Practitioner Faculty, presentation.

Merriam Webster Online Dictionary. (2014). *Culture*. Retrieved from http://www.merriam-webster.com/dictionary/culture

Murphy, S. (2006). Mapping the literature of transcultural nursing. *Journal of the Medical Library Association, 94*(2 Suppl), E142–E151. Retrieved from http://www.ncbi.nlm.nih.gov/pmc/articles/PMC1463039/

National Academy of Sciences. (2002). *Unequal treatment: What healthcare providers need to know about racial and ethnic disparities in health care, Institute of Medicine.* Retrieved from http://www.iom.edu/~/media/Files/Report%20Files/2003/Unequal-Treatment-Confronting-Racial-and-Ethnic-Disparities-in-Health-Care/Disparitieshcproviders8pgFINAL.pdf

Savery, J. R. (2006). Overview of problem-based learning: Definitions and distinctions. *Interdisciplinary Journal of Problem-based Learning, 1*(1). Retrieved from http://dx.doi.org/10.7771/1541-5015.1002

Schuessler, J., Wilder, B., & Byrd, L. (2012). Reflective journaling and development of cultural humility in students. *Nursing Education Perspectives, 33*(2), 96–99.

Sugerman, D. A., Doherty, K. L., Garvey, D. E., & Gass, M. A. (2000). *Reflective learning: Theory and practice.* Dubuque, IA: Kendall/Hunt

Tervalin, M., & Murray-Garcia, J. (1998). Cultural humility versus cultural competence: A critical distinction in defining physician training outcomes in multicultural education. *Journal of Health Care for the Poor and Underserved, 9*(2), 117–125.

United States Census Bureau. (2012). *Statistical abstract.* Retrieved from http://www.census.gov/compendia/statab/fed_reports.html

Wu, A., Burke, A., & LeBaron, S. (2007). Use of traditional medicine by immigrant Chinese patients. *Family Medicine, 39*(3), 195–200.

SUSAN STAATS

10. INTERNATIONALIZING COLLEGE ALGEBRA

Few undergraduate classes match the potential of college algebra to internationalize the university experience. The complexity and variability of the world's most pressing issues—of health outcomes, income, access to education, access to clean water—mean that a great deal of influential information is conveyed mathematically, usually as tables of values and graphs. Young adults who wish to become informed and active participants in global issues must learn to understand and interpret international perspectives through mathematics. At a time when postsecondary institutions are reevaluating undergraduate mathematics pedagogy, internationalization can help revitalize the curriculum.

College algebra in the United States is widely recognized as a troubled class. Students often experience extremely high failure and withdrawal rates, compelling them to retake that class multiple times (Small, 2006). In many states, college algebra and related pre-calculus courses disadvantage low-income students and students of color (Complete College America, 2012). Among the many reasons for the poor success rate of the class is its misalignment with student goals. In terms of typical course content, algebra has traditionally sought to prepare students for calculus and for math-intensive majors. However, in the United States, the class also became a standard general education requirement that students complete as part of their liberal education. As a result, college algebra is one of the most highly enrolled classes in the undergraduate curriculum in the United States, but only a minority of college algebra students follow the assumed pathway into STEM careers. The majority of college algebra students take the class as part of a social science or allied health science general education requirement (Herriot & Dunbar, 2009).

By internationalizing college algebra, we can draw upon the wide and deep data sets that are published annually on the world's central problems, and we can bring this knowledge to an extremely wide range of students. We can better align the class with the interests of the students who take it. When students in an internationalized college algebra class learn to trace trends and calculate comparisons under the guidance of a mathematics teacher, they will be able to correct mathematical misunderstandings, and so, to develop more accurate and critical global perspectives. This is why college algebra offers enormous, unrecognized potential to contribute to students' international knowledge.

The challenges to internationalizing college algebra are substantial, too. This chapter outlines these challenges and seeks to address them. I will outline sources of international data and provide examples of algebraic topics that can be supported by them. Another challenge is that mathematics faculty often do not have experience teaching international issues, and this may lower their interest or confidence in internationalizing their class. To this end, I provide case studies and ancillary sources—videos, readings, books—that faculty can use either as the basis of in- or out-of-class assignments for students, or as background material for their own development of international perspectives.

INTERNATIONAL PERSPECTIVES IN EARLY UNDERGRADUATE MATHEMATICS: PATHWAYS AND PITFALLS

International Curriculum in Undergraduate Mathematics Classes

Although efforts to internationalize undergraduate mathematics curricula are not widespread, some institutions have invested significantly in international content, usually in three places in the curriculum: in upper division courses for mathematics majors, in survey courses on mathematics for liberal arts majors, and in mathematics for elementary teachers. High-enrollment pre-calculus classes like college algebra have largely been ignored.

For many years, mathematicians have called for more attention to the history of mathematics (Anderton & Wright, 2012; Fauvel, 1991; Tzanakis & Arcavi, 2000). In many cases, this is taught in undergraduate or graduate classes for mathematics majors, although there is consistent interest in introducing history of mathematics at secondary levels, too. Attendant to this history is recognition of vast contributions to the field by non-European mathematicians (Appelbaum, Friedler, Ortiz & Wolff, 2009). Another approach to internationalizing mathematics classes is proposed by Arcadia University mathematicians, who are developing mid- and upper-level undergraduate classes on anthropological issues in mathematics and mathematics education, and on mathematical modeling of global issues, e.g., transportation and environmental issues (Appelbaum, Friedler, Ortiz & Wolff, 2009).

A long-standing approach in mathematics education that is highly committed to international perspectives is the field of ethnomathematics, established in the 1980s, largely through the efforts of Brazilian educator Ubiratan d'Ambrosio (d'Ambrosio, 1985). Ethnomathematics focused attention on both ethnographic inquiries into mathematical practices embedded within cultural activities and on curriculum development based on these practices. The field has produced lovely case studies of culturally-based mathematics (Ascher, 1991, 2006; Gerdes, 1998). The Pythagorean Theorem emerges from Angolan women's basketry craft. The mathematics of efficiency and optimization is recast in the Eulerian circuits of Southern African sand drawings and the narrative tradition that accompanies them. Ethnomathematics has documented varied base systems for counting along with the ways these are represented through the human body and through cultural objects, perhaps most famously in the Andean *quipu* knotted string bundles.

Ethnomathematics has most commonly made its way into primary and secondary schools as a means of creating a culturally-relevant curriculum (Bishop, 1998), and so, it is occasionally it is taught in classes on mathematics for elementary teachers. Ethnomathematics has also been the basis for liberal arts mathematics classes in some postsecondary institutions. These classes are typically taken as the single required mathematics course by a student whose major requires only exposure to rather than professional use of mathematics.

Many ethnomathematical case studies—though not all—rely on the mathematics of discrete systems rather than continuous systems of numbers. The positive integers, 1,2,3,4,…form a discrete system. College algebra is largely concerned with developing mathematical literacy around continuous number systems in which students consider numbers like 1.35, 1.36, and numbers in between, such as 1.357. Ethnomathematics case studies less commonly motivate investigations of the continuous number systems that figure prominently in algebra classes. A welcome case to the contrary is Eglash's Culturally-Situated Design Tools which allow students to use continuous variables to conduct computer modeling of cultural activities such as Native American Anishinabe house constructions, African American hair braiding, and graffiti art (Eglash, n.d.). Taken as a whole, ethnomathematics is a lively and exciting approach to internationalizing mathematics curriculum that has a relatively weak presence in college algebra classes in the United States.

Dilemmas in Internationalizing College Algebra

Scholarship on internationalizing the curriculum and on improving multicultural education in higher education share a concern with defining, developing, and reflecting on intercultural competence. Ippolito (2007), for example, takes the perspective that a major goal of internationalizing the curriculum is to improve intercultural understanding. Others suggest that cultural competence must be transformed into "the continuous critical refinement and fostering of a type of thinking and knowing—a critical consciousness—of self, others and the world" (Kumagi & Lypson, 2009, p. 783). "Critical consciousness involves a reflective awareness of the differences in power and privilege and the inequalities that are embedded in social relationships" (Kumagi & Lypson, 2009, p. 783). Even intentional teaching for intercultural and international understanding may fail to achieve these important objectives.

The process of internationalizing early undergraduate mathematics classes could fail to achieve either intercultural understanding or critical consciousness for several reasons. In the first place, a data-oriented approach to international issues runs the risk of essentializing people and their lives. Sifting through numbers does not yield an understanding of peoples' daily lives, struggles, or sources of agency. Furthermore, there may be insufficient buy-in from mathematics faculty, who may be unfamiliar with techniques of teaching for international understanding or who may be hesitant to take time away from existing curriculum to address international topics. Although many mathematicians collaborate on international research, this may not directly translate into intercultural understanding that can be expressed within or made relevant to the content of a particular mathematics class. There is a need for materials to build knowledge of the potential to motivate mathematical learning through international contexts, as well as materials that build contextual understanding, for topics that fit within undergraduate mathematics classes.

The following vignettes offer examples of algebra applications that use international perspectives (see also Staats & Robertson, 2009; Staats, Sintjago & Fitzpatrick, 2013). I've taught these applications in several contexts. I developed many of the contextualized algebra applications through teaching first-year seminars. These are small classes offered to students from any academic discipline in their first two semesters at the university; my seminars offered international perspectives credit and were intended to help students review basic math skills while learning about the Millennium Development Goals. I incorporated these applications frequently in college algebra classes which, in our unit, are typically offered to students majoring in education and in social services. Most of these students take the class as their only required mathematics class. In another case, my college algebra class was part of a learning community with an international focus. In the learning community model, all students in my college algebra class also enrolled in a World Literature class. This way of organizing curriculum lets students explore connections between two disciplines while building supportive social relationships with a cohort of peers. In our learning community, the algebra applications provided a wider comparative context for the personal stories of diverse communities, of change and struggle offered in the literature class.

Several factors make our classes fairly diverse, particularly compared to other units in large, research-oriented universities. Our campus is situated near large immigrant communities of Hmong, Latino, Somali and other East African peoples. Our college is home to the university's TRiO program, a federally-funded program to motivate and support students from disadvantaged backgrounds. Commanding English Transitions, one component of the TRiO program, serves English language learners. For some of these students, internationalized algebra applications let them use family histories and knowledge to interpret their algebra work. This approach to teaching algebra gives all students a chance to better understand the world contexts that have formed the diversity of our metropolitan area.

TEACHING ALGEBRA THROUGH AN INTERNATIONAL CONTEXT

Getting Started with International Data

The richest sources of data for an internationalized college algebra class are reports published annually by the United Nations Development Program. The United Nations Human Development Reports summarize data by country for a wide range of issues: basic health and health care data (e.g. incidence of key illnesses or tobacco use, availability of trained birth assistants); economic data (e.g. GDP per capita, GDP per capita growth rates); and environmental quality and sustainability (e.g. access to clean water and to sanitation, rates of deforestation). Since 2005, additional annual reports convey progress on eight key development issues known as the Millennium Development Goals (MDGs) (United Nations, 2014b). The MDGs are measurable benchmarks for progress on the worlds' most pressing issues. For example, between the years of 1990 and 2015, the Millennium Project hopes to:

- Halve extreme poverty of living on less than $1.25 per day.
- Reduce by ¾ mortality rates of children under 5 years old.
- Reduce by ⅔ rates of maternal deaths due to childbirth.
- Stop and reverse the spread of infectious diseases such as malaria, HIV/AIDS, and tuberculosis.

The MDG progress reports provide data in a form that is easily used in algebra classes: tables of values with two or three data collection years so that students can model the indicator with standard algebraic methods. Another useful data source is UNICEF's recent publication on income inequality, which provides income distribution for many countries organized by year and by quintile (Ortiz & Cummins, 2011). Gapminder.org offers customizable animations on global health, economic, and social issues; it is useful both as a means of looking up data and understanding change over time through the animations (Gapminder, n.d.). Because 2015 is the final year of the Millennium Project, the United Nations convened the Rio+20 conference to plan its successor, 17 Sustainable Development Goals to be assessed through 2030 (United Nations, n.d.). In coming years, there will continue to be current data on significant global problems that can inform international algebra classes.

Numeracy, Fractions and Proportional Reasoning

International data sets lend themselves easily to reviews of basic principles of quantitative literacy like numeracy and proportional reasoning. Engaging numeracy in a very direct way—reading columns of numbers in the Human Development Reports—raises awareness of disparities dramatically. In 2012, Japan reported 2.2 infant deaths per 1,000 live births; Sierra Leone reported 117 (Gapminder, n.d.). This demographic technique of offering data in normalized rates, e.g. cases per thousand, ten thousand or hundred thousand, will be new to many students. Infant mortality is expressed as the number of infant deaths in the first year of life per 1,000 live births. The maternal mortality ratio is often expressed in maternal deaths related to pregnancy out of 100,000 live births within a given time period. Students may discuss why normalized rates are used for these health data, potential problems of data collection, and why a different unit is used for maternal and infant health.

Students may compare the terminology that they know from algebra—rates of change—to demographic terminology of normalized rates.

Studying demographic indices is another way of reviewing fractions and proportional reasoning in college algebra. An index is a number derived from a formula that characterizes the relationship between a particular datum and its wider data set. The Gender Equality Index, the General Happiness Index, and the UNDP's Human Development Index are fairly well-known examples. The last of these ranks countries based on income per capita, life expectancy, and measures of educational access. Indices are widely used to represent data sets, and so they are one of the most useful but under-utilized potential topics for college algebra classes.

Table 1. Gender parity in education index for world regions.

	1990	2012
Sub-Saharan Africa	0.52	0.64
Northern Africa	0.65	1.12
Western Asia	0.63	0.95
Southern Asia	0.49	0.81
Eastern Asia	0.49	1.08
Latin American and the Caribbean	0.97	1.28
Developing Regions Overall	0.69	0.99

Several key misunderstandings in the interpretation of fractions can be addressed by reviewing trends in the Gender Parity in Education Index (Table 1). This index is formed by dividing the percent of school-age girls who attend school by the percent of school-age boys who attend school. A selection of regional trends in postsecondary enrollment is given by Table 2 (United Nations, 2014a, pp. 21–22). The target for gender parity in education is an index value between 0.97 and 1.03.

Discussion questions based on the Gender Parity in Education Index could include:

- In your high school and college experience so far, did young men or women tend to drop out more?
- What region has improved the most in gender parity in tertiary enrollment?
- In 2012, which region had the worst gender parity in tertiary enrollment?
- Can a fraction be greater than 1?
- Suppose that women's tertiary enrollment decreased in one of these regions between 1990 and 2012. What probably happened to men's enrollment?
- What social processes could account for the 2012 value of 1.28 for Latin America and the Caribbean?

Another index is the 20-20 ratio (sometimes called the 80-20 ratio or Quintile Ratio), which compares the incomes of the wealthiest 20% with the least wealthy 20% in a country. Students can compare trends in income inequality across countries using income quintiles in the UNICEF publication *Global Inequality: Beyond the Bottom Billion* (Ortiz & Cummins, 2011). For example, students could select two countries for comparison and calculate the 20-20 ratio for each year:

Table 2. Trends in the 20-20 Ratio for the United States and Brazil.

	Year	Quintile 1	Quintile 5	20-20 Ratio
United States	1990	46.6	3.9	11.9
	1995	48.7	3.7	13.2
	2000	49.6	3.6	13.8
	2005	50.1	3.4	14.7
Brazil	1990	64.5	2.4	26.9
	1995	62.5	2.4	26.0
	2000	61.7	2.4	25.7
	2005	60.0	2.9	20.7

Computing the 20-20 Ratio lets students discover for themselves changes in income inequality around the world. For example, calculating the 20-20 ratio for Brazil illustrates its position as one of the most unequal countries in the world. Still, under this measure, inequality in Brazil has dropped rapidly during a time period of increased inequality in the United States.

Linear and Polynomial Functions

Several of the MDGs have benchmarks that lend themselves to modeling with linear or polynomial functions. Between 1990 and 2015, Goal 1 aims to reduce poverty by half. Goal 4 is to reduce the under-five mortality rate by two thirds, and Goal 5 is to reduce maternal mortality by three quarters. The progress reports offer at least two data points on each of these goals, for example, the percent of people living on less than $1.25 per day in 1990 and in 2010 (United Nations, 2014a). A fairly easy algebra activity is to graph progress towards the goal, to assess whether the goal will be met in 2015, and to find the year in which the goal was, or will be, met. These questions require basic algebraic procedures that are typical of textbook questions.

In some cases, MDG reports offer three data points for these goals, for example, the maternal mortality goal in the 2013 and 2014 reports, the poverty goal in the 2013 report. This kind of data can support polynomial modeling with spreadsheets or graphing calculators, and it can support activities on concavity. For example, using MDG report 2013, students can generate comparisons between different regions.

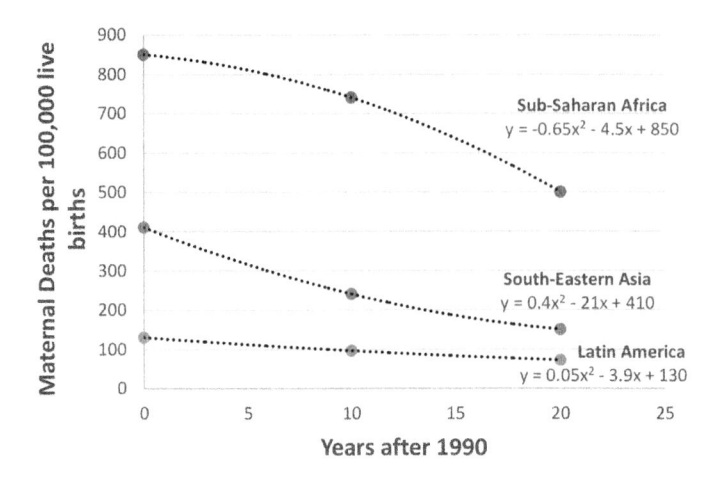

Figure 1. Maternal mortality trends in three regions.

The technical skill needed to produce this kind of chart is minimal, but it can support classroom discussion on important ideas in algebra, particularly for students who are taking the class to improve general quantitative literacy:

1. Why does the correlation coefficient equal 1 for these three graphs? How could realistic data fit a degree two equation perfectly?
2. How would you describe the concavity of each of these three curves?
3. Which region is doing best if you consider:
   - the slope of the line between the first and last point?
   - the concavity of the graph?
   - the absolute levels of maternal mortality rates?
4. If you needed to prioritize funding for maternal health, which region would you choose to receive the most funding? Why? What argument against your position might you face? What additional information would you like to have?

Logarithmic Functions

Extreme disparities in global health and economics mean that the numerical indicators often range across several orders of magnitude. In 2010, for example, the number of maternal death reports out of 100,000 live births was 1090 for Eritrea, 132 for Iraq, 11 for the Czech Republic, and 1.6 for Iceland (Gapminder, n.d.). In this situation, data is usually reported on a logarithmic scale in which the major grid lines are at 1, 10, 100, 1000, and so on, instead of a linear scale of 10, 20, 30 (for example). Economic indicators like GDP per capita also vary widely. In these situations, a logarithmic scale makes viewing data patterns much easier.

INTERNATIONALIZING COLLEGE ALGEBRA

I have often used graphics from Gapminder.org as students' first introduction to logarithms. Learning to read a logarithmic scale on a graph can create the sense that logarithms are useful, even necessary, in situations of extreme disparity. Figure 2 shows an example from a Gapminder screen shot (Gapminder, n.d., based on Dikhanov, 2005).

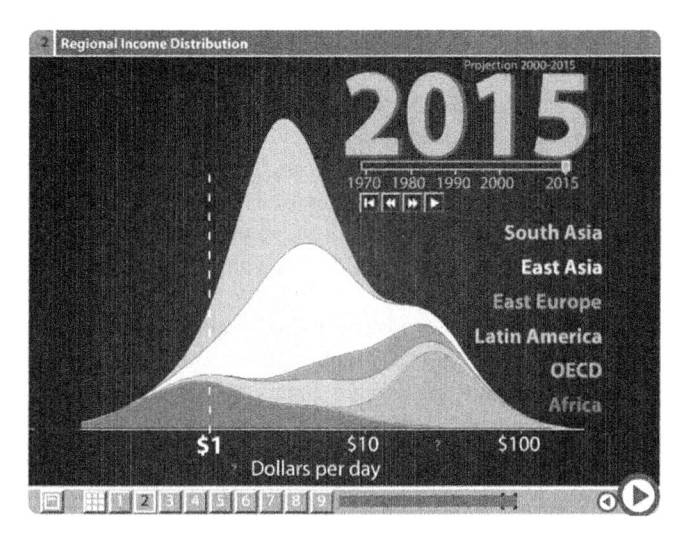

*Figure 2. Global income levels in dollars per day.
Free material from www.gapminder.org*

For students to "discover" the concept of logarithm through graphs like this one, I ask them to work on a series of math questions. First, students try to find the number that is halfway between $1 and $10 on the x-axis. Common answers are numbers like 4.5, 5 or 5.5. In the last case, the student has subtracted $1 from $10, taken half of it to get 4.5, and added it to 1. Although all these commonplace conjectures are wrong, they're based on some level of logic. Then students find the number that they think is halfway between $10 and $100. At this point, many students have a method that they believe will work, so I ask them to test it, by finding the number halfway between $1 and $100 on the x-axis. At this point, students may notice that their method does not corroborate the structure of the graph. Discussion eventually leads to recognition of the pattern of exponents, that $100 = 10^2$, $10 = 10^1$, and $1 = 10^0$. From here, students can determine that the number halfway between $1 and $10 is $10^{0.5} = \$3.16$, approximately the most common global level income that is predicted for 2015. The final stage of the lesson is to ask students to locate specific daily incomes on the x-axis, like $5 per day or $50 per day. The classroom discussion can then lead to equations like $\$50 = 10^x$. Solving this problem motivates the need for a new mathematical tool for calculating the unknown variable, $x = \log 50$. I have found that this sequence of problems creates mathematically interesting discussions, and it focuses students' attention on extremely low daily incomes in many parts of the world.

Gapminder.org offers an astounding amount of data on a wide range of global topics; presented through timeline animations that highlight trends and comparisons much more easily than scanning tables of data. One topic that can generate a great deal of discussion is the controversial relationship between income or income inequality within countries and public health indicators like infant mortality. Comparisons across countries suggest that inequality and infant mortality are related, but whether this relationships is causal or correlational is a subject of contemporary debate (Avendano, 2012). For example, a low-income family may benefit more from a small increase in income than a high income family, and this could have a marked effect on their children's health. If inequality decreases in this country, we may observe improved health outcomes. On the other hand, a country with high income inequality may spend more public money on health outcomes, so that income inequality has only a weak relationship on child health, and changes in income do not result in changes in health.

Students can debate these issues by using Gapminder to identify interesting cases, for example, to find countries with high income inequality and high public investment into health, like the United States and Brazil, versus countries that have lower income inequality and low public investment into health, like India. Figure 3 shows an animation from Gapminder on how a key health indicator—infant mortality—changes in comparison to personal income between 1990 and 2011 in Brazil, India, and the United States.

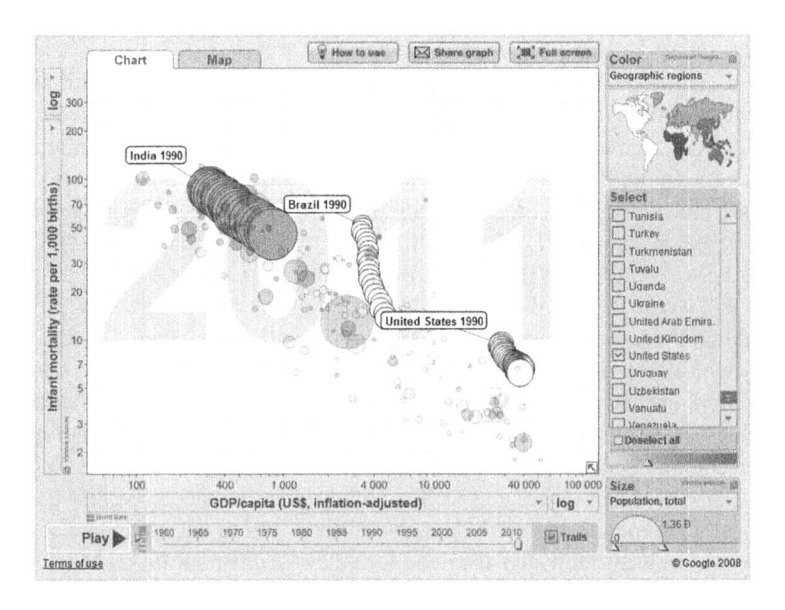

Figure 3. Does increasing income result in better child health?
Free material from www.gapminder.org

While data like these cannot resolve the relationships among personal income, a country's level of inequality, and health, they certainly can be the basis of classroom debate. The United States has clearly made the least progress on children's health issues of these three countries. Brazil, with lower incomes and even greater income inequality than the United States, has made tremendous progress on children's health issues. India, on the other hand, has grown economically in this time period, more than the other two countries, and this translated into some improvement for children's health, but not the dramatic changes as in Brazil.

Table 3. Testing linear and logarithmic models.

Brazil	Income	Infant Mortality
1990	3353	52
1995	3606	41
2000	3696	29
2005	3977	21
2010	4717	15
Linear Model	$y = -0.0253x + 129.64$ $R^2 = 0.7824$	
Logarithmic Model	$y = -3.6803x + 14.651$ $R^2 = 0.9129$	

Students can strengthen their understanding of logarithmic scales through this activity, too. The graph for Brazil looks linear. Students can scroll over the Gapminder screen to collect the data points, and then test whether the data is indeed linear (Table 3). The linear equation fits the data only moderately well, with a correlation coefficient of 0.7824. If students calculate the common logarithm of the data first, the model fits the data much better, with a correlation coefficient of 0.9129.

DISCUSSION: TEACHING DILEMMAS RAISED BY INTERNATIONAL ALGEBRA

Dilemma of Inaccurate Mathematics

Teaching algebra with international data poses several important teaching dilemmas. One dilemma is that mathematics teachers may feel frustrated or uncomfortable when working with data and methods that seem incomplete or inaccurate. Teachers and students may search for data that interests them and find that it does not exist. My own algebra classes, for example, often include students from East Africa whose families migrated to Minnesota as refugees. Conducting algebraic explorations using data from one's homeland can be very engaging, but students often find that data is not available from countries undergoing extreme conflict. Another source of frustration are standards of measurement change. In 2000, for example, living on $1 per day was a widely accepted standard for extreme poverty, but more recently, $1.25 per day (in 2005 dollars) is a more common standard. This reduces one's ability to work with published data from different years. Similarly, economic data published in different years may have been corrected for inflation according to different standards. As the context of a mathematics problem becomes more realistic, and as one begins to use data that represents real lives, a teacher may feel as if the results should also be more realistic and accurate than standard textbook algebra problems.

Still, recognizing limitations of data and methods can become an opportunity to develop a critical perspective on mathematics. After solving an internationalized math problem, students can reflect on a variety of critical questions, such as:

- How might this data have been collected, and how could collection methods compromise the data?
- What mathematical assumptions underlie our choice of algebraic method?
- If we make predictions using our method, what realistic factors limit the value of our predictions?
- If we are suspicious of our data, what is a realistic range of values for the data? If we rework the problem with this range of values, how much does it change our answer?

For the target audience, students who are taking algebra as a general education credit without the intention of going further with a STEM major, this critical reflection may be one of the most useful skills that students could develop in the class.

Dilemma of Stereotypes

Another teaching dilemma posed by internationalized college algebra is that studying data on economic and health inequalities can convey stereotypes of powerlessness and hopelessness among low-income people in other countries. This is particularly so for African countries, which predominate the extreme ranges of data sets on poverty and poor health outcomes for children and mothers. There is at least the tendency to look for trends over time, so that one does not see cultures, societies, peoples as static. Several of the contextual sources noted below can mitigate this problem, though, because they focus on innovations that were pioneered or significantly extended by people in non-Western countries.

Dilemma of Time Allocation

Just as with any technical aspect of teaching—conveying the week's schedule, passing out papers, reviewing previous topics—careful planning can make interdisciplinary class time meaningful. Once I recorded class discussions during a module that I taught on the epidemiology of infectious diseases (Staats, 2005). The mathematics involved creating a logistic model of the epidemic through numerical and graphical methods. After completing this foundational mathematical work, the class spent parts of the next three class days discussing contextual issues such as modes of transmission and geographical distribution of major infectious diseases; relationships between disease and poverty; and stereotypes of Africa. I reviewed the recordings for time spent discussing mathematics only, social issues only, and a mix of math and social issues; this assessment does not count time spend on matters unrelated to the epidemiology module such as new math topics and organizational talk. I found that we had spent just under 29 minutes on strictly mathematical topics, and just under 27 minutes on topics that were either social or a combination of social and math topics. In exit interviews, 48% of the students indicated that the epidemiology unit was the most memorable part of the class. This example illustrates that a mere 27 minutes—out of roughly 48 hours of direct classroom instruction—had a strong impact on students' impression of the class.

Dilemma of Assessments

A corollary to the question of allocating class time is the use of assessments. When I teach international algebra applications, or any interdisciplinary application, I have come to include test questions on all of the ideas—including social ideas—that were covered in class. I include these non-math ideas as part of review sessions before tests, so that students understand expectations. Sometimes, I have used longer take-home essay questions as a more significant assessment. For example, after a unit on the epidemiology of infectious diseases, students were asked to write three short paragraphs as if they were a journalist covering an HIV epidemic in South Africa. The three entries corresponded to three segments of the logistic equation model: when few people are infected and transmission rates are low; when transmission rates are at a maximum; and when nearly everyone is infected and transmission rates are low.

More often, though, I use assessment questions on tests that are short and generally factual, such as:

- Name three measurements that inform the United Nations Human Development Index
- Name a county with extremely low maternal mortality rates; and one with extremely high rates.

Students are accustomed to answering small, low-stakes questions like these in other classes. It is not a difficult transition for the student to answer them on a mathematics test if they understand that it is part of the class expectation.

DISCUSSION: CONTEXTUALIZING INTERNATIONAL ALGEBRA

The rich sources of data generated by the United Nations Millennium project and compiled by Gapminder.org can support teaching units throughout an entire college algebra course. Still, just doing the math may not develop intercultural understanding or critical consciousness. Further, a teacher may not feel comfortable teaching international algebra without developing personal knowledge of the issues. Both teachers and students need to be able to find sources to build contextual knowledge.

Once a teacher learns about a few case studies connected to a math activity, even spending one minute of an on-going discussion on this background can make the math more interesting and relevant for students. Below I will highlight some sources that I have found useful in building my own knowledge of international issues related to MDGs and other international algebra applications.

In particular, I have found the dozens of short international videos within the BBC Life series to be a very useful source for building a set of short examples that I can incorporate into the discussion of algebra activities on children's and mother's health. Many of these were produced shortly after the year 2000 to highlight the work of the Millennium Project, and so they are closely connected to the issues behind major data gathering efforts. At present, clips of some of the Life videos are available on the YouTube channel TVE Inspiring Change. I have used these videos to build my own knowledge, and I have assigned them to students, sometimes as out-of-class viewing assignments (most are around 25 minutes) and sometimes as short, in-class video clips.

Contextualizing Extreme Poverty

Reducing extreme poverty is the first Millennium Development Goal. A great deal of the world's collective progress towards this goal is due to China's rapid reduction of extreme poverty, making China an important case study in poverty reduction. China's commitment to a manufacturing economy halved its 1990 extreme poverty rate of 60% around the year 2002. This dramatic economic growth coupled with increases in income inequality are profiled in the Life series documentary *The Real Leap Forward* (Liu, 2005). An extremely personal and moving perspective on this economic growth is offered by Michel Peled's documentary *China Blue* (Peled, 2005). The film follows a young woman named Jasmine as she leaves her parents' rural home, travels with anticipation to a city, and secures employment in a blue jeans factory. Jasmine's tiring 20 hour work day amid growing disillusionment is heartbreaking. Mathematics figures prominently as the workers try to estimate their monthly piecework wages. I have used this film to create understanding of the personal toll of economic growth—Jasmine is about the same age as first-year college students—along with mathematics questions on estimating wages from the viewpoints of different figures in the film. Taken together, these films document the large-scale issues and the personal toll of dramatic economic growth.

An important but polemical source for contextualizing poverty is Collier's book on the "bottom billion," the portion of the world's population that live in countries that are not participating in global trends towards increasing income (2007). He identifies four poverty traps that limit economic growth: conflict, being a landlocked country with poor neighbors, possessing abundant natural resources, and bad governance. Collier's approach criticizes emphasis on international relief aid alone, in favor of a pro-business, neoliberal perspective on economic growth. He spends little attention on the drawbacks of growing an economy through manufacturing, ignoring, for example, the role labor unions could play in protecting workers like Jasmine. Still, Collier's book is math rich, and it helps mathematics instructors to develop a systematic framework for talking about international cases and issues in economics.

Contextualizing Children's and Mother's Health

Two of the Life videos examine children's health initiatives to increase Vitamin A consumption. Vitamin A supplementation is important for children because it can improve and strengthen immune systems and reduce susceptibility to commonplace illnesses like measles, diarrhea, and malaria. *Seeing is Believing* highlights Zambia's efforts to fortify sugar with Vitamin A, an approach that was pioneered in Guatemala (Pineda, n.d.; Television Trust for the Environment & Walker, 2002). It shows how the Zambian government worked with the single national sugar producer, in cooperation with counterparts in Guatemala, to improve Vitamin A access to the portion of the country—about half—that uses manufactured sugar. Around 90% of the country relies on maize that is ground into useable form in local mills; the video traces efforts to train locals in fortifying maize locally. The video *A-OK* takes up an alternative view, that nutritional programs should focus more on changing food production and use, so that people have sustainable control over their own nutrition (Tatham, 2000). It follows gardening, farming, nutrition, and cooking programs in Bangladesh and in Ghana. The video reviews controversies over genetically-engineered "golden rice" that produced high levels of Vitamin A.

The video *Dead Mums Don't Cry* highlights the work of Chadian obstetrician Grace Kodindo in caring for women during childbirth in a public hospital (Quinn, 2005). In Britain, the chance of a woman dying during childbirth is one in 5000; in Chad it is one in 11. The video gives insight into basic health issues for women, like the danger of eclampsia during childbirth and the need for rural areas to train birth attendants who can advise women of when their condition requires travel to hospitals. The stories are difficult to watch: families must visit pharmacies to purchase the medicines and supplies that the hospital lacks; families must organize their own blood donations while a loved one's operation is underway; a single doctor who must attend 45 births in one day. The film also follows Dr. Kodindo as she travels to Guatemala to learn about successes in reducing maternal deaths in a low income country. This important film documents the healthcare realities that account for shocking data disparities, and it highlights the difference that a few committed individuals can make.

Contextualizing Income Inequality

China Blue, with its deeply personal account of young female factory workers lives, offers one of the most accessible and touching contexts for understanding income inequality. Additionally, in the recent documentary film *Inequality for All*, economist

Robert Reich provides a historical context for income inequality in the US, arguing that strengthening the middle class will lead to a stronger economy (Chaiken, Dungan & Kornbluth, 2013). Short animations can easily be incorporated into classroom discussions and critiques, for example, on income of typical male workers vs. one percenters, wages vs. productivity, median male salary vs. household expenses.

Contextualizing Hope through Local Knowledge

One of the dilemmas of teaching international college algebra is that recognizing the depth of global disparity can confirm stereotypes that are common in the United States: that people in low-income countries lead powerless and hopeless lives. In part, the data itself can mitigate this problem, when students realize that the United States often does not lead the world in positive health and economic indicators. One of the advantages, too, of using the Life video series is that the videos usually portray diverse and local commentators—not only Westerners working for large international aid agencies, but local doctors, engineers, research scientists, and community volunteers discussing their contributions to strengthening their country's vitality.

The Life video series also documents programs that engage local communities in educational, health, and poverty reduction efforts. The documentary *Listen to the Kids!* profiles several young people campaigning for improvements in their communities in South Asia (Tatham, 2005). Deepak is a homeless child in India working with a program called Butterflies based in New Delhi (Butterflies Child Rights, 2011); this community of homeless children receive informal education in groups that convene on city streets; they develop and distribute newsletters, and administer a children's bank. Shati, a young girl in Bangladesh uses photography and direct intervention with families to campaign against young marriage and marriage dowries. The video *Lines in the Dust* outlines principles of participatory community education through the program Reflect, that guides communities in writing and mathematical literacy development programs (McGrogan & Broadbent, 2001; Reflect Action, 2009). For example, Ghanaian villagers draw graphs and timelines into the village sand to trace time spent working and resting by women and by men. Reflect uses a wide variety of visualization techniques—rivers for life processes, the roots and branches of trees for inputs and outputs of a significant situation. *Lines in the Dust* also highlights the use of theater to help communities in India to respond to pressure to undertake commercial cash agriculture. In general, participatory education involves many voices in community decisions, and demonstrates a method of building from local knowledge to community action without outsiders' decision-making.

In the social sciences and the humanities, an instructor who crosses disciplinary boundaries in these ways is often regarded as creative and inspiring. An historian who incorporates analysis of architectural trends, or a literature professor who lectures on the political background of a story are likely to be considered as good teachers. For mathematics instructors, however, crossing disciplinary boundaries is more controversial. Mathematics education has a historical focus on procedural skill, and there are unending, subtle, structural changes in algebra problems that create new challenges in skill development. The traditions of mathematics teaching suggest that it is preferable to spend class time posing a slightly new structure for, say, a factoring problem, than to develop background knowledge for an application that assists students in understanding why the application is important. Having a set of contextualizing materials available to teachers is a first step in learning to integrate disciplines in efficient and stimulating ways.

CONCLUSION

My university has provided several significant opportunities over the years to assist in my development of international algebra curriculum. I participated in two year-long faculty development communities organized by the university's Center for Teaching and Learning Services: Internationalizing the On-Campus Curriculum, and a Multicultural Education Fellowship. Being able to work with a cohort of people who value international perspectives gave me the courage to "think big" in my algebra classes, for example, to make the commitment to assessing non-mathematical content as part of the tests. My department has also offered supportive opportunities for internationalizing math curriculum, especially by allowing me to offer first-year student seminars. These small classes focus on innovative ideas, so that they are enriching for both faculty and students, but they do not generate a lot of tuition. I developed a great deal of my international algebra content in these seminars, which I now cycle into standard algebra classes.

Even with good institutional support and access to rich data sources, can internationalized college algebra create critical consciousness among students? This teaching project will need more faculty participants before we can begin to understand this question. Internationalized algebra curriculum can probably create a descriptive understanding of difference and inequality. Developing reflective awareness, one of the components of critical consciousness, requires attention to systematic processes of creating and continuing inequality. Incorporating contextual stories like the ones reviewed here will at least introduce students to processes of that create inequality and responses to them, like the Millennium Project and grassroots projects for community improvement. Introductory knowledge of international systems for poverty reduction could be developed elsewhere in an internationalized curriculum. Overall, college algebra is in an excellent position to contribute to the foundations of global understanding. Presenting international algebra applications in context restores human stories to tables of data, and a thorough and critical global understanding is impossible without engagement with numbers.

REFERENCES

Appelbaum, P., Friedler, L., Ortiz, C. & Wolff, E. (2009). Internationalizing the university mathematics curriculum. *Journal of Studies in International Education, 13*(3), 365–381.
Anderton, L., & Wright, D. (2012). We could all be having so much more fun! A case for the history of mathematics in education. *Journal of Humanistic Mathematics, 2*(1), 88–103.
Ascher, M. (2006). *Mathematics elsewhere: An exploration of ideas across cultures.* Princeton, NJ: Princeton University.
Ascher, M. (1991). *Ethnomathematics: A multicultural view of mathematical ideas.* Pacific Grove, CA: Brooks/Cole.
Avendano, M. (2012). Correlation or causation? Income inequality and infant mortality in fixed effects models in the period 1960-2008 in 34 OECD countries. *Social Science and Medicine, 75*, 754–760.
Bishop, A. (1988). Mathematics education in its cultural context. *Educational Studies in Mathematics, 19*, 179–191.
Butterflies Child Rights. (2011). *Butterflies: Protecting and empowering children since 1989.* Retrieved from http://www.butterflieschildrights.org
Chaiken, J., & Dungan, S. (Producer), Kornbluth, J. (Director). (2013). *Inequality for all* [Documentary film]. USA: 72 Productions.
Collier, P. (2007). *The bottom billion: Why the poorest countries are failing and what can be done about it.* New York, NY: Oxford University.
Complete College America. (2012). Remediation: Higher education's bridge to nowhere. Retrieved from www.completecollege.org/docs/CCA-Remediation-final.pdf.
d'Ambrosio, U. (1985). Ethnomathematics and its place in the history and pedagogy of mathematics. *For the Learning of Mathematics, 5*(1), 44–48.
Dikhanov, Y. (2005). *Trends in global income distribution, 1970–2000, and scenarios for 2015.* Human Development Report Office Occasional paper.
Eglash, R. (2003). *Culturally-situated design tools.* Retrieved from http://csdt.rpi.edu
Fauvel, J. (1991). Using history in mathematics education. *For the Learning of Mathematics, 11*(2), 3–6.
Gapminder. (n.d.). *Gapminder: For a fact-based world view.* Retrieved from http://www.gapminder.org
Gerdes, P. (1998). *Women, art and geometry in Southern Africa.* Trenton, NJ: Africa World Press.
Herriot, S., & Dunbar, S. (2009). Who takes college algebra? *PRIMUS 19*(1), 74–87.
Ippolito, K. (2007). Promoting intercultural learning in a multicultural university: Ideals and realities. *Teaching in Higher Education, 12*(5), 749–763.
Kumagi, A., & Lypson, M. (2009). Beyond cultural competence: Critical consciousness, social justice, and multicultural education. *Academic Medicine, 84*(6), 782–787.
Liu, J. (Producer & Director). (2005). *The real leap forward: Scaling up poverty reduction in China.* [Documentary film]. UK: Bullfrog films.
McGrogan, C. (Producer) & Broadbent, L. (Director). (2001). *Lines in the dust* [Documentary film]. UK: Bullfrog films.
Ortiz, I., & Cummins, M. (2011). *Global inequality: Beyond the bottom billion. A rapid review of income distribution in 141 countries.* New York, NY: UNICEF.
Peled, M. (Producer & Director). (2005). *China blue* [Documentary film]. USA: Teddy Bear Films.
Pineda, O. (n.d.). *Fortification of sugar with vitamin A.* Retrieved from http://archive.unu.edu/unupress/food/V192e/ch07.htm.
Quinn, T. (Producer). (2005). *Dead mums don't cry* [Documentary film]. UK: Bullfrog films
Reflect Action. (2009). *Reflect.* Retrieved from http://www.reflect-action.org.
Small, D. (2006). College algebra: A course in crisis. In N. Baxter, N. Hastings, F. Gordon, S. Gordon & J. Narayan (Eds.), *A fresh start for collegiate mathematics: Rethinking the courses below calculus,* (pp. 83–89). Washington, DC: Mathematical Association of America.
Staats, S. (2005). Multicultural mathematics: A social issues perspective in lesson planning. In J. Higbee, D. Lundell, & D. Arendale (Eds.), *The general college vision: Integrating intellectual growth, multicultural perspectives, and student development* (pp. 185–200). Minneapolis: CRDEUL, University of Minnesota.

Staats, S., & Robertson, D. (2009). International inequalities: Algebraic investigations into health and economic development. *MathAMATYC Educator, 1*(1), 6–11.

Staats, S., Sintjago, A., & Fitzpatrick, R. (2013). Kiva microloans in a learning community: An assignment for interdisciplinary synthesis. *Innovative Higher Education, 38*(3), 173–187. doi:10.1007/s10755-012-9235-y.

Tatham, D. (Producer). (2000). *A-OK?* [Documentary film]. UK: Bullfrog films.

Tatham, D. (Producer & Director). (2005). *Listen to the Kids!* [Documentary film]. UK: Bullfrog films.

Television Trust for the Environment (Producer). & Walker, C. (Director). (2002). *Seeing is Bbelieving.* [Documentary film]. UK: Bullfrog films.

Tzanakis, C., & Arcavi, A. (2000). Integrating history of mathematic in the classroom: An analytic survey. In J. Fauvel & J. van Maanen (Eds.). *History in mathematics education: The ICMI study* (pp. 201–240). Dordrecht: Kluwer.

United Nations. (n.d.). *Open working group on sustainable development goals.* Retrieved from http://sustainabledevelopment.un.org/index.php?menu=1549

United Nations. (2014a). *Millennium development goals report 2014.* Retrieved from http://www.un.org/en/development/desa/publications/mdg-report-2014.html

United Nations. (2014b). *End poverty: Millennium development goals and beyond 2015.* Retrieved from http://www.un.org/millenniumgoals/reports.shtml.

United Nations Development Programme. (2014). *Human Development Report 2014: Sustaining human progress: Reducing vulnerabilities and sustaining resilience.* New York, NY: Author.

Susan Staats
Department of Postsecondary Teaching and Learning
University of Minnesota

CATHERINE SOLHEIM, MARY KATHERINE O'BRIEN
AND SCOTT SPICER

11. ILLUMINATING A COURSE TRANSFORMATION JOURNEY

INTRODUCTION

Learning about families and culture are going to help me in my future career because I will have the ability to connect and relate to those who are different from me. It is a benefit to learn about different cultures because I am able to have a more mindful perspective of cultures other than my own. There is no universal definition of family.

The need to internationalize higher education is an imperative accepted by most college faculty. The challenge is that most faculty are not prepared for that task, having been trained primarily in their academic disciplines and lacking a solid grounding in international or intercultural content and pedagogy. I found myself in that exact predicament; I fully embraced the charge to internationalize and felt an urgency to transform my courses, but felt unsure about the process to do so.

In this chapter I will recount my journey, beginning with the impetus for internationalizing my undergraduate course and continuing through my development of requisite knowledge and tools for course redesign. I will discuss the way that I articulated elements of theory and pedagogy that shaped the course, the development of primary learning activities and their assessment, and will conclude with my personal reflection about the redesign process and outcomes. My goal is that readers will be inspired to internationalize their courses and learn potential strategies for accomplishing that goal from the journey I share in this chapter.

MY JOURNEY

The Impetus

Global and Diverse Families is an upper level undergraduate course offered at the University of Minnesota in the Department of Family Social Science. It is required for Family Social Science majors and also meets the University's liberal education requirements. I typically have 50 learners in the semester-long course. One might think that a course on global families would by its nature develop learners' sense of the world and their role in it. However, it was not necessarily the case, at least in the ways that would help them be more interculturally and internationally aware and agile, abilities required of our graduates as they work with families from cultures and backgrounds that are different than from their own. In fact, I was challenged to figure out how to operationalize the goal of developing intercultural competence in learners through this course.

For four years I taught the course using learning activities that are typically found in courses about families from a global perspective: learners read textbook descriptions of families from around the world, hear from culturally-diverse and international student guest speakers who talked about their experiences of family, conduct library research, and write a paper on a particular culture including pertinent aspects of family life such as dating and marriage, parenting, gender roles, and aging. At the end of the semester they share PowerPoint presentations with bullet points and pictures, focusing primarily on data that were found in scholarly literature. When taught in this manner, end of semester assessments revealed that learners were able to talk in broad generalizations about diverse families.... "Vietnamese families are...". "Dating in Korean culture is...". They were aware of cultural differences in families but had no sense of the variation of the experience of family within cultures or important ways that families differed across cultures. My concern was that what they were learning in this course would reinforce a monolithic understanding of families and culture. Then, when they encountered a family from a culture different than their own, they would apply that generalized knowledge to make assumptions and arrive at conclusions that missed unique family characteristics that might be very important to whatever challenge that family was experiencing.

I was also struck by how unconscious learners were about their own cultures or how their personal experiences of family had been deeply shaped by culture. In past semesters, *cultural obliviousness* seemed particularly apparent in European-American learners. However, even though learners from non-dominant cultures were aware of how their families and cultures were different from U.S families, they were not able to articulate the heterogeneity of family experiences within culture or how culture shapes the experience of family in cultures other than their own. Non-dominant culture learners compared their own culture's values with American values, assuming there was an agreed-upon set from both their own and others' cultures. For example, they would talk about their own cultural value of family and elders, saying that Americans didn't value family or older people as much as theirs did. In response, learners from the dominant culture pushed back, saying that wasn't true. I realized that learners, regardless of their own cultural backgrounds, were stuck in a very surface-level understanding of culture as it influenced families. They assumed that families of peers who looked like them were culturally similar and families of peers who looked different were culturally different. My observation of learners' under-developed intercultural competency was not surprising. As Bennett (2009) points out:

> In fact, cultural knowledge does not equal intercultural competence since a person can be an expert on a particular aspect of Chinese culture and yet be unable to negotiate with his Chinese counterparts. This gap between knowledge and competence may be due in part to being unaware of one's own culture and therefore not fully capable of assessing the cultural position of others. (123)

However common cultural obliviousness might be in U.S. undergraduate learners, I found surface-level generalizations about culture and family, learners' minimal awareness about themselves as cultural beings, and my inability to influence learners' understanding of these important ideas both disturbing and unacceptable in an increasingly globalized world. First, I was preparing undergraduates to work with families in a variety of settings such as homeless or domestic violence shelters, youth development and parenting programs, and transitional housing programs. I imagined them sitting down with a family whose culture or socioeconomic status was different than their own and making assumptions based on their generalized knowledge of another. For example, a U.S. born person working with a Somali family would work from a set of key assumptions about that family. Similarly, a Somali second-generation immigrant working with a European-American family would make assumptions based on their generalized knowledge of U.S. culture. This could lead to misunderstanding at best and discrimination at worst.

Second, their ethnocentric view of the world, and, for the majority of learners, their privilege as members of the dominant culture, seemed to affect their curiosity about how families had been and were being affected by poverty, natural disasters, racism, war and trauma, or governmental policies. For example, they might attribute causes of poverty solely to individual failures and be oblivious to the existence of structural inequality and racism.

Meta-Cognition / Awareness

As a fellow in the University of Minnesota Internationalizing Teaching and Learning (ITL) 2012-2013 program, I was guided through a process to develop an internationalized sense of "academic self" (per Sanderson, 2008), identify global learning outcomes, expand my teaching strategies, and develop course materials, activities, and assessments aligned with international, intercultural, and global learning. The ITL program providing me with incentive, intentional time, and space to systematically think about and make changes to the course.

This leg of my journey was perhaps the easiest for me due to my previous international and cross-cultural experience. Beginning with an initial cross-cultural immersion experience during young adulthood and continuing over three decades,

I became very aware of how my own cultural context had shaped and continued to shape me in many ways. However, I was challenged to translate that important developmental process and the knowledge I had gained from it into the classroom setting. After reading Cranton (2001), I realized that I needed to be more authentic by integrating 'self' and teacher. I consciously reflected on my own development process and the catalysts that prompted me to reflect and grow into a more nuanced intercultural self. I then used my own transformative process of learning about who I was as a cultural being to inform how I might shape learners' intercultural learning processes.

As one example, I became very aware that I was instinctively, but unconsciously, using a particular theoretical perspective and pedagogical approach to shape the course. Bringing that into my own consciousness moved me to intentionally affirm that the course is grounded in a social constructivist paradigm using a human ecology theoretical lens (Bubolz & Sontag, 1993). This means that I approach my teaching and students' learning with a frame that one's reality is constructed by interactions with others and our life experiences. Moreover, these interactions and experiences occur in nested and interdependent contexts – our families, our human-built environment, our socio-cultural environment, and our natural-physical environment. Therefore, our understanding of family and culture is socially constructed through observations of and interactions with others with whom we come in contact on a regular basis and through a variety of experiences that occur in multiple, layered, and interconnected contexts. By being explicit about my approach, learners seemed to make better sense of the overall structure and content of the course, and better understood my expectations of them as learners.

I was primarily concerned with how I could help learners be more aware and self-reflective about their own cultural identities and move toward a more ethnorelative and nuanced awareness of culture, globalization, and families. Research highlights the importance of self-knowing to the development of intercultural awareness. "First and foremost, cultural awareness involves processes of promoting the reflection upon one's own cultural norms and values, and on how these shape social identities of individuals and groups" (Eisenchlas & Trevaskes, 2003, p. 91).

The following paragraphs describe the three major assignments used in the course to engage learners in multi-sensory and technology-enhanced learning experiences and their respective assessment tools: 1) creating a personal culture digital story; 2) conducting an ethnographic interview and creating a digital narrative; and 3) engaging in 20 hours of volunteer service-learning in Twin Cities' community-based organizations that served diverse populations.

PEDAGOGY AND PROCESS: SUPPORTING STUDENTS' INTERCULTURAL LEARNING

Scholarly literature clearly supports the importance of scaffolding learning experiences to effectively develop intercultural competence.

The first use of an intercultural positioning system is to locate ourselves, to develop our own cultural self-awareness through understanding our cultural patterns. Only then can we begin exploring the gap between our values, beliefs, and behaviors and those of others. (Bennett, 2009, p. 27)

Informed Learning Goals, Assignments, and Scaffolding Decisions in the Course

I identified three primary learning goals for the course: a) to understand the role of culture in the experience of family, b) to become aware of ways that families impact and are impacted by global trends and issues, and c) to consider how they can use their skills and talents to support marginalized families achieve their goals. I share the graphic below at the beginning of the semester to communicate the three threads that are woven throughout the course. I also bring this visual back when the emphasis shifts from thread to thread, helping the learner keep the overall picture in mind while considering separate strands. (Insert image here)

Two assignments, the personal culture digital story and the ethnographic digital narrative, were completed sequentially, allowing learners to first build awareness of themselves as cultural beings before engaging with a person from a culture different than their own. The third major assignment involved volunteering through service-learning throughout the semester, submitting weekly reflections, and debriefing through class discussions. This assignment gave learners first-hand experience with people from diverse races, socioeconomic classes, cultures, and family structures.

ITL scholars including co-author Mary Katherine O'Brien exposed me to key research and teaching resources that influenced my thinking throughout the course redesign process. They were instrumental in helping me craft explicit and appropriate learning goals and create assessments to evaluate learner outcomes.

Crafting the digital media assignments was greatly influenced by my conversations with co-author Scott Spicer, media outreach librarian. Over a series of meetings, Scott pushed me to clarify the learning objectives for the assignment and offered suggestions for shaping the digital media dimension of it. His expertise was invaluable as I honed in on options that best fit what I was trying to accomplish. Moreover, he came to class to provide technical expertise in videography and media production, something about which I had little expertise and, with all the other demands of a faculty member, would most likely never fully attain.

Understanding Self as a Cultural Being: Personal Culture Digital Story

The personal culture digital story assignment, scheduled at the beginning of the semester, provided an initial opportunity to explore how culture shapes the experience and understanding of family. The learning objectives were two-fold, one content-related and one technology-related. The content objective was to identify who the learner was as a cultural being, noting how their background, experiences, values, and relationships had shaped their personhood. As noted earlier, this is a necessary and important first step in developing intercultural awareness. Theodore and Afolayan (2010) found that digital stories were effective in helping undergraduate teacher education learners become more culturally self-aware and thus more culturally competent. In the *Global and Diverse Families* course, creating personal culture digital stories gave learners an opportunity to examine themselves as cultural beings before they learned about a person from a culture different from their own through the subsequent ethnographic digital narrative assignment. The second objective was to provide a low-stakes technology assignment that allowed learners to practice technical skills needed to complete their ethnographic digital narrative assignment.

Learners used the human ecology framework (Bubolz & Sontag, 1993) to identify their culture by considering nested contexts and influences that had shaped who they are as persons – their family environment, their human-built environment, their socio-cultural environment, and their natural-physical environment. They first identified and described three salient aspects of their cultural self. Then they identified images or other visual artifacts that represented those three aspects. Many learners used pictures of family and friends. Some chose icons or symbols to represent religious or educational influences. Some shared images of their experiences abroad or maps of their hometowns.

The personal culture digital stories were created using iMovie, Windows Movie Maker, or PowerPoint. Learners were allowed to use a voice over narration for their stories or manual text captioning to guide the viewer and describe how the images portrayed their cultural influences. Most chose music that was either a favorite of theirs or that represented some aspect of their lives. Finally, learners published and uploaded their digital stories to the course management website. They viewed others' stories in class and analyzed them to identify key themes woven throughout their peers' stories. At the end of each class, we debriefed as a group by writing the key themes on a white board and discussing similarities and differences across stories.

Learning was assessed by asking a self-reflective question about how the assignment had deepened their understanding of cultural and global families. One learner shared an introspective response: "*The personal narrative was significant because it made me deeply analyze who I was as a cultural being.*" Another looked beyond his own story to connect with others: "*Watching the personal narratives was great to see that even though there are many Caucasian Americans in our society, they all have a very unique history that comes from many diverse cultures and traditions.*"

The assignment helped learners dig below the surface to see difference. One person shared: "*It really made me realize that just because someone looks and seems like they are in your culture, doesn't mean they have the same beliefs and values as you. People come from all different backgrounds.*" Reserving judgment until knowing a person was noted by a learner:

I learned that it is impossible to know who someone is or where they come from or their social class or what their ethnic and cultural background is just by looking at them and therefore shouldn't pass any judgment or make assumptions because they can be hurtful.

Finally, there was evidence that the intentional scaffolding of the personal culture digital story assignment prepared learners for the ethnographic digital narrative assignment. One learner noted: *"... the idea that self-reflection is essential in understand(ing) culture. Before we interviewed someone from another culture, we conducted our own digital narrative highlighting some of the ways that culture impacts our lives."* This assignment provided a low-stakes opportunity for learners to begin understanding themselves as cultural beings before exploring another's experience of culture. Moreover, it allowed them to learn how to access University digital media resources and to practice and gain confidence in the process of creating a digital media product to communicate their ideas using images, text, music, and voice.

Understanding of Culture and the Family Experience: Ethnographic Digital Narrative

The primary purpose of this assignment was to capture family narratives from individuals whose lives are shaped by diverse cultures so that learners could understand the variability of families' experiences within and across cultures. This was the most comprehensive assignment in the class that required learners to integrate and apply the concepts and skills cumulatively learned in the course. Additional purposes included developing learners' qualitative research and digital media literacy skills.

Learners acted as ethnographers, conducting research through a qualitative interview with a person from a culture different than their own. I encouraged them to focus on Minnesota's recent immigrant populations, but they were free to identify interviewees from their own social networks. As a result, cultural informants were from recent immigrant communities such as Hmong, Somali, Vietnamese, and Cambodian, international students from Russia, Malaysia, India, Israel, Tanzania, and China, and Native Americans. One learner interviewed a homeless youth who articulated how aspects of her homeless culture shaped the idea and experience of family.

Step 1. In teams of two, learners identified a person to interview. This information was submitted by week 3 of the semester, primarily to move learners to action early in the semester to avoid rushing this important assignment.

Step 2. Teams conducted preliminary demographic research on the culture and/or country of origin of their cultural informant. They also looked for research that provided some information about families in the culture/country of their informant, often from the anthropology literature. This information helped them shape the questions they would ask their cultural informant. Key points from their preliminary research were submitted in week 5.

Step 3. Teams submitted a draft of their interview questions in week 7 and received feedback from me. Initially, submitted questions tended to focus more concrete ideas related to culture such as food, holidays, etc. Learners needed a fair amount of coaching from me to craft good interview questions that went beyond the artifacts of culture and probed in more abstract ideas related to family dynamics and relationships such as values, beliefs, norms, dating and marriage, parenting and parent-child relationships, sibling relationships, gender roles, etc. Learners also needed help sequencing questions and writing probes to use to encourage richer descriptions from their informants during the interview. In this step they also outlined logistical plans for the interview including a) the roles each person would play, i.e., interviewing and video-taping, b) equipment they would use, c) where and when they would secure it, and d) the location the interview would take place.

Step 4. One class period was devoted to practicing the qualitative interview. After providing some initial tips related to interviewing, teams paired up and practiced asking each other the questions they had crafted. This helped them get comfortable asking questions and also allowed them to hear peers' questions that they might add to their own interview protocol.

Step 5. Teams conducted the interviews with their informants using personal equipment such as iPads or cameras, microphones, etc. that they checked out from the University's media lab. At the time of the interview, they requested suggestions for music and obtained pictures from their cultural informants to use in the narratives.

Step 6. Learners used a variety of software tools to edit their digital ethnographic narratives. At the start of the semester, learners indicated beginner to intermediate experience and comfort with media production processes. Accordingly, they were encouraged to use lower barrier, consumer-level video editing software tools to edit their ethnographic interviews, such as iMovie (Mac) and Windows Movie Maker (PC). Final Cut Pro X (Mac) has a slightly higher learning curve but additional functionality.

Step 7. Final digital ethnographic narrative videos ranged from 12-20 minutes, allowing for three to be presented, analyzed, and discussed within a 90 minute class period. As they watched, learners analyzed peers' narratives using a rubric that included four criteria, the same criteria I used to grade the assignment. The first criterion focused on the technical quality of the audio and video including how well it was edited. The second criterion assessed whether or not the narrative clearly provided the cultural context in which the person experiences family. This included providing some basic demographic data about the country, in addition to researched-based knowledge relating to general and family specific cultural aspects of the informant. A third criterion evaluated the overall effectiveness of the use of digital media to communicate key aspects of family, as well as the specific uses of music, images, video clips, and audio to engage the viewer. The final criterion, the one weighted most heavily in the grading rubric, focused on how well the narrative connected the dots between family and culture. Were topics about aspects of family life clearly explored? Were interviewers able to elicit solid descriptions of family life and how their informant's culture impacted who they were as individuals and family members? Viewers completed and submitted a rubric for each narrative. This process allowed them to critically evaluate the content and presentation.

Step 8. At the end of each class period and cumulatively over the weeks in which narratives were presented, I led large group discussions that encouraged learners to share their analysis across narratives: What were similarities and differences? Were there things shared that challenged your ideas of family? Were there aspects of the cultures presented that were new to you or that piqued your curiosity? Narrative creators were able to respond to questions and share additional background and insights that helped us understand what had been presented.

It was particularly helpful to have more than one narrative from informants from the same culture of origin to allow learners to see variation within as well as across cultures. I strongly encouraged learners to select key informants from communities of recent immigrants to the Twin Cities to increase the likelihood of having the ability to compare and contrast within culture. For example, we viewed three narratives from informants who were shaped by Vietnamese culture. Differences were quite apparent in areas of dating and gender roles across these young women's experiences. This allowed me to highlight the importance of not imposing assumptions based solely on an apparent cultural background.

Large group discussions were also critical to help learners unpack their reactions to what they'd seen and move to a deeper awareness of how others' ideas could potentially conflict with their own. When a learner verbally expressed a judgment about something a key informant or a peer said, I used questioning to help them consider the basis for their reaction. This gave them an opportunity to become more aware of when that occurred. I did not criticize their response, but rather encouraged them to reflect and consider whether or not their reaction was connected to their own cultural norms, values, and beliefs and how the informant's idea might similarly be shaped by culture. I helped them think through how they might reframe their observations as differences, and work to understand how the idea made sense in the particular cultural context of the informant, rather than move quickly to an unexamined judgment call. I found that these discussions were particularly rich when informants talked about dating, marriage, and gender roles in families and cultures that were quite different than those in dominant U.S. culture. As Bennett

(2009) stated, "Through exploration of our own position on cultural variables, we can identify similarities and differences with others and thus begin the process of building intercultural competence" (p. 127).

Step 9. After narratives were shown and analyzed in class, narrative creators individually submitted a self-assessment of their learning experience. They were asked a series of questions that helped them reflect on a) what they learned about family and culture, b) their own analysis of how culture shaped their informant's experience of family, c) what they enjoyed about the assignment, d) how they were challenged by creating the digital narrative, and e) what advice they would give to future learners about this assignment. Finally, they assigned points to their own and team member's contributions to the assignment. This helped communicate the need for accountability to the team and gave me a basis for adjusting points according to relative contribution if needed, always a challenge in assignments involving teams.

Viewing and analyzing the ethnographic digital narratives occurred during the last weeks of the semester. In addition to submitting individual rubrics, I used the final class synthesis (exam) to evaluate learning from this assignment. I asked them to choose three narratives and compare and contrast them in terms of similarities and differences in how informants' family experiences were shaped by culture.

Many learners' eyes were opened to the richness and diversity of cultures that were beyond their own experiences. However, this assignment not only helped them see 'another', it helped them think more deeply about their own culture, as these two students' words illustrate:

> Viewing the digital narratives. It was so neat to witness all of those different cultures. It also made me aware of my own culture and biases I had towards other cultures. I looked forward to "traveling the world" and learning about different perspectives just by sitting in class!

> The cultural identity of my being was challenged because I questioned how my cultural identity would come across if I were the one being interviewed. I do not identify with any or few ethnicities, which seems to occur among many American with European ancestry that dates back farther than I know, so I really had to think of how I identify myself.

Other learners were quite challenged by ideas, norms, or beliefs expressed by cultural informants. As mentioned earlier, I encouraged them to pay attention to times when something expressed in a narrative evoked feelings of discomfort, perhaps even shock or anger, to examine why that might be happening, how a different cultural perspective or practice might clash with their own, and to consider how they might handle their response and make sense of their reactions. I was pleased that several were able to write about that happening to them and even more pleased to read how they worked through their feelings to a non-judgmental response. One learner expressed this particularly well:

> In the digital culture stories we watched, some of the individuals expressed their belief in wife prices/dowries. I do not come from a culture where this is practiced and had learned this as a harmful practice in a social work course I took. This challenged my idea of marriage within this culture. I was originally shocked and could not believe this was still viewed as an acceptable practice; viewing women as a commodity, but after hearing more, my opinion changed. In learning more about the practice, I do not necessarily believe in it, but do have a better understanding of why it exists culturally and think more openly on the topic now. By challenging my view of marriage in this culture, I was able to enforce my own personal views on marriage and how it fits into my life culturally.

Importantly, only a few learners were cognizant of the research skills they were developing through this assignment:

> Asking good questions – it sounds basic, but I really learned the importance of asking a high quality question; one that opens doors for good discussion and digs down deep to the root of a feeling or belief. I learned more from [my friend for 3 years] in that hour-long interview than I ever have before.

This is an important learning goal to which I will pay careful attention in the future.

Digital Media Reflection and Decisions

It is important to note that there is a wide spectrum of student-produced digital media genres that allows instructors to adapt the use of digital media to fit an assignment's learning objectives. In this specific course, both digital stories and digital narratives were used. The ethnographic digital narrative differed from the digital story in a number of ways. For example, as described earlier, a digital story is often designed to communicate a personal story or at least a strong personal point of view from the perspective of the digital story creator. In contrast for the digital narratives, students were acting as ethnographers, so it was critical for these videos to communicate the voice of the interviewee. That necessitated more minimal crafting of narrative from the creator's point of view (acknowledging that all produced media has embedded some elements of creator bias, such as the questions chosen, how the video clips are edited and ordered, camera angles, lighting, etc.). Further, choosing the ethnographic narrative over the story approach for this assignment was appropriate for several reasons: a) It gave voice to those being interviewed – it was their story and it was important to honor it as such; 2) Interviewing and creating one informant's narrative gave learners an opportunity to have an in-depth conversation with someone from a culture different than their own and really focus on their informant, rather than thinking how they (the interviewer) would later communicate the story; 3) Viewing multiple narratives provided an opportunity for students to analyze cultural influences on family dynamics by hearing from cultural insiders, the primary learning objective for this assignment. This would have been harder to discover or even completely missed if presentations were composed from the creator's point of view.

Service-learning. Over the semester-long course, learners were required to volunteer a minimum of 20 hours in community agencies and organizations that served culturally and/or economically diverse children and/or families. My partner in this assignment was the University of Minnesota's Community Service-learning Center which describes service-learning as a "teaching and learning strategy that integrates meaningful community service with instruction and reflection to enrich the learning experience, teach civic responsibility, and strengthen communities. Students use what they learn in the classroom to address community-identified issues. They not only learn about practical applications of their studies, they also become actively contributing citizens and community members through the service they perform" (http://www.servicelearning.umn.edu, 2014). Sites offered for this course ranged from a drop-in center for homeless persons, recent immigrant adult tutoring in libraries, domestic violence shelters, etc. For most learners in this course, the service-learning assignment provided an opportunity to interact with people whose social addresses were very different than their own and to travel to unfamiliar neighborhoods across the Twin Cities metropolitan area.

Learners spent approximately two hours per week at their sites. Each week they responded to a set of questions about their experiences, examined through the lenses of the human ecology conceptual framework. For example in week two, learners responded to these questions: How does culture play out in your agency or organization - in the human-built environment, in the socio-cultural environment, in the natural/physical environment? What cultures and ethnicities are represented in this agency/organization and the people it serves? Is the diversity the result of past or recent immigration? If so, explain. Are staff and/or clients culturally different than you? How do you know; what evidence suggests that is so? What questions does the diversity represented raise for you in terms of service delivery? How does your agency/organization embrace and support cultural diversity? After responding to the questions, learners shared their personal thoughts and reactions to the service experience, providing rich descriptions and critical evaluations.

The eight weekly reflections gave me opportunity to monitor learners' experiences and whether or not they were fulfilling their commitment to our important community partners. I was able to respond to learners' frustrations and offer suggestions for dealing with them. I was also able to celebrate the positive experiences. In both cases, I tried to affirm what they were learning and normal and important parts of the process of interacting with others whose lives were very different than theirs.

At the end of the semester, learners were asked to reflect on their overall experience and articulate what they had learned about family, culture, and social justice through their volunteer experiences. The idea of learning through service to society's vulnerable families was new to some: *"Service-learning is an idea that*

I had never been exposed to before. The idea that people are in need all over the country and that I can help them simply by donating my time, is something really unique." Others appreciated the opportunity to meet people whose life experiences and cultures were very different than theirs. One learner wrote: *"My service-learning project was beneficial for me because it allowed me to interact with a group of people that I wasn't familiar with."*

Another shared:

> Actually interacting with people from another culture was a really great experience. I learned a lot about the Latino culture just by talking to the clients in the organization. It was really helpful in terms of broadening my knowledge and understanding of culture.

Some learners expressed frustration when situations or people at their sites were difficult but they recognized that they'd grown and learned about themselves and others by working through those challenges.

> Service-learning was important to me because it was hands-on and I was able to put myself in the situation itself with people different than me. This helped a lot because it really tested my patience and my acceptance, but I came out a changed person.

REFLECTING ON MY JOURNEY

Intercultural competence has increasingly been acknowledged as important in today's globalized reality. Bennett (2009) argues that is a key contributor to global and domestic effectiveness, and a prerequisite for "capably addressing issues of race, class, and gender" (p. 124). A recent Council of Europe report began with the words "Mutual understanding and intercultural competence are more important than ever today because through them we can address some of the most virulent problems of contemporary societies" (Barrett, Byram, Lázár, Mompoint-Gaillard, & Philippou, 2014, p. 2). Clearly developing intercultural competence is important for our future professionals and citizens. For me, it is an ethical imperative; my students will be launched into an increasingly diverse and complex world that requires perspective taking and the ability to "check" ones familial ethnocentrism at the door. My sense is that goal is applicable regardless of the disciplinary 'flavor' of ones' graduates. But developing intercultural competence is not easy. It's particularly challenging due to its process-oriented and developmental nature (Bennett, 1993; Deardorff, 2009), which presents an onerous task of creating authentic intercultural learning opportunities in the context of one course.

But the task is doable with an investment of time and the support of colleagues who have complementary expertise, in my case, in intercultural education and technology. I have three primary but interrelated lessons/recommendations to share with anyone undertaking the course internationalization task. First, it is critical to take the time to engage in self-reflection to consider how you have been shaped by your own culture and disciplinary training (Sanderson, 2008). This awareness can highlight areas in which you might be teaching from an ethnocentric position that neglects the consideration of multiple culture- and discipline-based perspectives that shape our knowledge base. Second, I encourage careful consideration and decisions about using the most appropriate pedagogical approach to shape the classroom environment and learning activities. After I embraced my social constructivist approach to culture and family, I was able to design and align learning activities to achieve course objectives and create assessments that reflected that pedagogical approach. This alignment contributed to a more authentic presence in the classroom. Third, I recommend Fink's (2003) model as a road map for the redesign journey. I had previously used this model to 'flip' a course and integrate a team-based learning pedagogy. It's probably fair to say that most faculty inherit learning goals for a particular course and probably don't pay a lot of attention to (re)designing a course to achieve those outcomes. The process of identifying course goals, designing learning activities to achieve them, and appropriately assessing learner outcomes is critical and worth the effort.

So, did I succeed in creating a learning environment that fostered the development of intercultural competence? I believe learners' reflections affirmed that this was indeed the case. In a self-reflexive mode, learners were asked to state their post-course location on the continuum of an ethnocentric to ethnorelative understanding of humans and relationships (Bennett, 1993), to discuss if they had moved as a result of their learning in this class, and if yes, how might they continue to develop intercultural sensitivity. Ideally, I would have preferred lo administer the Intercultural Development Inventory (IDI) (Hammer & Bennett, 1998) for more valid and reliable pre- and post-course comparisons, but it was cost-prohibitive. Learner reflections, however, provided evidence of their development of perspective taking which demonstrates movement toward the ethnorelative end of the IDI continuum. *"I learned that we cannot expect to fully understand someone who is different than ourselves unless we are willing to learn about their background and look at things from their point of view."*

Another learner demonstrated perspective-taking:

One of the most salient aspects of my learning in this course was my increased awareness of my own cultural perspective and how it shapes the way I view other cultures. Also it was emphasized to me that we must define our cultural selves and not define the cultural beings of others.

It was particularly rewarding when learners articulated that they were more conscious of how their reactions to ideas were culture-bound; they needed to consider new or challenging ideas in cultural contexts and refrain from rushing to judgment.

I have become more accepting of other views and willing to challenge my own views. I was raised with a specific religion and taught certain values in regard to gender roles, norms, etc. but now I question why I have always perceived these to be "right".

Similarly, one learner reacted to something she heard in a digital ethnographic narrative:

> My moral identity, religion and freedom felt like it was challenged by the matchmaker idea. I was very confused the first time I heard of it and immediately just thought it was weird. I did not give it a chance to understand why they did that and how it works for those who participate in it. I learned to not jump to conclusions and to listen to those of that particular culture explain the reasoning as to why they partake in matchmaking.

As stated at the beginning of this chapter, a strong motivation for redesigning this course was feeling an obligation to develop graduates who would bring intercultural awareness to their future work with diverse families. In their final synthesis (exam), I asked learners to speculate on how they would apply what they'd learned to their future professional careers, specifically to describe a) strategies they would use to understand themselves and others in their work, b) why this is important, and c) how their learning might contribute to their success. It was evident that learners saw potential application:

> One of the main concepts I've learned from this course that I will use in the future is not to make assumptions about individuals and to respect culture. There are so many elements that can affect how people act, think, contribute, and fit into their communities and this diversity should be respected and not judged by what appears on the surface. I've learned and will take with me that when dealing with individuals in this profession, and ideally in every profession, cultural background must be considered when trying to help people make decisions in their lives.

CONCLUSION

In conclusion, the process of transforming my *Global and Diverse Families* course has been worth the time and effort required. I am so much more confident in my teaching as a result of consciously integrating a social constructivist approach, consistently using a strong theoretical framework through which to consider course content, and integrating experiential learning, the use of digital media, and service-learning to effectively achieve learning outcomes. Although the transformation resulted in a course that requires more time, energy, and intensity than the previous version, I am deeply satisfied when I read learners' reflections. This final quote captures both the inward-focused self-reflection and the outward-focused consideration of another's culture that are primary goals for the course.

> I think I get stuck in this American bubble with my American ways and forget that other people may live life a different way, have a different way of thinking, treat family a different way, eat different foods, dress a different way. Even though I was always aware of other cultures, I think I always thought that my

way was the "right" way. I have become more ethnorelative in realizing that the way I live is not the only right way, but that there are so many different cultures and values that other people have that are also right. It will be important moving forward to keep that in mind and ask more questions to learn about people.

REFERENCES

Barrett, M., Byram, M., Lázár, I., Mompoint-Gaillard, P., & Philippou, S. (2014). *Developing intercultural competence through education*. Strasbourg: Pestalozzi Series No. 3, Council of Europe Publishing

Bennett, J. M. (2009). Cultivating intercultural competence. In D. K. Deardorff (Ed.), *The SAGE handbook of intercultural competence* (pp. 121–140). Thousand Oaks, CA: SAGE.

Bennett, M. J. (1993). Towards ethnorelativism: A developmental model of intercultural sensitivity In R. M. Paige (Ed.), *Education for the intercultural experience* (pp. 21–71). Yarmouth, ME: Intercultural Press.

Bubolz, M. M., & Sontag, M. S. (1993). Human ecology theory. In P. G. Boss, W. J. Doherty, R. LaRossa, W. R. Schumm, & S. K. Steinmetz (Eds.), *Sourcebook of family theories and methods: A contextual approach* (pp. 419–450). New York, NY: Plenum Press.

Cranton, P. (2001). *Becoming an authentic teacher in higher education*. Malabar, FL: Krieger Publishing.

Deardorff, D. K. (2009). Implementing intercultural competence assessment. In D. K. Deardorff (Ed.), *The Sage handbook of intercultural competence* (pp. 121–140). Thousand Oaks, CA: Sage.

Eisenchlas, S., & Trevaskes, S. (2003). Internationalisation at home: Some principles and practices. In A. Liddicoat, S. Eisenchlas, & S. Trevaskes (Eds.), *Australian perspectives on internationalising education* (pp. 87–102). Melbourne, Australia: Language Australia.

Fink, L. D. (2003). *Creating significant learning experiences: An integrated approach to designing college courses*. San Francisco, CA: Jossey-Bass.

Hammer, M. R., & Bennett, M. J. (1998). *The intercultural development inventory (IDI) manual*. Portland, OR: Intercultural Communication Institute.

Rizvi, F., & Walsh, L. (1998). Difference, globalisation and the internationalisation of the curriculum. *Australian Universities' Review, 41*(2), 7–11.

Sanderson, G. (2008). A foundation for the internationalization of the academic self. *Journal of Studies in International Education, 12*(3), 276–307.

Theodore, P. A., & Afolayan, M. O. (2010). Facilitating cultural competence in teacher education students with digital storytelling: Implications for urban educators. *Multicultural Learning and Teaching, 5*(2), 98–108. doi:10.2202/21612412.1070.

Catherine Solheim
Family Social Sciences
University of Minnesota

Mary Katherine O'Brien
Global Programs/Strategies Alliance
University of Minnesota

Scott Spicer
Library Coordinator Education Services
University of Minnesota

BARBARA GIBSON, MEREDITH HYDE AND TROY GORDON

12. SOCIAL MEDIA & INTERCULTURAL COMPETENCE

Using Each to Explore the Other

One would expect that travel and exposure would make a person more open to other cultures. We [study abroad students] often think we're much more open to new cultural experiences. Hence why we went abroad in the first place, right? When I first arrived in London I thought I was relatively open. I knew there were cultural differences out there and accepted that they exist and that we could coexist. Despite this, I think I'm going through cultural shock. I find myself thinking that there's no place like home and that I can't wait to get back. It's disheartening. I still want to travel, but I'm getting tired of it. From acceptance I've gone all the way down to defense. I'm constantly thinking about how American culture is more accepting and the better evil. Which is definitely not true. I don't think I've gotten to the point of thinking that American culture is THE superior culture, but I find myself constantly thinking, "Why doesn't Sainsbury sell more cosmetics?" or "There's no place like Target." I'd like to think if I stayed for longer I would once again be content and open to other cultures–it's just a phase. Hopefully in the matter of these next few weeks that will all change. It comes and goes in phases. Some friends tell me I'm being sensitive and I can see it. I can sense myself completely overblowing. I'd like to think if I stayed for longer I would once again be content and open to other cultures–it's just a phase. Hopefully in the matter of these next few weeks that will all change.
—Excerpt from student blog post, Nov. 2013

INTRODUCTION

Study-abroad semesters afford students a prime opportunity to develop intercultural competencies by living and studying internationally. But as numerous scholars have reported, international experience alone does not always equate to development (Bennett, 2004). The short time-frame of study abroad programs has often been noted as an obstacle to intercultural learning, as has the tendency for students to interact mainly with their compatriots. Increasingly, however, students' capacities to adapt to cultural differences abroad may be further compromised by a relatively new and influential practice: their propensity to stay connected back home – even to relate with the world around them by default – through social media (Wooley, 2013; Huesca, 2013). The vision of connectedness that social media seem to offer may become it's very opposite when students are abroad: an instrument of disconnection from any real engagement with cultural difference and the critical self-reflection it enables.

With this challenge in mind, Syracuse University's London Program took a unique approach designed to turn students' reliance on social media into a learning opportunity, creating a fusion course entitled 'Intercultural Communication and Social Media'. The course utilizes social media platforms and other technology to support the development of intercultural competencies, including increasing the students' cultural self-awareness, heightening cultural sensory perception, and fostering the ability to adapt thinking, behaviour, and strategies to achieve more effective communication. If living and working in a globalized world is to have practical and substantive meaning, we must be willing to link the teaching of intercultural awareness with intelligent and critical uses of the most common platforms of global communication.

The course and its assignments make use of the fact that the students are temporarily in a foreign country, travelling to other European countries throughout the term, and above all, eager to chronicle their study abroad experience via social media. Rather than imploring them to disconnect in order to experience 'authentic' local culture, the course instead asks students to learn to engage with these online platforms both as spaces of intercultural exchange and ultimately as tools for self-reflection.

First offered in 2013, this elective course is now in its third semester. Students participating in the course are in the UK for one 14-week semester. The class meets once per week for three hours, in a classroom setting at the Syracuse University London campus in the heart of London. Founded in 1971, the SU London program offers approximately 70 courses across 27 disciplines. Although most of the students are from Syracuse University, the program is open to any student enrolled in an accredited undergraduate program at an American institution.

COURSE DESIGN: WHAT INFORMED OUR APPROACH?

The course takes a multi-disciplinary approach, and utilizes Spencer-Oatey and Franklin's (2009) book "Intercultural Interaction" as a textbook, because it provides an excellent overview of frameworks from multiple disciplines. The course draws from a wide range of disciplines and frameworks, including the historically significant theories of Hall (1959, 1976), Hofstede (2005), and Trompenaars and Hampden-Turner (1997), as well as Bennett's Developmental Model of Intercultural Sensitivity (2004), and the more recent Cultural Intelligence framework developed by Earley and Ang (2003). Our approach is largely focused on the development of intercultural competency, defined broadly as "the capacity to interact effectively and appropriately in a variety of intercultural situations by successfully utilising one's intercultural resources (e.g. knowledge, skills, awareness, and attitudes)" (Berardo, 2005, page).

The overall course design includes a mix of lectures, discussions, research, self-reflection, simulations and exercises, individual and group work, and hands-on social media lab sessions.

The Weekly Blog: A Platform for Self-Reflection and Learning

The backbone of the course is the weekly blog, usually requiring a minimum of 250 words, (although some may utilize multi-media elements like photos, videos, or podcasts instead), and asking students to respond to prompts, link experience with scholarly theories, and reflect on their own learning.

Students are given instruction and hands-on help setting up individual intercultural journal blogs, utilizing the free WordPress platform. As the course progresses, they also set up accounts on Twitter and LinkedIn. Although a few students have previous social media experience with blogging, the majority do not, and while some have used Twitter and LinkedIn to some extent, most are not expert in their use. From the beginning, we discuss social media cultures, examining communication and behavioural norms and the underlying values that are observable across media.

Weekly blog topic assignments ask the students to incorporate concepts covered in the classroom or assigned readings, and to reflect on their own experiences and feelings. The blogs are assessed for quality of content (demonstrating depth of thought), application of concepts, and execution (meeting the accepted standards of the social media platform), and feedback is provided as needed. Following is an example of one of the blog topic assignments, and an excerpt from one student's post:

Blog topic #6. After completing the reading on Cultural Intelligence (Earley & Mosakowski, 2004) and taking the mini CQ self-assessment within the article, reflect on your own intercultural communication competencies and areas that might need further development.

> P. Christopher Earley and Elaine Mosakowski talk about Cultural Intelligence or CQ and how there are ways to adjust ourselves so we can be prepared in a global workplace or any intercultural scenario. They talk about three components of cultural intelligence: the cognitive, the physical, and the emotional. These components are also referred to as the Head, the Body, and the Heart. These elements are what makes up our behaviors and interactions in a new cultural setting. I took the Cultural Intelligence self assessment and scored the breakdown of where I stand in my own personal Cultural competencies.
>
> Cognitive Cultural Intelligence aka The Head: I definitely lack in this area automatically because your cognitive intelligence has everything to do with

> mentally preparing oneself for a new cultural experience. If you are prepared then you are less likely to hit roadblocks and awkward situations. It's all about being prepared to exit your comfort zone. It seems that I am less likely to automatically try to relate to another culture I'm very average in how I will adjust myself after having an experience. Cognitive CQ = 3.75/5
>
> Physical Cultural Intelligence aka The Body: This area was my strongest suit by far. I already know from my experiences in London that I will adapt to the local culture such as I will keep to myself on the tube and while walking down the street I don't really make eye contact with strangers often. I admit that when I say "sorry" upon accidentally bumping someone while rushing through mobs of people it doesn't really sound too much like me, in fact it might have a little accent twist on it. Even in Italy I tried to use my limited Italian as much as I possibly could in order to fit in ever so slightly. Physical CQ = 4.5/5
>
> Emotional/Motivational Cultural Intelligence aka The Heart: My emotional cultural intelligence tied with my cognitive intelligence and I guess I can see why. My weakest point by far is that I am only slightly confident that I can deal well with people from different cultures. Can you blame me though, if I'm not properly immersed/prepared in any way I'm bound to feel at least a little out of place. Sure I am alright at adjusting to change but my confidence levels aren't going to be at peak levels when I am not quite sure what is going on around. Emotional/Motivational CQ = 3.75/5
>
> Maybe I'm not a natural as profiled by Earley and Mosakowski as the one that is strong in all three areas and is culturally competent. If I had to place myself on their scale I would say I am in between the provincial who works best with people that they are similar to and the analyst who observes their surroundings and tries to understand where they are and how they need to present themselves before making any sudden movements. I know that I can improve on my ability to keep my eyes open as well as my mind and it is totally normal to do some research because that will totally change the experience that you have for the better.

The blog also serves as an excellent source for topics for in-class discussions, as well as for spotting trends and diagnosing common issues that may arise during the study abroad semester (as detailed later in this chapter).

Field Assignment One: Emerging from the Bubble

> Being an abroad student I am learning about these cultures and how fascinating they can be, yet I feel as if I don't even really get a chance to exit the US bubble while studying and living with Americans, at least it doesn't seem that easy.

The first and often most challenging difficulty to overcome in teaching any intercultural communication course to a largely monocultural group is the lack of exposure to other cultures' perspectives. In this respect, study abroad programs would seem an ideal opportunity to help students gain intercultural experience. The reality, however, may be that students spend almost all their time abroad surrounded exclusively by fellow students from their home campus. This "expat bubble" effect can actually heighten ethnocentric thinking and behaviour. One example of this, observed by a student in the Twitter posts of fellow students during a weekend trip to France was the frequent use of the hashtag "#englishplease".

It is vital to begin the intercultural learning abroad by helping students get out of that bubble. The first assignment, then, adopts a 'field research' approach by requiring students to look up from their screens and engage face-to-face with people of different cultures. Students are asked to conduct brief, in-person interviews with a minimum of eight people, each from a different country (this is easily achieved in London's multicultural environment, but the assignment could be modified for a more homogeneous location), asking each for an example of something that makes a good impression in their culture, and something that makes a bad impression. In class, students discuss and compare notes about what they found; they are then asked to expand on their research and discussion in responding to their first required blog topic:

> Write about your field research findings and your thoughts regarding how culture influences our perceptions of others. Can you relate your findings to any of the frameworks or models covered in the readings or lectures? Reflect on any insights you've gained about yourself from learning what people from other cultures think.

One of the most common surprises students experience from this exercise is learning that in many cases, the things that may be viewed negatively in other cultures are things they consider positive. For example, several students were told that boasting about one's accomplishments or drawing attention to oneself makes a bad impression, and that humility and self-deprecation makes a good impression. This kind of "ah-hah" moment can serve as the beginning of awareness that not only do other cultures do things differently, they may think and feel differently.

Field Assignment Two: The View from Outside the Fishbowl
(Developing Cultural Self-Awareness)

Much of the course emphasises developing cultural self-awareness, which is defined as an awareness of one's own cultural influences, tendencies and biases, and awareness of how one's own culture may be perceived by members of a different culture. This definition includes aspects of both cognitive and metacognitive knowledge identified under a variety of terms in numerous studies across disciplines, including Early and Ang (2003), Bennett (2004), Adler & Bartholomew (1992), Rosen et al. (2000), Cant (2004) and Gudykunst (1998).

This is particularly difficult to achieve while inside your own culture, as reflected in the saying "the fish is the last to notice the water." So again, although study abroad semesters are an opportunity for students to get outside their own cultural aquarium, many study abroad campuses may simply create small fishbowls, with a focus on looking outward, observing the foreignness of others. Students' constant connection back home via social media essentially serves as a trans-Atlantic pipeline to the home water supply.

Our second field assignment aims to give students a view from outside their own fishbowl. This time, students work in pairs to create a brief questionnaire designed to learn how Americans are perceived by others. They choose their own data collection method, with a requirement to collect data from a sample of at least 10 people (all non-Americans). Some utilize online surveys, others choose face-to-face interviews. Some use open-ended questions, others create multiple-choice lists of positive and negative descriptors (i.e., confident, arrogant, friendly, pushy).

Their findings are almost always shocking and upsetting to them, and their initial reactions are generally defensive, with almost every write-up including references to "unfair" or "incorrect stereotypes". This tendency is often observable in students' tweets and blog posts, as can be seen in this excerpt:

> I love being from New York and wouldn't ask to live anywhere else in the world. I think a lot of the stereotypes people from other countries have about Americans were a lot of the time wrong. Well not completely wrong. Yes, Americans can be loud, obnoxious, wasteful, etc. But so can people from other countries. It's not All Americans. You can't group people from a certain culture and say they are all that way. Yes some Americans are loud that doesn't mean I am loud. It's wrong to group people with a category that doesn't belong to them. But this did make me think how sad it is that most countries have a lot of negative stereo types about Americans. People said we were poorly dressed, had bad manners, were loud, and all types of negative things.

This initial shock is usually followed by new insights, and in general, based on the blog posts over the first half of the semester, students seem to make good progress. However, in weeks seven and eight a clear pattern has tended to emerge, with many of the blog posts again containing ethnocentric and defensive statements. Individually, the sentiments might be viewed as minor set-backs, but taken collectively, all appearing at about the same time in their study-abroad term, the posts provided an indicator that this could be a symptom of "culture shock."

We believe the second field assignment is, in effect, speeding up the process that normally might take place over a period of many weeks or months. And without focused discussion and self-reflection, this exposure to the view from outside the fishbowl can result in increased ethnocentrism rather than increased cultural self-awareness. Students without the opportunity to reflect that this course offers might become 'stuck', as it were, at this point.

It is at this point that the blogs become doubly valuable, as not only a medium for self-reflective writing, but also a means for reviewing and evaluating their own and each other's thinking as they go through this process, thereby adding a metacognitive component. As common themes emerge across several students' posts, we use the opportunity to explore them further in classroom discussions. It is a good point to revisit Bennett's Developmental Model of Intercultural Sensitivity (DMIS) scale, and ask students to reflect on their journey. Earlier in the semester, when the model is first introduced, students inevitably place themselves on the ethnorelative end of the scale. When faced with the evidence of their own blog posts, which contain statements that clearly demonstrate denial, defensiveness, or minimization, they realize they overestimated themselves. They come to recognize that it's not necessarily a uni-directional progression, but a circuitous journey, as can be seen in the following blog post excerpt:

> Personally I'm kind of at a crossroads. As I noted in my last blog post I feel both ethnocentric and ethnorelative all at once. There are times where I feel very mindful of my surroundings and the different cultures I'm interacting with, and then there are time where I feel like I'm completely rejecting the entirety of differences displayed before me. It's interesting to think that exposure can have a multitude of effects. It can open your eyes or prompt you to completely reject the outside world. Or I think the more normal behavior is it's a cycle of both. Ultimately it's all a matter of time. In class we discussed the amount of time it takes to get fully adjusted to a new culture. Inherently there are always ups and downs constantly occurring, but with the passage of time comes a familiarity. You begin to expect the feelings of depression or elation and because you've become familiar with them, you're better able to cope with the situation. Unfortunately, four months is nearly not enough time to start getting into a cycle of familiarity.

Group Assignment: Utilizing Film to Develop Cultural Sensory Perception

One of the core intercultural competencies we focus on is cultural sensory perception (Gibson, 2014). This term is preferred to "cultural sensitivity," which is often misinterpreted to mean something like "don't offend the natives," akin to political correctness. It is defined as the ability to recognize when cultural differences are in play, utilizing a range of senses to spot verbal and non-verbal cues. The new term incorporates Hammer, Bennett, and Wiseman's (2003) definition of intercultural sensitivity as the "ability to discriminate and experience relevant cultural differences" (p. 422), Brislin's (2006) definition of cultural intelligence as "being skilful at recognizing behaviours that are influenced by culture" (p. 41) and Earley and Mosakowski's (2004) reference to a "seemingly natural ability" to accurately interpret culturally unfamiliar cues (p. 139).

This competency is normally developed over a long period of time, and requires exposure to unfamiliar cultures. To speed up the process, the course assigns a group project that utilizes films. Small groups (ranging from two to five students) are formed, and each team selects a video DVD from a selection provided. The assignment is to analyse the film from an intercultural communication perspective, applying one or more of the theoretical frameworks covered in the course, and present their analysis to the class. The presentation may include showing and discussing selected scenes from the film. Students are advised that it will be necessary to watch the film multiple times in order to do this well, and to watch it at least one time as a group, stopping scene-by-scene to discuss observations and reactions. Evaluation criteria includes: ability to identify cultural differences in communication, behaviours and values; application of concepts/theories to analysing cultural differences; and self-awareness and reflection that demonstrates an understanding of team members' own cultural biases in evaluating the behaviours and values depicted in the film.

Interestingly, students have reported that one of the most difficult things about this assignment is that it can't be done while multi-tasking, with their attention divided between multiple devices. This discovery highlights for them that cultural sensory perception requires a level of mindfulness that they rarely give to anything. It helps them explore how closely they pay attention to face-to-face interactions, and question whether they may be missing verbal and non-verbal cues, a competency considered vital to successful intercultural interaction (Spencer-Oatey & Franklin, 2009):

> This project definitely required a higher level of mindfulness because I was trying to pick up on certain things. When I watch a movie for pure enjoyment I think my level of mindfulness is at zero. I don't pick up on cultural differences when watching movies, I just notice that things are different. For example in the movie I watched the young girl's parents didn't want her to go away to college. In my family it isn't an option, you have to go to school. If I was just watching that movie for leisure I probably wouldn't have attributed the difference to her culture. I liked watching the movie with a high mindfulness level and I think now that I have done it I will subconsciously do it when watching movies in the future.

Research Assignment: The Fusion of Intercultural Communication and Social Media

Throughout the course, social media platforms are studied not merely as technological tools but as cultures and subcultures, paying attention to values and norms evident in each one, and how users adapt their communication style to the particular platform.

The final assignment brings it all together, as students develop individual research projects that either analyse social media to study intercultural communication, or study the culture of social media. Students are encouraged to choose a topic that interests them personally. They may utilize any of the theoretical frameworks covered in the course, and draw their data from any social media platform.

Working in small groups in the classroom, students brainstorm topics and possible methodologies, and receive feedback from the rest of the group as well as individual feedback from the instructor. Students then submit a brief research proposal and are given further feedback before beginning data collection. The resulting product is a research report of 1500 to 2500 words, and a brief classroom presentation of their findings.

A few of the topics researched by students in the course so far have included:

- Women, the Hijab, and Twitter
- Syncopated Communication and Identities: Blogging in China
- A Little Privacy Please: Differences in usage of Facebook between generations
- Connectivism versus Celebritism
- Comparing Norms of Self-promotion in Facebook & LinkedIn
- Social Media and its Impact on Culture Shock
- How Values and Norms are Learned on Twitter
- Caption That: A Study of Gender, Selfies, and Word Choice
- Are Cultural Values and Differences Evident Through Social Media Usage Between Indonesian and American Users?
- Trompenaars' Theory of Specific/Diffuse as Applied to the Social Media Platforms of Spanish and American Students

The titles show the broad range of approaches, topics, and methodologies selected. Following are four examples of recent projects that demonstrate the different ways this assignment can be applied.

One student chose a topic that utilized social media to study her own culture and gain insights into her own use of social media, as well as the impact social media has on culture. Her project examined how American Facebook users communicate with family members on the platform, how those exchanges differed when communicating with non-family Facebook connections, and what impact online communication might have on family relationships.

Another student chose to explore to what degree study abroad students' social media use enhances the development of new relationships abroad. Her project examined the Facebook accounts of 16 fellow students during the term. She found they had "friended" 133 new people during the semester, ninety percent of whom were Americans (the majority were from the same study abroad program). Only 14 out of 133 new Facebook friends added were locals in the host country or other locations. Her conclusion was that although most students began the study abroad semester with the anticipation of making new friends in a foreign country, the overwhelming majority of their online activity remained focused within their home country culture.

One project was designed to analyse differences in the type of Facebook profile pictures of people from different national cultures. The methodology involved the analysis of 1,138 profile pictures of 30 Facebook users from five different countries of origin, including the UK, USA, Russia, Puerto Rico, and China. Analysis consisted of reviewing profile photos uploaded in the past three years and assigning categories. Following are two excerpts from her findings:

> Facebook profile pictures do reflect cultural values that we subconsciously represent in the way we look and pose, and how we want ourselves to be represented for the public. Trompenaars and Hampden-Turner's fundamental dimension of culture state that some cultures are more individualistic than other, communitarian cultures. My research has shown that participants who come from Eastern cultures tend to focus less on their face and are more likely to default to a picture of them surrounded by friends or family, whereas Facebook users from Western cultures tend to crop out other people and emphasize their own face.

> I noticed a pattern with [students studying abroad]. One particularly prominent example was one of the participants who is originally from the UK but then moved to Hong Kong. His Facebook image changed completely from a typical Western cultured Facebook user with mostly portraits and close-ups of his face, into a more Eastern-culture driven kind of representation, where he is usually surrounded by his friends and fellow students.

Taking a more sociolinguistic approach, another project, titled "An Observational Study of the Uses of the "N" Word on Twitter," studied the Twitter activity of eight young Black British and American people, observing differences and similarities in how the word is used, and whether it is used more casually by Americans than British young people:

> When observing the relationship between the practise of oversharing and the use of social media as a communication tool with the re-appropriated use of the word "nigga" by young Black people, the question of how it is being used, and who is using it become key. Within the United States there is an established norm, Black people are 'allowed' to use the 'N' word regardless of medium. However, the creation of worldwide communities via social media has increased access [...], leading other communities to 'claim' or create their own context around the word.

> The hypothesis of the study was that subjects from the US use the word more casually in their daily communication than their UK counterparts. However, this hypothesis was proven wrong within this study. When looking at the usage of all the subjects, their usage of the ward was similarly casual, using it in everyday interaction between individual Twitter users and their Twitter community as a whole, especially because their profiles are public. However, where differences come into play are with the cultural context in which the

word has become a norm for users to not only feel comfortable enough to publicly use the word on social media, but also dictates the frequency in which the word is used.

It should be noted that the emphasis for the assignment is not on producing serious academic research, but on applying course concepts which are new to them to the more familiar world of social media. Evaluation is based on the following criteria:

- Well-developed research plan, research method is appropriate to the research question.
- Implementation follows the plan, meets standards of credibility and ethics.
- Draws on one or more theoretical approaches covered in the course, and demonstrates an understanding of the theories in relation to the research topic.
- Demonstrates a good understanding of the social media platform chosen.
- Research report is well written and complete; arguments and conclusions are supported by the findings.
- Report utilizes multiple, credible references, and properly cites all sources.
- Presentation is informative and insightful.

Overall, this research assignment has proved to be an excellent learning activity, and has produced interesting and unique work. Based on the experience of the first semester, more support was built in to the planning stage, including workshop sessions on data collection and data analysis methods. We found it essential to require the written research proposal far enough in advance to allow for individual feedback from the instructor before data collection begins. Students have found that much of the research proposal can then be incorporated into the final report. Student feedback on this assignment has been positive, with many stating that it sparked an interest in further study of intercultural communication.

CHALLENGES AND RECOMMENDATIONS

Like the social media that inspired it, the course is continuing to evolve. Research to measure the course's effectiveness in developing intercultural competencies has begun, utilizing the Cultural Intelligence Scale (CQS) assessment tool for both pre- and post-course measurement. However, the question of whether such self-assessments provide useful findings is arguable, for the very reason noted earlier with regard to students' placement of themselves on the DMIS scale. Pre-assessments may be over-inflated and post-assessments may reflect students' new understanding that their journey has just begun. Perhaps more useful would be a post-assessment that asks the student to identify where they now think they were at the beginning, and where they are now.

The fusion of such distinct topics presents challenges, and the constantly changing nature of social media adds additional challenges. But it also provides a rich source of content and data which may allow further research into how educators can use new technologies to support the development of intercultural capabilities. Although most undergraduate students are heavy users of one or more social media platforms, that may not equate to expertise, especially when pushed to utilize new platforms or functionalities. We found it helpful to provide brief basic how-to sessions for each platform, and to build in lab sessions that allow students to get hands-on help. Overall, when using social media to support learning, it's important to engage students in communicating with the professor and each other via your chosen social media platforms. Creating incentives can help overcome reluctance to engage in class-related online interactions. For example, to encourage students to monitor Twitter posts with the course hashtag, before the first session the professor posted the following tweet on her own Twitter feed:

> In case any of my new #CRS400 students are paying attention, first to retweet this wins a prize.

The prize, announced in the first session, was a "get-out-of-blogging" pass, which would allow a student to skip one blog post of their choice. With a total of 14 required weekly posts per student, this became a coveted prize, and ensured that students read all posts carrying the hashtag. Similar incentives were used almost weekly, and the timing of the professor's posts varied.

Especially in a study-abroad environment, where students are living in short-term accommodation and may have limited internet connectivity, expect occasional problems with technology that prevent them from posting on time. It is also useful to have students reflect on the anxiety that this being cut off often produces.

The rapidly changing landscape of social media also presents challenges to the professor to keep their own social media knowledge up-to-date. Platforms that were ideal and free last year may be inaccessible the next, and learning the ins and outs of the latest tools and trends can be time-consuming. One way of overcoming this is to assign a group project that requires each team to research and master one tool or platform and present a how-to session for the rest of the class. It is important to note that this course took place in an English speaking program, and that offering it in another language culture might offer other challenges and opportunities.

CONCLUSION

In today's digital age, incorporating social media into the curriculum is becoming essential to engaging students, but beyond that, it represents an enormous resource that can be tapped for helping students develop intercultural competencies and prepare them for a global work environment. The rapidly changing nature of the social media landscape may present its own intercultural challenges to those of us who are "natives" of a more traditional academic culture. But our exploratory ventures with this course have convinced us that both students and professors can benefit from utilizing social media to move beyond our cultural comfort zones.

REFERENCES

Adler, N. J., & Bartholomew, S. (1992). Managing globally competent people. *Academy of Management Executive*, 6(3), 52–65.

Bennett, M. J. (2004). Becoming interculturally competent. In J. S. Wurzel (Ed.), *Toward multiculturalism: A reader in multicultural education*. Newton, MA: Intercultural Resource Corporation.

Berardo, K. (2005). *Intercultural competence: A synthesis and discussion of current research and theories*. Retrieved from http://www.yumpu.com/en/document/view/4541721/intercultural-competence-a-synthesis-and-discussion-diversophy Last accessed 7 August, 2013.

Brislin, R., Worthley, R., & MacNab, B. (2006). Cultural intelligence: Understanding behaviours that serve people's goals. *Group & Organization Management*, 31(1), 40–55.

Cant, A. G. (2004). Internationalizing the business curriculum: Developing intercultural competence. *The Journal of American Academy of Business, Cambridge*, 5(1/2), 177–182.

Earley, P. C., & Ang, S. (2003). *Cultural intelligence: Individual interactions across cultures*. Palo Alto, CA: Stanford University Press.

Earley, P. C., & Mosakowski, E. (2004). Cultural intelligence. *Harvard Business Review*, 82(10), 139–146.

Gudykunst, W. B. (1998). *Bridging differences: Effective group communication* (3rd ed.). London, England: Sage.

Hall, E. T. (1959). *The silent language*, New York, NY: Doubleday.

Hall, E. T. (1976). *Beyond culture*, New York, NY: Doubleday.

Hofstede, G., & Hofstede, G. J. (2005). *Cultures and organizations: Software of the mind* (2nd ed.). London, England: McGraw-Hill.

Hammer, M. R., Bennett, M. J., & Wiseman, R. (2003). Measuring intercultural sensitivity: The intercultural development inventory. *International Journal of Intercultural Relations*, 27, 421–443.

Huesca, R. (2013). How Facebook can ruin study abroad. *Chronicle of Higher Education*, 59(19). Retrieved from http://chronicle.com/article/How-Facebook-Can-Ruin-Study/136633/

Rosen, R., Digh, P., Singer, M., & Phillips, C. (2000). *Global literacies: Lessons on business leadership and national cultures*. New York, NY: Simon & Schuster.

Spencer-Oatey, H., & Franklin, P. (2009). *Intercultural interaction: A multidisciplinary approach to intercultural communication*. Basingstoke: Palgrave Macmillan.

Trompenaars, F., & Hampden-Turner, C. (1997). *Riding the waves of culture: Understanding cultural diversity in business*. London, England: Nicholas Brealey.

Wooley, S. (2013). Constantly connected: The impact of social media and the advancement in technology on the study abroad experience. *Elon Journal of Undergraduate Research in Communications*, 4(2). Retrieved from http://www.studentpulse.com/a?id=822.

RECOMMENDED FILMS FOR GROUP PROJECT

Ae Fond Kiss…
Anna and the King
Bend it Like Beckham
Bread & Roses
Brick Lane
East is East
Japanese Story
Like Water for Chocolate
Monsoon Wedding
My Big Fat Greek Wedding
Rabbit-Proof Fence

Real Women Have Curves
Red Dust
Snow Falling on Cedars
The Joy Luck Club
Water
Weeping Camel
West is West
Whale Rider
Witness
Yasmin

Barbara Gibson
Syracuse University, London

Meredith Hyde
Syracuse University, London

Troy Gordon
Syracuse University, London

ADAM JAGIELLO-RUSILOWSKI

13. DEVELOPING DIVERSITY-RELATED COMPETENCES IN CREATIVITY WORKSHOP FOR TEACHERS

INTRODUCTION

Last year, we had the privilege of working with Dr. Adam Jagiello-Rusilowski. He was an invited expert on a panel and in a workshop on the topic of engaging diversity in undergraduate classrooms in Warsaw, Poland. His leadership as a scholar and instructor in the field of culturally relevant and engaged pedagogy has been evident in a wide range of contexts, including: direct work with youth and community theatre, advising Polish government agencies and Soros Open Society Institutes in Central and Eastern Europe on youth policies promoting civic and cultural participation and social inclusion of the marginalized groups, research as a part of the international EU-supported project, "Drama Improves Lisbon Key Competences in Education." We were pleased when Dr. Jagiello-Rusilowski accepted our invitation to participate in this volume. The focus is on his integration of pedagogical principles and instructional activities from Odyssey of the Mind with Janusz Korczak's work with sociometric techniques to facilitate intercultural learning and mindful global citizenship. Through this interview, Dr. Jagiello-Rusilowski brings his wealth of experience working and researching with, and advocating for youth to the practices we can use in our own classrooms. Given the complexity of the project and research he is describing, we opted for an interview format as the most accessible for readers who might be unfamiliar with it.

Tell us a little bit about the Creativity workshop at your University in Gdansk?

The "Creativity workshop for EFL teachers" was offered as a required course to the third year students of Early Education with English (Faculty of Social Sciences, University of Gdansk) and all international students of education or psychology. The creativity course met three hours each week for the entire spring semester. It was graded as Pass/Fail as it focused specifically on the development of skills and attitudes versus a theoretical subject. The creativity course was taught in English, so all students needed to be able to understand and speak English, however, students understood and spoke English with differing degrees of confidence and fluency.

Who were the students that participated in the workshop?

The creativity workshop participants were made up of 45 Polish female students and 18 international students from Russia, Ukraine, Spain, Finland, Italy, USA, China, and Vietnam. The Polish EFL students spoke English very well and many had travelled and/or worked abroad in other European education systems. After graduation many went and taught in Norway or Sweden in urban, multicultural contexts. The 18 international students who choose to register for this course were interested in a field related to education. While they are not pre-service teachers they were interested in applying the idea of creativity to contexts both inside and outside of a formal educational context. For example, some were hoping to apply what they learn to facilitate corporate intercultural leadership training.

What were the outcomes or goals for the workshop?

The main goal of the course was to give all the students an opportunity to experience creative problem solving in diverse teams and translate that experience into the development of their intercultural competencies. More specifically for the Polish students of early education, the course was intended to provide an environment for critical inquiry on how language training could also include intercultural learning. It was hoped through creativity exercises students participated in within the course that these could reduce fear of the other and empower students to cross cultural barriers, and enhance their creative output.

What should we know about the social context in Poland that gave rise to this workshop?

Poland is a well-educated nation that often fails to meet the criteria for civil society, such as interpersonal trust, membership, performing functions in organizations, and a positive attitude towards democracy (Czapinski, 2009). While the number of Polish college and university graduates has doubled, supporting the development of democratic citizenship through better education and training and contributing positively to most economic indicators, the social fabric remains among the weakest in Europe (citation?). One important context for considering intercultural learning is through creativity and educational drama.

From a cultural perspective, mainstream Polish communities value social ties with family and close friends of similar backgrounds. This kind of "bonding capital" is basic but may hinder community development or in extreme cases lead to manifestations of xenophobia or even racism when it is not augmented with "bridging capital" (willingness to cooperate with distant friends and workmates). Only then is the specific community able to build the most precious kind of social capital referred to as "linking". Environments based on trust, transparent law and participatory inclusive social mechanisms are difficult to find in Poland. However, the few Polish innovators and their micro communities effectively push for cultural change in their environments, especially promoting diverse perspective taking in problem solving, non-hierarchical relations for knowledge sharing in education, workplace and life-style in general.

Polish elites agree that the only way to increase the prosperity of the country is to create, attract and sustain more agents of innovation. This requires engagement with diversity and intercultural learning of a larger sector of the society than just the creative class themselves (science, business and culture pacesetters). They acknowledge, therefore, the need for changes in educational programs to build stronger linking social capital across generations or cultures (Szomburg 2012). The mission is reflected in the new Polish Qualification Frame for higher education under the general label of social competences. The translation of the intent into actual teaching practice and validation of the new learning outcomes has become, however, a long and slow process for our university systems.

What were some of the current challenges that the workshop sought to address or respond to?

Polish students look at the concept of social capital from the perspective of employers. They are aware that reaching out to people of different nationalities and cultures, mobilizing distant resources and being engaged by dissimilar others should be part of their education. Yet, fewer than 2% of the student population in Poland have used EU funded mobility schemes (e.g., Erasmus student exchange program, international practicum, volunteering) or intentionally interact with international students. On the other hand, almost every second university student have benefited from low cost airline bargains allowing short trips, weekend or summer jobs abroad. Those who had the chance to interact with peers from other countries list their intercultural networking experiences among their most valuable assets for employability. They report that the most challenging situations involved problem solving with people of different backgrounds and communication styles. Finding original solutions was self-rewarding, therefore not actually associated with learning. They regret, however, that these experiences cannot be considered as part of new learning outcomes, validated or recorded by their universities (Jagiello-Rusilowski, 2013). They would need educational feedback from their teachers and more structured reflection in terms of changes in personal attitudes s to be able to actually connect the new competences to their previous learning and future careers (Mikiewicz 2011).

Abstract concepts of social capital or innovating must be grasped on more experiential level by Polish students, teachers and most importantly faculty. Some academic staff participate in numerous international (EU funded) Research and Development projects. They report such experiences from their international work as opportunities to learn how to look at problems from diverse perspectives, generate alternative solutions and try them out in interdisciplinary teams tapping into richer resources but also overcoming communication barriers stemming from cultural differences and stereotyping. Engaging with diversity is meaningful for faculty in the context of teamwork oriented towards discovery or creative solutions that would have never been possible as a result of individual effort (Jagiello-Rusilowski & Pentilla 2012).

Can you tell us a bit about the research and experience that informed your vision for and development of the workshop?

The idea for the workshop came from my over 20 years of experience as the coach, judge and international liaison for Odyssey of the Mind – a program that teaches young people innovative thinking and problem solving. It is implemented in over 40 countries mainly in USA, Europe and Asia. Odyssey of the Mind was developed by Dr. Samuel Micklus, professor of Creative Design at Rowan University, who encouraged his students to take risks to come up with innovative technical solutions. He developed five different divergent problems (generating unlimited number of unpredictable solutions) and variety of spontaneous tasks encouraging young people to use collective thinking under time pressure. A competition and series of tournaments were set up to compare the creativity of the teams by specially trained judges. The presentations took the form of theatre sketches and the program developed its own (sub)culture based on respect for diversity, freedom of thinking and opinions, breaking stereotypes and prejudice, human solidarity, development of imagination and vision of better human relations and standards of living creatively with limited resources of nature.

The program assumes that some individuals will be more motivated to work on problems which require imagination, team effort and risk taking rather than knowing the only correct answer. It is a team effort on divergent challenges that allows the participants with various interests and skills or cultural backgrounds to work together toward a successful solution to a problem. By giving students divergent problems, you are offering them the opportunity to learn to ask non-obvious questions, generate ideas, evaluate them, combine in unusual ways, and to negotiate with teammates. They learn to try out their solutions, analyze faults and try to correct them. They also develop team-working skills like active listening, drawing on team's diversity, tolerating ambiguity and risk taking with applying previous knowledge. They learn commitment and to depend on each other, as well as budgeting time and money.

The conceptualization of the creativity workshop at University of Gdansk was also informed by research on the role of trust in multicultural teams solving problems creatively. Activities aimed at building a team and developing affect-based trust ensure first-hand experience of comfort, self-disclosure, and rapport with representatives of distant cultures allowing the participants to share knowledge and solve problems creatively (Chua, 2010). Another kind of trust is based on experience of others' competence. This cognition-based trust allows team members to deal with cultural barriers when they realize that a specific problem cannot be solved just from the same-culture perspective. Creative problem solving gives more opportunities to show competence than field-specific problems, but more importantly encourages cultural idea exchange. Experience of "flow" (Csikszentmihalyi 1996). is self-rewarding and reduces psychological strains such as anxiety and stress during cross-cultural interactions (Takeuchi, 2005).

What Polish pedagogical traditions influenced the foundation for the workshop design and pedagogy?

Polish teachers, particularly those of early education are often inspired by a pioneer innovator of intercultural education, Janusz Korczak, a pediatrician, pedagogue, researcher, humanist and an author. His life and work ended abruptly but the legend which began in August 1942, when he was killed with the 200 children of the Jewish orphanage from the Warsaw ghetto, in Treblinka Nazi German concentration camp, continues. His pedagogy and concept of research in education was not derived from any specific ideological or philosophical perspectives but was created as a tool to improve the learning environment in the interests of children. He understood that teachers can be the driving force for inclusive, intercultural education. Being a humanist, he believed in the uniqueness of each child and the particular historical, social, cultural, and political context of each setting. The combination of these two characteristics led Korczak to the conclusion that a coercive authority or remote, impersonal theory cannot rule over a personal knowledge and understanding of children or their relations with each other and significant adults.

Korczak argued that the teacher should be an autonomous thinker and a lifelong inquirer. He insisted that the teacher should respect a young learner as an actual person rather than as "a man to be, somebody of the future" (Korczak 1967). He was a pioneer in using drama as a tool for dialogical engagement of teachers and students in educational enquiry. He experimented with status, choosing real life dilemmas for the young learners and allowing them to speak from multiple perspectives, including the voices of authority they could have assumed. Korczak's research documents that the less exposed to intercultural interactions the children had been the more they benefited from role and perspective taking, liberating themselves from limiting patterns of language and behavior. He also found sociometric techniques much more friendly for students who did not feel very confident in verbal communication but were willing to take ownership of their learning.

Based on your research findings, can you describe the core activities of the workshop? Which activities were critical to supporting students' development of social competencies?

Throughout the semester students did a variety of trust-building exercises., which challenged them to listen attentively (so that they could re-phrase what they heard), notice things, and compare what they observed. All of these skills, students learned were part and parcel of the creative process and effectively engaging diversity so as to develop an innovative, quality product. They were followed by proper sessions of creative problem solving in which team members were posed a divergent problem, generated responses, elaborated them collectively, tested and improved the solutions before the final presentation receive feedback. Most instructional methods of the course were adapted from the Odyssey of the Mind coaches' and judges' training workshops.

One example of a trust-building exercise was called Vampire. All students had to share their nicknames and then learn each other's nicknames. The instructor (the Vampire) would approach a student (victim) and another student would have to react in a calm manner to protect the other student being "attacked" by saying their nickname. This fun exercise generates quite a bit of excitement. These kinds of activities work for exploring the idea of responsibility and ability to control emotions when one is frightened or scared. Activities in which students are actively/ physically engaged, help participants focus, and become more aware of specific aspects of behavior and the direct outcomes.

After every activity, we engaged the students in a discussion about how they felt during the activity. In the discussion following the Vampire activity, we reflected upon one's emotions and the how emotions interact with our concentration, recall and how you interact with one another. We discussed how when you were scared or felt rushed, you were less likely to remember the person's nickname and be able to protect them from the Vampire. We then explored their physical reactions during different parts of the activity, and how it affected communication and ability to contribute to group work.

Can you provide more elaboration on a specific activity: what did it consist of, how was it scaffolded within the course design, how did students respond?

One exercise is called, "*Are you pulling my tail?*" In this activity, the team's task is to *construct a structure which will be as long as possible* but will stay intact (together) on the floor when pulled by a judge for one foot. It also must symbolize a character with a tail. Various limitations and parameters are provided and the activity allows only 20 minutes total before judging/evaluation. The activity was preceded by a survey on self-efficacy and followed by a reflective activity that asked group members questions such as: what roles did you manage to explore during the activity? Which behaviors of others helped you generate and test creative ideas? What pressures were useful and which hindered creativity?

The average level of the students' self-reported self-efficacy about their social competence (knowledge, skills, and attitudes) was 27 out of 100, however, the following differences between students' identified nationality were found:

- American, Italian, and Finnish students self-reported self-efficacy scores were above the overall average;

- Russian, Ukrainian, and Spanish students' self-reported self-efficacy scores were below the overall average. Interestingly, some of these students self—reported 0 values on the sentences:" I am able to engage in teamwork problem solving" and "I am able to tolerate ill-defined problems."
- Polish students' self-reported self-efficacy scores were above the average in the knowledge category but below the average in the other two categories.
- The highest overall self-reported score was for the sentence: I am able to offer activities building trust, focus, and cooperation while the lowest self-reported score was for the statement: I am able to overcome the fear of spontaneous manifestation of my own diversity.

During the reflection activity, students pointed to the educational experiences as the main source of the differences between them rather than nationality. Students from Poland, Russia and Spain took the opportunity to manifest their skepticism about the learning outcomes of the course. They gave vivid examples of creativity being discouraged or openly punished by teachers in their schools and intercultural competences gained from informal learning passing completely unrecorded at their universities. Polish students voiced serious doubts about investing in creativity methods for teaching school subjects if the testing system expects the pupils and later students to know the correct answers only. The students from Russian Federation shared their fear of being challenged to contribute to diverse teams working creatively. They would rather read about applied creativity and problem solving then actually experience it with the foreigners who will not have much chance to find out about Russian culture anyway. In fact already at the beginning of the second session they showed the instructor a long list of publications in Russian on applied creativity methods in education. They seemed confused about the course and instructor's expectations of them to contribute with their social competences. They considered themselves "clients" of the university "receiving papers," that is formal qualifications for teaching.

The Chinese students felt that the creativity course violates their basic beliefs on how you learn a foreign language. For them, they believe that through hard work and obedience to the teacher, they will learn the necessary content and skills. Spontaneity and multiple solutions in a classroom, in their opinion, threatens the status of the teacher and confuses the students. The course, however, could have value for the Chinese teachers themselves who should understand foreign students better and help them adapt better to the culture they joined.

Vietnamese students supported the perspective of teaching language through the authority and professionalism of a teacher equipped with a good handbook. They disagreed, however, with the Chinese belief that language is an imposed element of cultural adaptation. For the Vietnamese students acquiring new language is gaining mobility, a key to educational and personal development through interaction with other cultures. Finish, Italian, and American students tried to persuade the group to open up more to the experiences offered by the course, sharing their beliefs about the benefits from working in diverse groups and listening to different perspectives. The opportunities for hands-on tasks and finding original solutions were valued by this group of students' more than typical academic work. They also shared their motivation to develop intercultural competencies during their university years. They argued that the ability to mobilize diverse human resources, to overcome barriers, and create new value in professional teams are things that employers seek when recruiting.

Towards the end of the term, after completing several more projects and activities, participants were asked to reflect on the experience as well as to come back to their self-efficacy questionnaires and expression of their beliefs in the form of sociometry. The average level of self-efficacy beliefs about achieved learning outcomes of the course was higher but the following differences remained:

- American, Italian, and Finnish students self-reported above the average beliefs level
- Students from Russia and Ukraine self-reported below the average but at least no 0 values were marked on any sentences
- Polish students self-reported above the average in the knowledge category but their views on their ability to change (over 50%) in the value to overcome the fear of spontaneous manifestation of my own diversity.

The participants of the Creativity Workshop at University of Gdansk found their work gave them an opportunity to apply the knowledge both about creativity and intercultural learning. They reported that cumulative impact of the workshop was that it encouraged them to reflect back on some activities they experienced themselves during the workshop sessions and analyze them from the perspective of their prospective language pupils. They reported how the trust they developed helped overcome many obstacles for the teamwork during the design process. Numerous assumptions were challenged e.g. about the dominance or even superiority of host country culture or English speaking students. The participants admitted that if it was not for the long process of building a strong community of learners the final project would have experienced more strains and cultural barriers. What seemed childish games and funny but irrelevant divergent tasks proved in fact a necessary investment in affect-based trust. The positive emotional attitudes towards diversity increased the task orientation and experience of flow during the team organized meetings. As a result the students felt more ownership over their ideas and appreciated feedback from their peers. Most of them reported being better prepared for future intercultural interactions and gaining valuable insights into creative problems solving process in diverse teams.

Did you encounter resistance or dissonance?

This particular pilot use of creativity activities for intercultural learning assumed a balanced local-global perspective. It subscribes to understanding of intercultural education as overcoming barriers between particular individuals or groups with identification of the source of the division both in the cultural and economic/ political agendas. Facing these barriers may cause different forms of fear (Bash, 2012). University students will tend to mask the fear and resist typical warm-up icc breaking activities as something not matching the status of higher education institution. My advice is to use your authority and rationalize the activities quoting the adequate research or employers perspective when necessary. Skipping the "silly games" will appear always tempting or even sensible but yielding it may actually jeopardize the creative processes and miss the opportunities for intercultural learning.

Another source of resistance to engaging in the activities offered within creativity workshop for intercultural groups is students' sensitivity to unexpected manifestations of status among themselves and by the teacher. They try to limit the risk of losing the status and therefore prefer to stick to their cultural identities and pattern of behavior not always encouraging linking to intercultural resources in problem solving. The creativity workshop proposed that language (also a foreign one) is an important social resource but people can use other means of communication with distinct implications for how to conceive of intercultural relationship. The main requirement is that participants perceive one another in terms of potential contributions rather than subject positions. Equipped in affection-based trust and creative problem techniques students will recognize themselves in dynamic categories and roles rather than self-defining ones. They are, therefore, much more liberated to respond to the unique requirements of the situation and can afford a more expanded sense of intercultural relation.

What reflections or takeaways would you highlight for those who plan to do a similar workshop?

Describing the creativity workshop with the mission of spreading it as a good practice faces one particular problem. The most useful description should linear and clear in terms of steps and approaches used as possible. The actual class, however, should not follow a linear plan as the instructor will always remain sensitive to the group dynamics and their responses to the activities and reflections that follow. Students gradually should take ownership over the class and the instructor should be consistent with this approach, therefore, to the extent in which the learning outcomes would still be achieved, let the students lead the process, especially in terms of pace of learning, the space set up and the choice of particular activities.

The main recommendation from the practice of Creative Workshop with international students training as language teachers is for the instructors to engage interculturally themselves. This means to become interested in the cultural "burden" or "wings" the student bring into classroom. Students will be more motivated to take risks and share their knowledge and creative ideas with peers from even distant cultures once the trust is built within the learning community but more importantly when the participants are helped with reflection on the meaning of their new competences for building social capital on personal and community level. The weaker social capital they have at home the more "edging in" they will require from the instructor and the group as the learning community to transform their skepticism about creativity to enthusiasm for intercultural collaboration.

What did you learn from doing the workshop?

As faculty members, we tend to assume that what is at the core of our authority in the classroom is our specific field competence, in particular theoretical knowledge. A good class is based on clear presentation of information, logical sequence of arguments, evidence, sometimes critical questions we pose as class leaders. We also tend to think of students as a unified and passive group, an audience to appreciate our expertise. The experience of facilitating Creative Workshop has taught me that students get really involved in a class if they experience cognitive dissonance and get help from the instructor to deal with it by testing their existing competence, constructing new knowledge, developing new skills or changing attitudes. This workshop provides a two-fold opportunity for dissonance: one is the divergent problem itself the other is the cultural shock. The most challenging part is the attitude students bring to the class. If they think of themselves too highly, they cut themselves off from the help they need; if they undervalue their capacities they do not even try to seek solutions.

The creative workshop has taught me that as a teacher I have personal resources to leverage the situation with students' attitudes by organizing the experience of "Flow" and giving them the right feedback after the activities. Thanks to the intercultural make-up of this class, what I learned was that quality of learning depends heavily on quality of relations within the community of students and the instructor. Even the most tricky barriers and negative attitudes can be transformed with the patience, commitment to trust-building and sense of humor of the instructor. Students will follow you into real challenges if you create a safe environment and support them with feedback.

REFERENCES

Bash, L. (2012). Intercultural education and the global-local context: Critiquing the culturalist narrative. *Issues in Educational Research*, 22(1), 18–28.

Beiner, F. (1997). Korczak's pedagogy of respect. *Dialogue and Universalism*, 7(9–10), 143–152.

Chua, R. Y. J., Morris, M. W., & Ingram, P. (2010). Embeddedness and new idea sharing in professional networks: The mediating role of affect-based trust. *Journal of Creative Behavior*, 44(2), 85–104.

Czapiński J. (2009). Kapitał społeczny. In J. Czapiński & T. Panek (Eds.), red. *Diagnoza Społeczna 2005. Warunki i jakość życia Polaków* (pp. 204–214). Retrieved from http://www.diagnoza.com/.

Eden, S. (2000). *Henryk Goldszmit – Janusz Korczak: The man, the educator, the writer. Jerusalem.* Israel: Janusz Korczak Association in Israel.

Efron, S. (2005). Janusz Korczak. Legacy of a practitioner-researcher. *Journal of Teacher Education*, 56(2), 145–156.

Csikszentmihalyi, M. (1996). *Creativity: Flow and the psychology of discovery and invention*. New York, NY: Harper Perennial.

Jagiello-Rusilowski, A. (2013). *Formalne i pozaformalne przestrzenie nabywania kompetencji spolecznych*. Research report for Instytut Badan Edukacyjnych, Warsaw.

Jagiello-Rusilowski, A., & Pentilla T. (2012). Validating innovation competences as learning outcomes. *International Conference on Engineering Education (ICEE) Proceedings*, Turku (pp. 218–225).

Korczak, J. (1967). How to love a child (J. Bachrach, Trans.). In M. Wolins (Ed.), *Selected works of Janusz Korczak* (pp. 254–279). Washington, DC: National Science Foundation. (Original work published 1914)

Mikiewicz, P. (2011). *Social capital and education*. Wyzsza, Wroclaw: Dolnoslaska Szkoła.

Moretti, E. (2013). *The new geography of jobs*. New York, NY: Houghton Mifflin Harcourt.

Szomburg, J. (2012). *Postawy i umiejetnosci kluczem do rozwoju Polakow i Polski*. Wolnosc i Solidarnosc nr 50 (pp. 11–19). Gdańsk: Instytut Badań nad Gospodarką Rynkową.

Takeuchi, R., Wang, M., & Marinova, S. V. (2005). Antecedents and consequences of psychological workplace strain during expatriation: A cross-sectional and longitudinal investigation. *Personnel Psychology*, 58(4), 925–948.

Woolcock, M. (2001). The place of social capital in understanding social and economic outcomes. *Canadian Journal of Policy Research*, 2(1), 1–17.

APPENDIX 1

Learning outcomes of creative workshop (Jagiello-Rusilowski)

Knowledge	Skills	Social competences
Students distinguish creativity as a process resulting in novel solutions that enhance learning where traditional methods fail from common sense perception of creativity in the classroom	Students transform convergent problems into divergent ones, apply creativity criteria and differentiate original ideas from common responses to a problem	Students contribute and show appreciation for novel ideas from peers, actively listen to capitalize on collective brainstorming
Students relate psychological processes of creative problem solving to the facilitation of language learning as well as crossing barriers between individuals from diverse cultures	Students are able to offer activities building trust, mindfulness (focus) and collaboration for diverse groups.	Students engage in teamwork, respond to initiatives, mobilize own and peers' resources, sustain task oriented action. They are willing to face uncertainties of working with individuals from diverse cultures
Student identify needs of learners, describe roles needed for creative teamwork, explain motivation processes for creative communication	Students match language needs with creative challenges and type of feedback/evaluation for optimal motivation	Students negotiate preferred roles, leverage status, share ideas, offer and accept constructive feedback during and after problem-solving
Students relate theories of creativity to principles of constructing divergent problems for language learning	Students construct divergent tasks for language learning	Students tolerate ill-defined tasks, are able to alternate perspectives on motivating others to be creative, are willing to share experiences of "flow" (Csikszentmihalyi, 1996)
Students give examples of strategies for intercultural communication facilitating creative teamwork	Students are able to offer indicators of effective intercultural cooperation	Students overcome barriers, show sensitivity to diversity as peers and facilitators of creative problem solving in a language classroom

SAHTIYA HOSODA HAMMELL, ROSE COLE, LAUREN STARK,
CHRISSIE MONAGHAN AND CAROL ANNE SPREEN

14. ON BECOMING A GLOBAL CITIZEN

*Critical Pedagogy and Crossing Borders in and
out of the University Classroom*

The scope and complexity of global initiatives have dramatically increased at institutions of higher education (Altbach & Knight, 2007). Many colleges and universities conceptualize their programmatic and curricular responses to these calls for internationalization around global citizenship education (Deardorff, 2006; Morais & Ogden, 2011; Musil, 2006; Nussbaum, 2006). However, despite the increasing focus on internationalization in education policy and programming, neither university nor high school curricula have been sufficiently able to address how to prepare students to participate in their communities as active and engaged citizens. Moreover, there is little consensus on what "global citizenship education" actually is or should be and how students should experience it (Green, 2012), especially outside of study abroad programming (Lewin, 2010).

In some ways, global citizenship education can function as a just and equitable approach to internationalizing campuses: by de-centering elitist understandings of global experiences and de-emphasizing global travel as key ways to approach cultural engagement, global citizenship education can avoid the usual critiques of study abroad and international service learning (Green, 2012; Lewin, 2009; Engle & Engle, 2003; Musil, 2006; Butin, 2010; Siaya & Hayward, 2003). Conversely, the term "global citizenship" itself is so broad as to include many competing, if not divergent definitions. For example, "global citizenship" may be defined as global activism and global reform (Schattle, 2009; Urry, 2000); global cosmopolitanism (Appiah, 2008; Schattle, 2009; Urry, 2000); global hybridity (Rhoads & Szelényi, 2011); or global management and global capitalism (Falk, 1994; Schattle, 2009; Urry, 2000). Yet, educating for global capitalism is quite different from educating for global activism (Davies, 2006). As such, it is crucial for institutions to understand the underlying assumptions of global citizenship education and to take a critical approach to global citizenship initiatives.

However, what does a critical global citizenship pedagogy look like in an undergraduate setting? What are useful ways to approach the pedagogy and curricula of global citizenship education? The purpose of this chapter is to provide answers to these questions using empirical findings from a qualitative case study that documents and describes the processes and approaches of a university course on global citizenship.

CRITICAL GLOBAL CITIZENSHIP: MINDFULNESS AS A PATH TO RESPONSIBILITY

While the majority of the chapter will be devoted to detailing the design and implementation of a global citizenship course, we first present a theoretical model for "mindful global citizenship," and suggest that this model offers a conceptual framework for the pedagogy of globalization and citizenship. By designing global citizenship curricula using mindfulness as a theoretical frame, we argue that higher education actors will be better able to support the commonly stated core aims of internationalized undergraduate education: fostering the cultural understanding and critical thinking necessary for responsible civic engagement (Chickering, 2003; Hutcheson, 2011; Tilak, 2008).

We suggest, and will subsequently demonstrate, the ways in which our approach to mindful (vs "mindless") global citizenship practice helped to prepare undergraduate students to act as responsible citizens in an increasingly complex world. Our pedagogical aims build significantly on concepts of social justice, which consider civic learning as responsible activism that recognizes the individual's connections to social issues in their own community and throughout the world (Davies, 2006; Rhoads & Szelényi, 2011; Schattle, 2009). In describing this framework we explain how mindful global citizenship education aligns with anti-oppressive pedagogies such as anti-racism, social justice pedagogy, critical pedagogy, multicultural and human rights education, and suggest that this strand of emancipatory education aligns closely with the concept of mindfulness education.

Our application of mindful global citizenship education was developed using Langer's research on mindful education. Langer (1997), defines mindfulness as "the continuous creation of new categories; openness to new information; and an implicit awareness of more than one perspective" (p. 4). For Langer, uncertainty lies at the heart of mindful education, allowing students to evaluate and respond to new information without relying on existing stereotypes or preconceptions (p. 15). Conversely, she defines mindlessness as "entrapment in old categories," "automatic behavior that precludes attending to new signals," and "action that operates from a single perspective" (Langer, 1997, p. 4). These definitions are useful to revisit in order to begin to illustrate how we apply mindful global citizenship education as an alternative to "mindless" global citizenship education.

Teaching and Learning Global Citizenship and Human Rights Course

Seventeen university students (both undergraduate and graduate) were enrolled in Teaching and Learning Global Citizenship and Human Rights (TLGC) course in the Fall semester; six undergraduate students from the Fall cohort enrolled in an internship for the Spring semester, which corresponded with the year-long elective at the high school. As the university students in the internship would be responsible for mentoring the six project teams in the high school course (one university student per team), we intentionally kept the internship course small in number.

In designing a collaborative global citizenship education initiative between the university and the local high school, we wanted to encourage critical thinking and intercultural understanding amongst course participants (both undergraduate and graduate students) in TLGC through a three-pronged integrated approach to pedagogy, utilizing: 1) readings and in-class discussions; 2) weekly experiential class visits to a corresponding course entitled "Becoming a Global Citizen" taught at a local high school; and 3) reflective assignments and discussions that provided a foundation for their weekly class visits. It is important to note that participants in the high school course represented a range of students who were diverse in ethnicity, ability, class, and nationality. Approximately half of the students were US born and participated in Advanced Placement (A.P.) courses as well as in afterschool clubs such as Amnesty International and Model United Nations and half were resettled to the US as refugees and/or immigrants from a wide range of countries (e.g. Afghanistan, Bhutan, El Salvador, Liberia) and were enrolled in the English Language Learner (ELL) program. Thus students' knowledge of global phenomena varied from theoretical/conceptual to personal/experiential. The high school teacher who collaborated on the design of the course explained the importance of offering this detracked, university-high school collaboration:

> About 10% of [our high school's] students are born in another country. Teaching about global citizenship provides a wonderful opportunity for refugee and immigrant students to draw upon their experiences, cultures, and languages as a powerful resource, to teach their American born peers about global issues from a personal perspective. At the same time, it provides an environment for English Language Learners and native English speakers to engage in meaningful dialogue with university students on issues that are important to all of them.

Both courses were designed to create a collaborative, transformative learning environment where a diverse group of high school, undergraduate, and graduate students were able to learn from each other's unique life experiences, academic training, and perspectives. Additionally, in bringing together a group of students with different racial, ethnic, class, and linguistic backgrounds, as well as different legal and social status, this course aimed to both reveal and break down existing socially-constructed categories (e.g. refugee/migrant, legal/undocumented, exchange/ELL, elite or honors/at-level, general/ special education) allowing students to recognize and ultimately challenge these categories and their social and economic salience. This goal is reflected in a statement on transformative learning presented to university students at the onset of the course:

> There is no singular model or standard for what actually constitutes transformative education, but generally speaking, transformative education seeks to rupture students' worldviews, complexify all that is typically represented as simple, destabilize understandings of Truth, and allow students to see society from the center, as a coherent whole, and therefore act in such as way so as to change that reality. (Lukacs, 1971, p. 69)

For those of us on the research team, our hope was that these benefits would extend far beyond our classroom, into the high school and broader community and potentially advance democratic citizenship.

The readings for the university course included a wide range of academic literature on social justice, human rights, and global citizenship education pedagogies. Building on Freire's concept of the "banking model of education" (2000), we directly challenged this model in the undergraduates' pre-course packet. We explained in the packet that the course is not designed as a "traditional classroom setting, with a teacher who is considered to be an 'expert." In the first weeks of the course, we also discussed our expectation that the classroom was a space for democratic co-learning with the high school students; we asked all students to try and let go of the "expert-learner" model of education, and to strive to build meaningful relationships with everyone in the room. We encouraged students to keep open minds and welcome uncertainty as it was the first time the course had been offered and to be willing to try new approaches depending on what was and was not working. All course participants provided regular feedback, formally and informally, on the lessons, concepts, and approaches taken in the high school course that resonated or alternately did not resonate with them in the high school classroom. As we began to frame the curriculum and teach the course, we made several general observations that provided insights into the research approach, which included capturing and describing the exceptional level of student ownership, engagement, and unique aspects of non-traditional learning that were taking place.

As a result, several questions began to arise:

- In what ways can mindful global citizenship education better support internationalization efforts within higher education?
- How does mindful global citizenship education "work" in an undergraduate setting?
- How can mindful global citizenship be implemented in a higher education setting? What are the requirements for implementation? What are the challenges to implementation?
- How does mindful global citizenship education promote the critical thinking and cultural understanding necessary for responsible civic engagement in undergraduate students?
- What are some of the outcomes, challenges, and limitations of global citizenship education as an approach to an undergraduate experience?

DATA COLLECTION AND ANALYSIS

We utilized a qualitative, case study approach that included participant observation, semi-structured interviews, and focus groups taken throughout the academic year with course participants. Participant observation in the form of field notes collected by members of the research team (observing the university students) and the university students (observing the high school students) were particularly rich sources of data that represented a multitude of perspectives. The field notes were structured by a fixed set of questions, including: 1) describe the activities that you facilitated or participated in today; 2) what conversations of moments did you observe that stood out to you? Why? Do you see any connections between what we've read and discussed in-class at the university and what you experienced at the highs school? We analyzed university students' weekly and summative reflection papers as well various forms of online correspondence (e.g. posts on the course forum, email correspondence) via a coding rubric (comprised of emergent themes generated during first-round coding of the data). All research team members participated in the coding process and arrived at consensus upon emergent themes designations on the coding rubric.

MAKING GLOBAL CITIZENSHIP EDUCATION "WORK": CURRICULUM AND PEDAGOGY OF MINDFUL GLOBAL CITZENSHIP

Mindful Global Citizenship Curriculum

During the first semester of TLGC, students attended class together on Tuesday mornings and then each signed up for one weekday to attend the high school class. The major impetus for the first semester was having the university students learn about human rights, citizenship, identity, and inequality and then create activities and lessons that they would teach at the high school (Appendix A), and post on the classes' weblog as an engaging tool for an audience that we imagined would include other educators and students (Appendix B).

Our joint university-high school course was also designed to support critical thinking and intercultural awareness and understanding through a series of reflective, collaborative, and open-ended topics and assignments. To support the development of undergraduate and graduate students' ability to recognize infinite differences and alternative perspectives, we assigned writing assignments such as field notes, reflective essays, and reading responses. These skills were also encouraged in personal interactions, weekly course discussions and informal conversations at lunch after the high school class, and monthly dinners with the course instructors (also research team members) and high school teachers. These assignments were also intended to support the importance of uncertainty in transformative learning that breaks down existing hierarchies.

Additionally, the university course was designed to increase students' comfort and ability to help facilitate the following skills and competencies commonly associated with global citizenship education:

Table 1. Global citizenship education: skills and competencies.

Knowledge and understanding	Skills	Values and attitudes
• Social justice and equity • Diversity • Globalization and interdependence • Sustainable development • Peace and conflict	• Critical thinking • Ability to analyze arguments • Persuasive writing • Ability to challenge injustice and inequalities • Respect for people and things • Co-operation and conflict resolution	• Sense of identity and self-esteem • Empathy • Commitment to social justice and equity • Value and respect for diversity • Concern for the environment and commitment to sustainable development • Belief that people can make a difference

The high school curriculum was dynamic, flexible, and designed to introduce the high school students to core themes commonly associated with global citizenship education (listed below). Lessons were hands-on and highly interactive; no two days were alike. The weekly course content and themes for the first semester (and corresponding lesson plans for the high school) depicted below provide an overview of some of the significant units and events that the first part of the year addressed. The original list of themes were co-created by members of the research team in conjunction with the high school teachers involved in the creation of the class.

The flexibility of the curriculum and new ideas brought in with guest speakers and current news events enabled us to be responsive to the needs of the class, and we found ourselves delving more deeply into concepts that students struggled with and/or resonated with. Looking for the points of engagement that built on or challenged the experiences of students fostered the most interactions for students and constantly called upon them to apply previous topics covered in the course. One of the university students described our curriculum model this way, validating that the goals of this model mapped onto the lived experience of the students:

> We've taken the time to come together with localized news topics from countries around the world. This combination of academic material and current/present events effectively connect what can seem like distant, abstract concepts with living, breathing people. I think the same has been done with our experiences in the {high school} class. In both classes we've had conversations about diversity, identity, democracy, human rights, and developed innovative ways to engage with these ideas.

Table 2. Curricular themes and events.

Content and Themes	Selection of Special Units and Events
• Identity • Participatory research • Citizenship • Social justice • Equity • Diversity • Human rights and education rights • Globalization and interdependence • Sustainability Development • Policy making • Peace and conflict	• Local immigration issues: viewed a documentary *9500 Liberty*, helped high school students write policy briefs to prepare for a Skype conversation with a US Senator. • Oral histories: seminar with representatives from Voice of Witness (a nonprofit book series with a mission to illuminate human rights abuses through oral histories) and facilitated high school students taking each other's oral histories to make a video for diversity week. • Workshops: participated with the high school students in workshops with professionals on team building, youth participatory action research, youth activism and visionary practice, social movements. • University visits: hosted research days and field trips (organized student leaders and faculty members as interviewees and guest speakers for the visiting high school students).

Another described how the topics both engaged and empowered the students to think beyond the classroom to their possible impact on the world:

> In our class discussions and readings. we've touched on large-scale ideas and social issues. We have the opportunity to share with high school students these broad based ideas, and they share with us their own unique perspectives and stories. We've had conversations about poverty, child labor, genocide, and a number of other social injustices. The workshop that we attended that integrated Amnesty International presented the students, and myself, with the tangible hope of being able to do something about everything that we've been exposed to this semester. In our class. I think the overarching theme has been a push for systematic change and the improvement in the livelihood of our fellow citizens of the world.

For many of the university students, it was their first time working with or mentoring high school students and the first time they had been introduced to some of the themes covered in the high school course. Initially, several expressed surprise and curiosity as to how the course would work. During an interview, one of the undergraduate students expressly identified the challenge to her academic experience as the reason she enrolled in the course to begin with:

Even though participants in the first semester were intentionally looking to push themselves, the reality of moving past their habitual mindlessness remained a challenge. It was not until the second semester, when the university students enrolled in the course for internship credit (without grades) that they began to find themselves achieving mindful global citizenship. During the second semester, the structure of the university course shifted; university students were responsible for mentoring the high school students and assisting with their community-based, action-research projects. These projects (short-documentary films shown at the high school) enabled students to consider the ways in which the "global" issues they learned about in the first semester of the course translated into "local" problems. Topics included segregation, homelessness, sustainability, and immigration. The undergraduate students mentored and supported the high school students as they developed their research questions, gathered and analyzed data, and put together their final documentary films.

Mindful Global Citizenship Pedagogy

As previously stated, our model of mindful global citizenship intentionally utilized a three-pronged integrated approach to pedagogy: connecting knowledge acquired through in-class readings and discussions to experiences in the corresponding high school course with reflection that allowed students to consider changes in their own understandings over time. We suggest that this tripartite, integrative praxis is essential for mindful global citizenship, replacing more traditional approaches to service learning or civics that narrowly define civic engagement (Nicoll, 2013). Most programs rely on either academic content or field-based experience, with very few linking the two, while emphasis on reflection is even more rare. However, a combination of theory and reflection divorced from field experience makes it difficult to foster critical engagement with the ways in which theories of global citizenship translate into practice in classroom settings; alternately field experience and reflection disconnected from theoretical understandings of global citizenship might lead students to presuppose that there is "one right way" of experiencing global citizenship education and also leave them without a deeper understanding of intentions that underlie the curricula and pedagogy of global citizenship courses. Finally losing reflection means that global citizenship is presumed by proximity and leaves room to promote mindlessness as core beliefs and assumptions may be left unexamined. While all three parts of praxis are inextricably linked to each other, we will discuss each separately to give some shape to the student experience. Together the three mutually reinforce mindful global citizenship for transformative outcomes.

Knowledge. Our understanding of praxis required us to honor the knowledge that undergraduate students shared with each other and their high school colleagues, as well as the knowledge they co-constructed throughout their time together. One intentional way to foster these parts of our integrative praxis was through the once-weekly seminar. Again, reflection and field-based experiences were crucial to the seminar, but this format allowed students to process the books and articles they were reading and ground their understanding of the theoretical language necessary to discuss their experiences. The seminar was intended to model social justice and mindfulness practice for the students, emphasizing open mindedness, encouraging flexibility, helping students wrestle with uncertainty and giving them space to process shared experiences.

The seminar also helped us as instructors and researchers to better understand the challenges to mindful global citizenship that students were encountering because of their location along the spectrum from mindlessness to mindfulness. Specifically, time in the university classroom illuminated points of mindlessness for undergraduate students: discomfort with uncertainty of all kinds; anxiety about grades and expectations; extreme reliance on dichotomous categorization; inability to adopt other perspectives; and automatic behaviors that precluded full engagement with a democratic classroom (both at the university and as mentor-facilitators in the high school).

For example, one student articulated a question that is representative of his peers' discomfort with uncertainty: "How do I teach kids at the high school things that *I'm* not comfortable thinking about?" He, and other students were challenged by having to confront their own assumptions and teach something for which they might not have a definitive answer for questions that could arise. Students also initially relied heavily on their perceptions of rigor in the academic classroom and many were consistently anxious about the need to create curricular units for the high school classroom that ended with traditional assessments. Even those comfortable with the concept of differentiated instruction struggled with meaningful differentiation and differentiated assessment that went beyond allowing extra time on the same assignments or dictionary access. In response, we continually emphasized the importance of non-traditional learning methods and outcomes and modeled this in the university classroom by continually adjusting our pedagogical approach throughout the course to intentionally facilitate opportunities for all students to contribute in meaningful ways, to have opportunities to share and reflect together, and to unpack biases and preconceptions. As university students who have achieved at a very high level within the traditional, didactic, performative paradigm of mindlessness, concerns about the rigor of the course surfaced frequently. Encouraging this dissonance and challenging students to reflect on their own discomfort with non-traditional assessment was central to expanding students' previous world views.

Experiences. Topics for the course were not just content from the curriculum, but based on the life experiences of all students. For example, university students interviewed the high school students as part of an oral history unit. In doing so, they learned about the wide-ranging experiences of the high school students, some of whom had previously lived in refugee camps, been child soldiers, had children of their own, or faced discrimination in the local community. In the first semester, many of the university students were overwhelmed by hearing the high school students' lived experiences. However, by the second semester, they demonstrated an awareness of the importance of sharing lived experiences in a global citizenship classroom. As one student explained in her field notes:

> Watching Asha grapple with the possibility of bringing her own personal story into the [her] group's project made me think back to the beginning of the year and appreciate how far we have come since then. I don't think Asha [a student who emigrated as a refugee from Kenya] is used to having an opportunity to bring her personal history into her schoolwork, so I think that is simultaneously an exciting and scary concept.

Relationships, specifically "push-pull" relationships, deeply characterized the experiences in and out of the classroom. We pushed students to question and change their beliefs, attitudes, and approaches. But at a certain point—the tipping point (or points), we allowed ourselves as educators to be more pulled by where students wanted to go. Tipping points are when students begin to see the complexity in issues and stop looking for the "right answers" or the "other side" and when educators apprehend that students are using their own critical eyes to explore complex problems. In the TLGC course, though students were initially resistant to critical pedagogical approaches, by the end of the year they felt increased confidence in their own uncertainty and "unknowing" and began to trust themselves to have the authority to explore and critique their own experiences. One member of the research team observed in her field notes:

> Sometimes you don't see the big change during the course, but for us we began seeing major changes between the first semester and the six students who carried on in the second semester. We really let the students (initially some of whom had been among the most vocal resisters enrolled for a second semester!) take the reins, line up speakers, and coordinate students' projects (while stepping in occasionally when needed to assist). We saw these students talking and acting different[ly] and begin to push the high school students similar to the ways in which we had pushed them during the previous semester.

Reflection. The three-pronged approach was crucial for mindful global citizenship education, and in many ways functioned cyclically: as students reflected on their experiences and synthesized their knowledge of the world with those of their peers, they achieved new insights that informed their classroom experiences and their reflections. Our approach built in many opportunities for reflection. Students wrote reflective essays (which were confidential between themselves and the instructors) and made forum posts (which were publicly shared with their peers, and which their peers commented on). Students were also expected to submit field notes about their experiences in the high school class. Additionally, focus groups and more casual meetings at an instructor's home and during field trips (when the high school students came to campus) provided an opportunity for reflective discussions facilitated by instructors. It was through these reflective activities that we were able to see the evolution from mindless to mindful global citizenship among the undergraduate students as they relied more and more on themselves as possessors of knowledge.

We highlight one activity that both the university and high school students reflected upon as being particularly significant in facilitating their own critical awareness. To help students process and make sense of listening and interpreting different perspectives, students participated in a "Stages of Awakening" activity. This was designed to help students understand the ways they emotionally process difficult information that challenges previously held beliefs. Students were asked to pick a particular theme or topic from the course and reflect on the ways they were processing that topic, and how they wish they were processing it (e.g., "I'm very angry at the plight of refugees; I want to accept it as a reality and then feel impassioned to undertake change; I'm going to gather more information and meet with Human Rights Watch to see how I might get involved"). One can see the ways that knowledge, experiences (like the stages of awakening activity) and reflection are linked through the following forum post from an undergraduate student:

> It was good to practice articulating feeling powerless and to discuss how one moves out of that first stage of awakening. These tools can be helpful in regard to the rest of the class, because the material that we're discussing in both the university and high school classrooms can at times be completely overwhelming. When we spend so much time learning about income disparity, funding inequity, conflict minerals, waste and pollution, and other examples of what is wrong in the world, it can be easy to become bogged down, to give up hope and feel like you have absolutely no control over the situation. While we probably can't change these issues all by ourselves, we can use the Stages of Awakening model to become aware of the individual impact we can have and the power we can gain from working with others to find solutions. In a way, Thursday's lesson provided a defense mechanism from the paralyzation [sp] that threatens to take over when we spend so much time reading about and discussing the seemingly insurmountable problems of the world.

We often pushed the students by encouraging them to take intellectual and emotional risks with the high school students and stressed the importance of building meaningful relationships. We also brought in a number of speakers that helped to provide tools for them to work with students on tough or uncomfortable issues (e.g. Voice of Witness, UpStander, trainer/facilitators on teaching diversity, human rights activists, and Amnesty International), while allowing them to recognize that it will always be a work in progress. During our seminars we provided opportunities for them to reflect on why they were challenged by the course. One student stated,

> I think that today demonstrated that efforts to create a "critical classroom" … have been working. The students seem comfortable questioning everything, including supposedly "good" reforms aiming to resolve social issues. It is important to be critical of our own reform efforts even when they have good

intentions, and the students certainly demonstrate their understanding of this concept today with the questions that they asked the two speakers.

Another student was able to recognize how her experiences at the high school took her outside of her comfort zone and, through the use of reflection during her field notes, she analyzed the cause of her feelings and the inherent cultural relativism present in applying her context to others:

> There was one point during the class when the activity became very disorganized and it seemed like everyone was talking at the same time. I began to compare this classroom to my own high school classroom and briefly thought that my own high school classroom [was better] because of how organized it was. Then I thought of…how problematic my comparison was…it was just a very different way of managing a classroom than my teachers managed us. Furthermore, my classroom was about one-twentieth as diverse as this CHS classroom, which lends itself to a lot of differences in classroom environment that I cannot understand as a product of an entirely homogenous classroom environment.

ASSESSMENT

We used alternative, performance-based assessment measures to recognize the range of authentic learning happening and to mitigate the potential to fall back into mindlessness. Developing new assessment models was essential to help students break out of their mindless patterns of understanding related to achievement and success derived from the traditional classroom models to which they were most accustomed. One of the students described her thinking about the effects of this pressure on the students' action research projects:

> When a student from a nondominant social or cultural group joins mainstream education, they feel as if they must lose part of their culture or identity in order to succeed in that dominant system. It feels like this is happening somewhat with the documentaries. When these films were first being discussed, the students had very creative and exciting ideas about how they would complete their project and how they would represent the diversity of experiences that immigrants have … however, as the actual due date for the assignment got closer, they simply wanted to know how they could pass the assignment. Because the assignment is graded and they know they must "succeed" on the assignment, they limited their [vision]…What was interesting is that this was done without anyone telling them that they had certain requirements to fill. The TAs and mentors in class always emphasized that the documentary should not fill out a set checklist; however, the students were not comfortable with this so they limited themselves. It makes me wonder how social justice

classes, which necessarily do not follow mainstream education, can ever work against the pressures of the dominant system that emphasizes strict metrics and requirements.

This insight about the role of assessment in the high school was particularly gratifying in light of the fact that many of the university students in the first semester expressed concern that we were not evaluating their performance with traditional assessment models. At the beginning of the first semester, we asked the students to take responsibility for writing one lesson plan that corresponded to one of the topical themes of the high school course. Students did this, though expressed frustration if their lesson was not incorporated or was utilized on a different day (as a result of changes to the high school schedule or occasions when concepts needed more time to be taught than anticipated). The students initially seemed most concerned that if their lesson was not utilized their grades would suffer, despite repeated assurances that this was not the case. We pushed them during in-class discussions to reflect on why they were adamant their lesson be utilized on the particular day they had planned for, even if it was not best for facilitating the high school students learning and would be better utilized later. As a result, by the middle of the semester we decided to change this requirement and instead stressed the importance of students' familiarizing themselves with the topic theme of the week through outside readings. Students expressed discomfort at this change and also openly began expressing skepticism, self-doubt, and uncertainty at using social-justice oriented or critical pedagogy despite noting sometimes with surprise that high school students were really engaged by what we were doing. In another activity students carried out called "Nexus", they created a Venn diagram illuminating the intersection of "passion," "skills," and "what the world needs." The undergraduates heard from, and were surprised by, some of the high school students – "I asked Neha [a Tamang student from Nepal who grew up in a refugee camp] to describe some issues dealing with their topic thinking he wouldn't respond or wouldn't really say much, but he did. He had obviously been listening when I thought he wasn't."

Students struggled throughout the first semester with an assessment model based upon their own reflections and participation. However, by the second semester, students enrolled in internship course began to voice opinions about assessment that ran contrary to those they had held the first semester. As one student stated:

> Just as we have talked about how standard assessments might not be best-suited to each and every student, every aspect of our dominant cultural value system might not be best-suited to each and every student. Everyone's priorities and values differ slightly, and that is okay, but I think we often fail to demonstrate that to school-aged kids.

CONCLUSION

In this chapter we presented a model of global citizenship education that can be adopted across a wide range of higher education settings with minimal or no adaptation by leveraging the richness and diversity that already exists on campuses and in classrooms. We suggest this model can better support meaningful and deep internationalization efforts within higher education by bringing global issues into local classrooms and in doing so avoid traps of mindlessness that befall many global citizenship initiatives. However, the design of this course requires sustained reflection and reflexivity on the part of course facilitators, processes that are time-intensive and more often than not reliant upon intuition rather than clear-cut information. To critically engage in themes of war, environmental degradation, and migration (to name but a few) is to promote continued dissonance to students' (and at times facilitators') previously held views and there is no one-approach fits all strategy. As facilitators, we drew upon our individual and collective knowledge and experience to devise meaningful activities that addressed students' continually evolving needs. We hope the ideas and experiences presented in this chapter offer insights to those planning or facilitating their own global citizenship courses but recognize that implementation strategies and impacts will vary from one classroom to the next as well as from year to year in the same classroom.

Ultimately, students enrolled in the university course demonstrated an increased willingness to critically engage with complex, challenging "global" topics (e.g., war, migration, environmental degradation), openly reflect on their own dissonance and discomfort with many of these themes, change their previously held beliefs with regards to assessment, and perhaps most importantly build meaningful, lasting relationships with members of their local community who come from all corners of the globe. By the end of the first semester, we had seen changes in almost all of the students. On any given day, you could walk into the classroom and find students sitting in small groups, engaged in conversation about anything ranging from human rights, to where they wanted to go to college because they could make connections between what they were learning and the world they lived in. By the conclusion of the second semester, students' hope in the promise of this course mirrored our own when we designed it. "I believe the high school students (and all of us students in general) will leave this class with a greater understanding and a new perspective of what it means to be a global citizen, the kind of injustices people just like us experience around the world everyday, and, not just the hope that things will change, but the tools needed to come together and be a part of that change."

REFERENCES

Appirah, K. A. (2008). Chapter 6: Education for global citizenship. *Yearbook of National Society for the Study of Education, 107*(1), 83–99.
Altbach, P. G., & Jane, K. (2007). The internationalization of education: Motivations and realities. *Journal of Studies in International Education, 11*(3–4), 290–305.

Butin, D. W. (2010). *Service-learning in theory and practice: The future of community engagement in higher education.* New York, NY: Palgrave Macmillan.

Chickering, A. W. (2003). Reclaiming our soul: Democracy and higher education. *Change: The Magazine of Higher Learning, 35*(1), 38–44.

Davies, L. (2006). Global citizenship: Abstraction or framework for action? *Educational Review, 58*(1), 5–25.

Dearfordd, D. K. (Ed.). (2009). *The SAGE handbook of intercultural competence.* Washington DC: Sage.

Engle, L., & Engle, J. (2003). Study abroad levels: Toward a classification of program type. *Frontiers: The Interdisciplinary Journal of Study Abroad, 9*(1), 1–20.

Falk, R. (1998). Global civil society: Perspectives, initiatives, movements. *Oxford Development Studies, 26*(1), 99–110.

Freire, P. (2000). *Pedagogy of the oppressed* (30th Anniversary edition ed.). London, UK: Continuum.

Green, M. F. (2012). Global Citizenship: What are we talking about and why does it matter. *Trends and Insights for International Education Leaders,* 1–3.

Hutcheson, P. (2011). Goals for United States higher education: From democracy to globalisation. *History of Education, 40*(1), 45–57. doi:10.1080/0046760X.2010.514868

Lewin, R. (Ed.). (2010). *The handbook of practice and research in study abroad: Higher education and the quest for global citizenship.* New York, NY: Routledge.

Lukacs, G., & Lukacs, G. (1971). *History and class consciousness: Studies in Marxist dialectics* (Vol. 215). Cambridge, MA: MIT Press.

Musil, C. M. (2006). *Assessing global learning: Matching good intentions with good practice.* Washington DC: Association of American Colleges.

Morais, D. B., & Ogden, A. C. (2011). Initial development and validation of the global citizenship scale. *Journal of Studies in International Education, 15*(5), 445–466.

Nicoll, K., Fejes, A., Olson, M., Dahlstedt, M., & Biesta, G. (2013). Opening discourses of citizenship education: A theorization with Foucault. *Journal of Education Policy, 28*(6), 828–846.

Nussbaum, M. C. (2006). Education and democratic citizenship: Capabilities and quality education. *Journal and Human Development, 7*(3), 385–395.

Rhoads, R. A., & Szelényi, K. (2011). *Global citizenship and the university: Advancing social life and relations in an interdependent world.* Stanford, CA: Stanford University Press.

Schattle, H. (2009). Global citizenship in theory and practice. In R. Lewin (Ed.), *The handbook of practice and research in study abroad: Higher education and the quest for global citizenship* (pp. 3–20). London: Routledge.

Siaya, L. M., & Hayward, F. M. (2003). *Mapping internationalization on US campuses: Final report, 2003.* American Council on Education.

Tilak, J. (2008, December). Higher education: A public good or a commodity for trade? *Prospects, 38*(4), 449–466.

Urry, J. (2000). Global flows and global citizenship. In E. F. Isin (Ed.), *Democracy, citizenship and the global city* (pp. 66–78). London: Routledge.

APPENDIX A

Sample high school lesson plan (formatted using schoolwide norms)

Global Citizenship		Daily Lesson Plans
Module:	National vs. Global Citizenship	
Day:	Monday, September 23	
Objective (SWBAT):	Different concepts/ models of citizenship	
Activities	**Instructions**	**# of minutes**
Do Now: Survey	As students arrive, they will be handed a survey at the door that they should sit down and fill out immediately.	15
Opening: National Citizenship	Watch this video: Is citizenship nationality? https://www.youtube.com/watch?v=PFsQaRVh0e8 Have students answer the questions on the worksheet/online survey (link found on the blog) and then share with their group.	10
Group Work: Global Citizenship	Read this article: What's a World Passport? By Daniel Engber Have students answer the questions on the worksheet/online survey (link found in the blog) and then share with their group.	10
Closing: Class Discussion	Each group should share the most interesting thing that they discussed in their groups with the whole class. After each group has spoken the floor should be opened up to general responses to each other's insights.	10
Homework:	N/A	
Reflection	We have all been a situation where someone has made an assumption about our nationality or we have made an assumption about someone else's nationality. How did this make you feel? Are there good/bad ways of asking people about their ethnic/national background?	

APPENDIX B

Sample blog post that corresponds with lesson

Monday Sept. 23- National vs. Global Citizenship

Leave a reply

Today we are going to look at different types of citizenship, focusing on national versus global citizenship. Let's start with a definition:

Citizenship *denotes the link between a person and a state or an association of states. It is normally synonymous with the term nationality although the latter term may also refer to ethnic connotations. Possession of citizenship is normally associated with the right to work and live in a country and to participate in political life.*

In today's lesson plan HumanRightsandCitizenship we will start by taking a 15min survey.

We will then watch this short clip on national citizenship:

After watching this video all students will take a survey on national citizenship in order to explore what exactly it means. For anyone who cannot fill out the Google form, the Worksheet can be downloaded as a Word doc. After filling out the survey students will discuss their answers in small groups.

Next students will read the article Whats a World Passport? by Daniel Engber. This article introduces the concept of a world passport, but also reveals some of the problems associated with it. When done reading, students will fill out another survey. After filling out this survey students will discuss their thoughts on the two different types of citizenship and the strengths and weaknesses of each.

229

JANE JACKSON

15. "UNPACKING" INTERNATIONAL EXPERIENCE THROUGH BLENDED INTERCULTURAL PRAXIS

Shortly after returning home, while my experience was still fresh and profound, I was overflowed with numerous things that I wanted to share with my friends; yet, many times I just swallowed my words due to my friends' uninterested response. Without reflection, many parts of my experience were hidden and more and more of them were fading away... Only after taking this course could I realize the importance of reviewing our experience. Being an exchange student is a challenging, enriching, alarming, enlightening, and thrillingly unusual experience... By reviewing my experience, I learned to value the friendships and new discoveries I made. I got to know myself better and became more optimistic and thankful.

—Post-sojourn reflective essay, Lena

The words above were penned by a participant in an intercultural transitions course that I developed at my university in Hong Kong to help undergraduates make sense of their international experience. While much has been written about the importance of adequate pre-sojourn orientations (Bennett, 2008; Jackson, 2006, 2012; Bathurst & LaBrack, 2012) and ongoing support during stays abroad (Jackson, 2008, 2010; Lou & Bosley, 2012; Paige & Vande Berg, 2012), the reentry phase (e.g., reentry/reverse culture shock) has been accorded relatively less attention. This is changing, however, as more and more international education scholars recognize the need for intervention to help returnees process their sojourn and reentry experiences, and make sense of conflicting emotions and their evolving sense of self (Mendelson & Citron, 2006; Meyer-Lee, 2005; Szkudlarek, 2010). This chapter provides an example of an initiative designed to enhance, consolidate, and extend the learning of student sojourners. While the course is offered in Asia, the methodology employed could be adopted or modified for other settings.

The primary purpose of this chapter is to offer insight into the benefits of guided, critical reflection for student sojourners/returnees. After describing *Intercultural Transitions* and summarizing the findings related to three offerings, I focus on the intercultural journey of a single participant to better illustrate the learning process. Instead of briefly touching on the trajectories of multiple participants, we follow the evolution of Lena (a pseudonym), a multilingual Hong Kong Chinese student who joined *Intercultural Transitions* after a yearlong sojourn in Sweden. She was selected for this case study as she experienced significant gains in intercultural competence and self-awareness during the semester-long course, and her rich oral and written narratives offer valuable insight into the potential impact of guided critical reflection.

While the developmental trajectories of students vary and a single case study cannot be representative of all returnees, we can still learn a great deal by examining the journeys of individuals like Lena. In particular, her storied experiences and my analysis elucidate the complex notions of intercultural competence, reentry culture shock, and identity reconstruction in relation to guided, critical reflection, drawing attention to multifarious internal and external elements that influenced her unique journey.

THE INTERCULTURAL COURSE: DESIGN AND DELIVERY

Intercultural Transitions: Making Sense of International Experience was inspired by my education abroad research: ethnographies of short-term sojourners and mixed-method investigations of international exchange students (Jackson, 2008, 2010, 2013a). When I designed this elective, 14-week, credit-bearing course, I aimed to deepen and extend the intercultural learning of undergraduates with recent or current international experience. The course draws on multiple theories, including the Intercultural Development Continuum (Hammer, 2012), Kolb's (1984) experiential learning model (Passarelli & Kolb, 2012), and Mezirow's (2000) transformative learning theory.

The Intercultural Development Continuum (IDC)

The Intercultural Development Continuum (IDC) (Hammer, 2011, 2012), an updated version of the Developmental Model of Intercultural Sensitivity (DMIS) (Bennett, 1993, 2012), guided the selection and sequencing of course materials and activities, as well as the monitoring of the participants' intercultural development. Within this framework, intercultural competence is defined as "the capability to shift cultural perspective and appropriately adapt behavior to cultural difference and commonalities" (Hammer, 2013, p. 26). The IDC centers on one's perception and response to cultural difference and the constructs of "monocultural mindsets" and "intercultural mindsets" (Hammer, 2012). According to Bennett (1993), if one has a monocultural or ethnocentric mindset, "the worldview of one's own culture is central to all reality," (p. 30), whereas an intercultural/global mindset (ethnorelative orientation) is associated with "being comfortable with many standards and customs" and "an ability to adapt behavior and judgments to a variety of interpersonal settings" (p. 26). Intercultural/global mindsets and ethnorelative worldviews are thought to be much more effective in scaffolding the attitudes, knowledge, and actions that facilitate successful intercultural communication and acculturation in unfamiliar linguistic and cultural environments (Bennett, 2004, 2008; Hammer, 2012).

The IDC theorizes that people progress from ethnocentric stages (Denial, Defense) through Minimization (a transitional orientation) to more ethnorelative stages of development (Acceptance, Adaptation, and Integration) as they acquire intercultural competence (Hammer, 2009a, 2009b, 2012). *Denial* measures a worldview that simplifies and/or avoids cultural difference. *Polarization: Defense/ Reversal* measures a judgmental orientation that views cultural differences in terms of "us" and "them". In *Defense,* "us" is viewed as superior, whereas in *Reversal* (R) "them" is superior and "us" is maligned. *Minimization* (M) measures a worldview that emphasizes cultural commonality and universal values. With limited cultural self-awareness, individuals in this transitional phase may not pay enough attention to cultural difference. *Acceptance* measures a worldview that can comprehend and appreciate complex cultural differences (e.g., values), while *Adaptation* identifies the capacity to alter one's cultural perspective and adapt one's behavior so that it is appropriate in a particular cultural context. Individuals do not necessarily progress from one stage to the next in sequence. Negative intercultural experiences (e.g., perceptions of racism, contested identities, severe language and culture shock) may trigger ethnocentric tendencies and pull one back to a lower level of intercultural sensitivity.

Linked to the IDC, is the Intercultural Development Inventory (IDI) a cross-culturally validated, psychometric instrument, which measures intercultural competence (Hammer 2012). While "located outside the IDC", the IDI also measures Cultural Disengagement (CD), that is, "the degree to which an individual or group experiences a sense of disconnection from a primary cultural community" (Hammer, 2012, p. 119).

Experiential Learning and Personal Transformation

In experiential learning theory (ELT) learning is viewed as "the process whereby knowledge is created through the transformation of experience. Knowledge results from the combination of grasping and transforming experience" (Kolb, 1984, p. 41). Optimally, in this learning cycle, individuals gain concrete experience (e.g., intercultural interactions abroad), reflect deeply on this experience, draw lessons from it (conceptualize ideas), and put their new understandings into practice. ELT offers a model for interventions in education abroad learning due to 'its holistic approach to human adaptation through the transformation of experience into knowledge' (Passarelli & Kolb, 2012, p. 138).

ELT is in accord with the IDC and Mezirow's (2000) notion of personal transformation in adult learners who fully engage in the process of critical reflection and meaning-making. The latter suggests that emotional reactions to crises (e.g., culture shock) can serve as catalysts for 'frame shifts', resulting in significant personal growth. This resonates with Hammer's (2009a) view of cultural adaptation as "the capability of shifting perspective to another culture and adapting behavior according to cultural context" (p. 209). A growing number of intercultural educators (Bennett, 2004, 2008; Brockington & Wiedenhoeft, 2009; Vande Berg et al., 2012) recognize that intercultural experience coupled with guided critical reflection can move students to higher levels of intercultural competence. All of these theoretical understandings informed the design of *Intercultural Transitions*.

Course Design and Activities

In this learner-centered course, the class size is capped at 25 and an eLearning platform is used to nurture a sense of community and create learning spaces that extend beyond the classroom walls. In a supportive environment, the participants are encouraged to critically examine their own (and others') international experience in relation to theories and models of intercultural competence, intercultural transitions, culture shock/adjustment, intercultural citizenship, and identity reconstruction. Guided reflection encourages them to question their assumptions and actions, and connect their experiences to theoretical concepts. Readings (e.g., sojourner accounts), discussions (face-to-face and online), and reflective writing tasks (e.g., online forum chats, blogs, essays) prompt the participants to become more mindful of the ways in which their own attitudes influence the way encounters unfold. As they share experiences and 'unpack' their intercultural learning, they are prompted to push past stereotypes and set new goals for the enhancement of their intercultural competence.

With the support of Teaching Development Grants, I have tracked the intercultural development of 55 participants in three offerings of the course and gathered their views about various elements, including computer-mediated activities. Pre- and post- IDI results revealed that, the groups as a whole acquired a higher level of intercultural competence by the end of the semester, moving from the low to the high end of Minimization, the transitional phase. Thematic content analyses of the qualitative data (e.g., open-ended questionnaires, reflective essays, Forum chats, post-sojourn interview transcripts) were generally in accord with the IDI results, suggesting that guided, critical reflection (in class and online) helps propel students to higher levels of intercultural competence (Jackson, 2013b).

AN ILLUSTRATIVE CASE STUDY: LENA'S STORY

The remainder of this chapter centers on Lena's developmental trajectory. Pre-course data for her case study consisted of: her application to join the exchange program (e.g., an essay outlining her sojourn aims and expectations) and the Pre-International Exchange survey (an in-house instrument) that is administered to outgoing international exchange students at my institution (Jackson, 2011). The data collected during the *Intercultural Transitions* course consisted of: three reflective essays, weekly online forum posts/blog entries, the PowerPoint file/handout she developed for her oral presentation, and questionnaire surveys, including the IDI that was administered at the beginning and end of the semester.

Lena's post-course data included a questionnaire and a 150-minute semi-structured interview with a Hong Kong Chinese research assistant. By her choice, the interview was conducted in Cantonese and then translated into English during the transcription process. Efforts were made to retain the nuances and emotions of her discourse in the translation, which was checked by two bilingual research assistants. All of Lena's written narratives (e.g., application essays, blog entries, forum chats, essays) were written in English and excerpts are in their original form.

Throughout the course, I also kept detailed field notes and they were also entered into the NVivo database that was developed for the course. This qualitative software program facilitated the development of Lena's case by organizing and triangulating data from a variety of types and sources (Bazeley & Jackson, 2013).

It is also important to note that, following the research ethics guidelines of my institution, all of the participants in *Intercultural Transitions*, including Lena, were invited to provide written consent for me to analyze and report on their data after the course ended. They were assured that their participation (or non-participation) would not impact on any grades, and anonymity was assured.

Lena's Profile

When I first met Lena she was a final-year English major with a minor in translation (English-Chinese). A bright, young woman, she had a Grade Point Average of 3.5 (above average), and was also fluent in several languages: Cantonese (her mother tongue), Putonghua (Mandarin), and English. Lena also acquired a basic knowledge of Swedish during her sojourn. Prior to travelling to Sweden, all of Lena's close friends were Hong Kong Chinese and she had not taken any intercultural communication courses. She was the first member of her family to study abroad.

When she applied to join the academic yearlong exchange program in Sweden, Lena wrote the following in her application form: "I want to live in an entirely different culture and see how I perceive my role as a Chinese." Later, in her first essay in the *Intercultural transitions* course, she offered more insight into her motivation to venture abroad:

> Studying abroad had always been my biggest yet farthest dream. Since primary school, I had heard people praising its benefits. Their positive comments strongly convinced me to acquire international experience. I did not have the chance to accomplish this before entering university due to inadequate opportunities provided by my school and the unsatisfactory economic condition of my family. Nevertheless, the desire for studying abroad never diminished in my heart. I wished to experience the benefits that my friends proudly claimed; I wished to step out of my comfort zone and become a mature lady; I wished to explore the magnificent world and gain precious real life experience through travelling. Fortunately, the exchange program could help me to accomplish my dream. With my parents' strong encouragement and my enthusiasm, I eagerly applied.

While in Sweden, Lena took courses in mass media, psychology, introductory Swedish, and English literature. In the first semester, although she lived in a campus dormitory, where the majority of residents were locals, she spent most of her leisure time with two female exchange students from Japan and France. In the second half of her stay, she also interacted with exchange students from Hong Kong who were at the host university for that semester. Lena travelled a great deal and visited 17 European countries with her friends.

When the sojourn ended, she returned to her home university to complete the remaining credits needed for her Bachelor of Arts degree. After working in the city for a few years, she aspired to pursue postgraduate studies abroad in the field of communication.

Intercultural Competence: Pre-course

At the beginning of the *Intercultural Transitions* course, Lena completed the Intercultural Development Inventory (IDI). In this survey, the Perceived Orientation (PO) indicates where the individual places herself along the Intercultural Development Continuum (IDC) (either Denial, Polarization (Defense/Reversal), Minimization, Acceptance, or Adaptation) (Hammer, 2012). Lena's Perceived Orientation (PO) on entry was 117.0 (Acceptance), indicating that she believed that she was very interculturally competent.

The Development Orientation (DO) indicates an individual's "primary orientation toward cultural differences and commonalities along the continuum *as assessed by the IDI*" (Hammer, 2009b, p. 5). The DO is the perspective that the individual is most likely to draw on in intercultural encounters. Similar to the PO, the DO can be "Denial, Polarization (Defense/Reversal), Minimization, Acceptance, or Adaptation" (Hammer, 2009b, p. 5). Lena's DO on entry was 80.0 in Polarization (Defense/Reversal), an ethnocentric stage of development. This meant that the Orientation Gap (OG), the difference between the PO and DO, was 37.0. As a difference of 7 points or more indicates a meaningful gap (Hammer, 2009b), the results signify a significant overestimation of her intercultural competence when she began the course. This finding was similar to many of her peers.

An IDI profile also indicates the Trailing Orientations (TO) that are not yet resolved (Hammer, 2009a). In times of intercultural stress or conflict, trailing issues can pull individuals back from their DO for coping with cultural difference. For Lena, no worldviews were fully resolved at this stage, suggesting that she could revert back to lower levels of intercultural competence when under stress (e.g., acute culture shock). Finally, Leading Orientations (LO) indicate the next step to take in the enhancement of intercultural competence, in terms of the intercultural continuum. As her Developmental Orientation (DO) on entry was Reversal, her LO were Minimization, Acceptance, and Adaptation.

Post-course

At the end of the semester, Lena again completed the IDI. The results revealed that her Perceived Orientation (PO) was 131.91 (Adaptation), while her Developmental Orientation (DO) was 111.58, in the high end of Minimization. The Orientation Gap (OG) was 20.33. As for Trailing Orientations (TO), all of her worldviews were resolved and the Leading Orientations (LO) for Lena were Acceptance and Adaptation.

The IDI results show that she had made significant advances in intercultural competence during the semester, with a dramatic gain of 33 points, moving from Polarization (Defense/Reversal), an ethnocentric stage of development, to the high end of "Minimization", the transitional phase. She had resolved all of the issues that had pulled her back in times of intercultural stress. While still overestimating her level of intercultural competence, the OG was reduced by 16.67 points, indicating that she had become more mindful of her limitations.

Cultural Disengagement: Pre and Post-course

As well as measuring intercultural competence, the IDI also identifies "Cultural Disengagement" as a separate scale, which indicates "the degree to which an individual or group is experiencing a sense of alienation from their own cultural community" (Hammer, 2011, p. 476). When Lena joined the course, she received a score of 1.9, indicating that she felt very detached from her cultural group and was not involved in "core aspects of being a member of a cultural community" (Hammer, 2011, p. XX). After the 14-week course, her score had moved to 4.1, indicating that she had become much more connected to her cultural group and was experiencing less identity confusion.

Insights from the Qualitative Data

The analysis of the qualitative data offered insight into the impact of critical praxis on her intercultural awareness and sensitivity and helped to explain the IDI results. As Lena unpacked her international experience and learned about the stories of her peers and other sojourners, she revisited her reaction to cultural difference and the challenges she faced adjusting to life in Sweden. Much to her surprise, her return home was also far from smooth.

The data for Lena's case is extensive; however, due to space limitations, what follows are selected excerpts that draw attention to key elements in her intercultural journey.

Culture shock in Sweden

In one of her first blog entries, Lena wrote about the culture shock she experienced as she struggled to adjust to different "ways of being" in Sweden:

> Living and studying in Sweden for one year is definitely the time I experienced the biggest culture shock. When I look back now, I can still recall the mixed feeling of excitement as well as discomfort. This feeling was particularly intense during the first few weeks… The most obvious culture shock that I experienced was the intimacy with strangers. Instead of shaking hands, hugging and kissing cheeks are what Westerners (especially Europeans) do when they meet strangers. At the beginning, I felt quite awkward and uncomfortable because this custom is very different from the traditional Chinese one. Although I knew this practice before I left home, it was still quite hard to accept once I faced it in reality, so most of the time I just stood there, observed, and responded passively according to what other people did to me. Gradually, I realized hugging and kissing cheeks was their way to show friendliness and hospitality to strangers. I started to appreciate this practice as these small physical movements could show huge warmth and bring friends closer together.

Throughout the semester, cultural differences in physical contact and intimacy were dominant themes in her writing as well as in class discussions.

Romanticized Visions of Sweden and Reluctance to Return Home

In Sweden, most of the students in her residence hall were host nationals; however, Lena had limited social contact with them and attributed this to different interests and habits. While she had initially found it challenging to adjust to unfamiliar cultural practices, in her first essay, it was evident that she had developed a deep affection for the host nation:

> Despite culture differences, I fell in love with Sweden uncontrollably. The beautiful nature was one of the most irresistible things. The blue sky was glittering because of the afternoon sun; the fresh air was fragrant with scents from the sea and the hills. I was totally amazed when I first saw this beautiful scenery! Whether feeling the soothing spring breeze, watching the almost unsetting summer sun, seeing the crimson autumn leaves, or shivering under the heavy winter snow, I was astonished by the almighty power of the creator and I felt unprecedentedly close to nature. I was further impressed because the Swedish appreciated and cherished the beauty of nature…Every family implemented waste separation. In our dormitory, all students were very self-disciplined and practiced waste separation, too… Swedish politeness and hospitality also impressed me. They treated everyone as their friends. It was very common to see them greeting or giving strangers an amiable smile. It

would be embarrassing to do so in Hong Kong as some might be suspicious of your intentions. Although a new learner of Swedish life and culture, locals never ignored me. Instead, they offered me help voluntarily. Once I held two heavy bags of food and was rushing back to my dormitory in a rainy day without an umbrella. A very generous stranger came to help me carry those bags and offered me his umbrella. Although I could barely understand him as he spoke in Swedish, I was very touched. I am the lucky one because I met so many nice people when I was abroad. What people gave me might only be a nod or a smile, but these tiny actions meant a lot to me. They calmed me down, gave me support, and united us as one family.

Lena felt welcomed in the new environment, even if she did not develop close friendships with any Swedes and spent most of her free time with other international exchange students. This is significant as host receptivity can play a key role in the adjustment process and impact the intercultural learning of student sojourners (Jackson, 2012; Vande Berg et al., 2012). Some of her peers, for example, perceived their hosts to be cold and unfriendly and chose to avoid intercultural contact altogether, which limited their exposure to the host culture and language, and hampered the development of their intercultural communication competence.

Lena fell "in love" with Sweden and the freedom the sojourn afforded her; not surprisingly, she was not keen to leave: "As the date of my return home approached, I realized it was time to say good-bye to my friends abroad and my 'temporary' home. Farewell parties gave me sadness rather than joyfulness; packing intensified my sorrow because I couldn't put Sweden into my suitcase and take it back home with me. I was reluctant to leave (essay #2)." Her lack of enthusiasm about returning home contrasted with that of her classmates who had never really adjusted to the host environment and spent much of their sojourn connecting with friends and family back home via Skype, QQ, and/or Facebook.

A Difficult Reentry: Reverse Culture Shock and Cultural Disengagement

Much to her surprise, Lena's return to Hong Kong did not go well as she suffered a great deal from reentry or reverse culture shock, which Gaw (2000) defines as "the process of readjusting, reacculturating, and reassimilating into one's own home culture after living in a different culture for a significant period of time" (p. 83-84). Instead of feeling at home, she felt disconnected from the city, as she explained in her first essay:

Reverse culture shock took place right after I arrived at the Hong Kong International Airport. Walking into the arrival hall, a sudden flush of strangeness came upon me. The contaminated smell of air caused by the noisy crowds stressed me out; the nonchalant gaze of the people annoyed me; the comparatively small size of people embarrassed me; the ubiquitous bilingual signs and trilingual broadcasting was the only thing that drew me closer to my home but at the same time I could feel that I was very much distanced from my mother tongue. I missed not hearing Swedes talking and learning every single word like a baby. Reuniting with my family after leaving home for one year was undoubtedly one of the most pleasant things. Yet, I was unexpectedly calm when I saw them in the airport. Not because I wasn't delighted to see them, but because I didn't know how to respond. Should I run towards them and give them a big kiss like what I did in Sweden when I met my friends? Or should I just come over to them, give them a big smile and start to chat with them like I had never left home? This confused me because the hugging and kissing culture was, for me, something 'European', but I was back home, returned to a place where my traditional parents might not entirely comprehend this culture. Finally, I did not hug and kiss them. I only behaved like the 'old' me. But inside, I knew this position of the 'old' me was being challenged. I was shocked by this transformation. I felt more like a traveller visiting a new destination rather than a home comer returning home.

In Sweden, Lena had grown accustomed to different social norms and, after she returned to Hong Kong, she initially felt out of sorts in her home environment. Although acting like her former self, internally she felt "transformed."

When she entered the *Intercultural Transitions* course several months after her return, Lena was still struggling to readjust to life in Hong Kong. Talking and writing about her feelings and listening to the stories of her peers who were also experiencing reentry shock helped her to process her conflicting emotions. In her second essay, she disclosed more about the challenges she faced as her "new self" became reacquainted with her "old home":

After living in Sweden for one year, I was finally home. At first, blissful thoughts about being back in Hong Kong, long-awaited reunions with family and friends outweighed any nostalgia for Sweden. This euphoria was short-lived. Within a few weeks, I found myself in the depths of despair instead of at the anticipated peak of ecstasy. I discovered some changes that made me doubt my long-trusted home, changes that were a tiny influence on others but meant a lot to me. I became easily irritated. I realize now that I was overwhelmed by reentry shock and experiencing frustration, alienation, disorientation, and helplessness without understanding exactly why… While abroad, I had never imagined the situation of heading home. Last year, I travelled through Europe exploring different corners of it. I thought I had flown so far and so high to the carefree paradise that I did not have to return home. Returning home and going back to one's origin isn't that easy, is it? It is discouraging to go all the way back regardless of the remarkable footprints we have left throughout our journey; it is exhausting to start anew when all the things around us have changed tremendously and we have no idea what is going on. My reentry experience was no exception. I didn't expect to be as disoriented as when I went to Sweden because I was returning home to the warm and familiar place where I was brought up and lived for more than twenty years. Yet, the power of reverse culture shock was unexpectedly strong. Facing countless reentry challenges, I became a stranger at home; it was only after many trials and errors that I was able to readjust my 'new' self to my 'old' home.

The "power of reverse culture shock" affected her attitudes towards her peers. In the months before joining *Intercultural Transitions,* this "stranger at home" longed for interactions with people who had international experience and feared that her "new self" would slip away.

Hong Kong versus Sweden

In the first half of the course, similar to many of her peers, Lena's written and oral narratives were replete with "us" vs. "them" discourse, as she frequently compared the host culture with her home environment, as in the following excerpt:

I admire the Swedish not only for their friendliness, but also their positive attitude towards occupations. In Hong Kong, one's status is reflected by one's occupation and income. Those who earn lower income such as cleaners and waiters are often looked down upon. Sometimes, the low income group is even stereotyped as having unpleasant personality and poor hygiene. In Sweden, people are not judged by their occupation. All jobs are seen as equal and everyone's effort is equally appreciated because they all contribute to the well-being of the society. Instead of working as a private tutor like most Hong Kong students, my Swedish friends work as part-time hospital cleaners. I could not imagine my parents' and friends' response if I am a hospital cleaner. They might feel ashamed and order me to quit the job. However, my Swedish friends did not face any criticism and prejudice. They could pursue their career freely and happily. I felt much honored to study in this civilized country... *(essay #1)*

Clearly missing Sweden, Lena continued to exalt the wonders of "this civilized country", while complaining about a myriad of problems in Hong Kong. In the post-course interview, she talked about her negative attitude and acknowledged that she had been quite "judgmental and intolerant" on reentry: "When I first arrived home, I just couldn't help comparing Sweden with Hong Kong. The more I compared, the more I became critical of Hong Kong culture and longed to go back to Sweden." In her second essay, she wrote about her struggle to adopt a more balanced view:

Once I relaxed a bit, the negative emotions, including the anxiety, the doubt, and the fear, began to dissipate. I've relaxed my tense emotions, as well as my cynical criticism towards my home culture. As I became more relaxed and less stressed, I was not irritated as easily and could think more objectively. I'm now able to step backward and perceive things from diverse perspectives rather than just from my subjective lens. Instead of idealizing everything overseas and disdaining everything at home, I now possess a more balanced view that takes both places into consideration. I can distinguish both the merits and drawbacks, both the upside and the downside of different cultures in an objective way. This open-mindedness is indeed one of the most important lessons that I've learnt... Apart from being less judgmental of different cultures, I've become less critical of my friends when I started to put myself into their shoes. I realized that some might be jealous that I'd been abroad, or resentful that I'd left. They might feel insecure that I have 'overgrown' them. Others might feel rejected or heartbroken when I kept on talking about how wonderful my exchange experience was. It was even worse when I compared Hong Kong with Sweden all the time. They might wonder if I still cared about them, and if I preferred staying in Sweden rather than being back home with them. I realized that they also had to readjust to having me back.

Attributing much of her malaise to reentry culture shock, Lena expressed remorse for the way she had treated her family and friends: "It was terrible to realize how judgmental and intolerant I was. The readjustment process took a long time" (post-sojourn interview).

Breaking Down Stereotypes

As she worked through her experiences and emotions in the *Intercultural Transitions* course, Lena reflected on her attitudes toward cultural difference both at home and abroad. In her first essay, she disclosed that stereotypes of Europeans had unduly influenced her sojourn, as if a "pre-installed computer system" had been controlling her mind. In the pre-sojourn orientation sponsored by her home university, the images that were conveyed to her by local returnees affected her perceptions of host nationals as well as other Europeans:

Before going to Sweden, I attended a sharing session with returnees who had just come back. The information they gave me affected my judgment right before I experienced things in person. Comments like 'Don't go to too many parties; Westerners are really crazy.', 'French are arrogant; they speak their mother language all the time because they think it's more superior than other languages.' kept lingering in my mind when I was in Europe. As time went by, I found that I had stereotyped Europeans according to the returnees' subjective opinions. I didn't know how it happened. It was just like a pre-installed computer system controlling my mind, telling me which group of people were unfriendly, which group of people were barbarous, etc. (essay #1)

Through readings, lectures, and guided critical reflection in discussions and writings, Lena became more aware of the harmful effects of stereotyping and resolved to stamp out this habit. Interestingly, she was also determined to encourage her friends to avoid this reductionist practice: "I'm glad that I've witnessed gradual improvement in my intercultural competence. I'm now more sensitive to stereotypes and brave enough to remind my friends not to use stereotypes to judge other people" (essay #3).

Benefits of Guided, Critical Reflection

After a semester-long period of structured reflection, Lena offered her views about what she had gained from this process:

> Reflecting on our international experience and sharing it with each other through Moodle has been a very rewarding experience…Questions encouraged me to widen my understanding of how to approach thought processes related to my intercultural interactions. The process of interactive sharing and constant reflection during the course enabled me to have deeper, more critical understanding of myself and people from other cultural backgrounds… Not only have I learnt new theories and models and tested them with my international experience, I am able to integrate my experience into my daily life and set realistic goals to enhance my intercultural learning. (essay #3)

Lena believed that she had gradually become more self-aware and reflective, and this claim was supported by concrete examples in her narratives. More self-critical, she recognized that she was not as open-minded as she had assumed when she joined the course. In particular, she realized that she had a tendency to resort to 'us' vs. 'them' discourse when exposed to unfamiliar 'ways of being':

> After in-depth reflection, I am able to use intercultural theories and new ideas to explain my behaviors abroad. Surprisingly, I discovered that I was not as open-minded as I thought. Although the returnees told us to be more open-minded to cultural differences, I failed to do so. Many times I was trapped in my self-constituted box because I possessed an 'ethnocentric' mindset instead of an 'ethnorelative' mindset. I clung to my own cultural worldview and used my own cultural values as the standards to evaluate others instead of understanding behaviors from others' cultural frame of reference. I upheld a strong defense of my own worldview and the 'us' versus 'them' notion was apparent. Failing to recognize that different cultures have different ways of looking at and valuing life, I adopted an imbalanced view which made me magnify drawbacks and blind me to merits. For example, I attributed the short working hours in Sweden to people's laziness rather than appreciate the virtue of a more relaxing lifestyle; I despised my Swedish friend's choice of being a hospital cleaner as this is regarded as a disgraceful job in Hong Kong. I failed to appreciate the equality of all persons regardless of their occupation. I criticized people's intimacy with strangers as shameful behavior that contradicted the traditional Chinese virtue of li (etiquette) but I failed to understand this was indeed a kind of li in Swedish society. Through self-reflection in this course,

> I finally discovered the primary obstacle to my integration of alternative cultural elements into my worldview: I lacked a genuine openness, which is a prerequisite. (essay #3)

Acknowledging the merits of continuous reflection, Lena noted that enhanced self-awareness and self-regulation in real-world intercultural interactions could lead to richer, more meaningful relationships with people who have a different linguistic and cultural background.

Keeping International Experience Alive

It is not unusual for returnees to "shoebox" their international, intercultural learning once they return home (Jackson, 2012; Szkudlarek, 2010). Lena conceded that this is what she would have done if she had not been prompted to revisit her experiences in *Intercultural Transitions.* In her final essay she explained:

> Not only did in-depth reflection reveal my shortcomings, it awakes me to the fact that I have insufficient reflection on my international experience no matter if I was abroad or at home. In Sweden, I wanted to keep a diary so that I could recall my experience anytime. I started this plan with enthusiasm but it ended as a failure owing to my laziness. Shortly after returning home, while my experience was still fresh and profound, I was overflowed with numerous things that I wanted to share with my friends; yet, many times I just swallowed my words due to my friends' uninterested response. Without reflection, many parts of my experience were hidden and more and more of them were fading away. Only after taking this course could I realize the importance of reviewing our experience. Being an exchange student is a challenging, enriching, alarming, enlightening, and thrillingly unusual experience and, undoubtedly, reviewing it is one of the most feasible ways to alleviate fears of forgetting it like it has never happened. By reviewing my experience, I learned to value the friendships and new discoveries I made. I got to know myself better and became more optimistic and thankful.

The process of writing and talking about her intercultural experiences helped keep her international experience alive and encouraged her to incorporate new understandings into her daily life and current intercultural interactions. Sharing experiences and learning about different ways to respond to cultural difference inspired her to assume more responsibility for her own personal growth: "Listening to the stories of others motivated me to set specific goals for self-improvement and enrichment" (essay #3).

Further Steps Toward Intercultural Competence

Near the end of the course, Lena resolved to further enhance her intercultural competence. In her final essay she wrote: "Cultivating intercultural competence is now my first and foremost goal. I want to be able to communicate effectively in another language cross-culturally and have a diverse and knowledgeable worldview. I wish to exhibit cross-cultural sensitivity and adaptability and, ultimately, carry this competence throughout life." Lena was determined to nurture her curiosity and suspend judgment about unfamiliar cultural norms and practices, until she had gained more first-hand exposure and understanding:

> The first step is to foster attitudes that motivate me to develop intercultural competence: what inspires me to want to learn about others? Curiosity is a critical factor. For curiosity to thrive, I have to suspend assumptions and judgments, leaving my mind open to multiple perspectives. It is important to recognize that I carry a particular perception because of the way I was brought up and that others brought up in a different environment carry a different perception. When I face situations that contradict my perception, I shall ask, "What do I see here? What might it mean? What else might it mean?' and most importantly, 'What might others think it means?" For instance, I felt weird when everyone abroad asked "how are you?" and answered "I'm fine, thanks. And you?" I thought it was fake and superficial because almost everyone was repeating the same thing. I felt no sincerity in it. Only after I cast off my assumptions could I understand the rationale behind it and appreciate its merit. (essay #3)

In this final essay, Lena provided further evidence of critical self-analysis, when she described how her fears of cultural difference had hampered her intercultural development:

When I pondered my international experience, I discovered that what stopped me from suspending my assumptions and judgment was the fear that I had to surrender my personal and cultural integrity once I accepted other cultural elements. My original culture was so ingrained in me, it made me feel secure and superior and, therefore, I did not want to lose it. I felt that embracing new cultural elements meant being disloyal to my original culture. Now I understand that upholding the notion of superiority and inferiority will only fasten myself in a self-constructed prison without any positive progress.

Encouragingly, Lena also revealed concrete plans to leave her "self-constructed prison" behind, by putting into practice the intercultural knowledge and skills she had acquired during the semester:

> I've been seeking ways to train my intercultural skills. Being a buddy of incoming exchange students is a golden opportunity. I can improve my listening skills by listening to different accents, and raise my observation skills by paying attention to their cultural-specific facial expressions and gestures... I'm glad that I've witnessed a gradual improvement in my intercultural competence and hope other people can also realize that this is important and pursue it. Although still a novice at intercultural competence, I hope my determination to enhance

it can influence future exchange students so that they can start developing an awareness of their own core values and assumptions before going abroad. I'm looking forward to advising them so they can benefit from what I've gained from this course. (essay #3)

Becoming an Intercultural Citizen: A Life Long Process

When students enroll in *Intercultural Transitions*, the IDI results generally indicate that they perceive themselves to be very open-minded and significantly overestimate their intercultural competence, and Lena was no exception. On entry, she believed that she possessed an ethno relative mindset and advanced intercultural communication skills. As she revisited her sojourn and reentry experiences and learned about intercultural theories, she recognized areas that she needed to work on to be become truly intercultural. By the time she penned her third essay, she viewed the development of intercultural competence as "a lifelong process."

> What this course has offered me is out of my expectation. Not only am I able to recall my international experience through reflection, I've discovered my strengths and weaknesses and set the practical goal of enhancing my intercultural competence. As developing intercultural competence involves a lifelong process, I realize the importance of regular engagement in reflective practice like what I've been doing in this course. I know enhancing intercultural competence is challenging, but what I value most is the continuous learning, growth, and development throughout the entire journey. I'm now ready for the challenges ahead.

In an online forum discussion near the end of the semester, Lena was also able to articulate what it means to be an intercultural citizen. In her post, she stressed the need to eliminate "prejudice and apathy" and embrace a more open-minded, "global mindset."

> Whether a person is an intercultural citizen or not has nothing to do with his cultural background or how many countries he has been to. Rather, it is something related to the global mindset of the individual- the generous dimension of his mind to the existence of different cultures and perspectives, and the evaporation of negative attitudes such as prejudice and apathy… Being observant is the first step to becoming an intercultural citizen. If we are observant enough, we can recognize differences in people from different cultural backgrounds and incorporate some of these differences into ourselves. Knowing about differences without exploring why they exist means apathy; it will only intensify the differences and the distance between 'us' and 'them' will become more obvious and unchangeable… When I first went to Sweden, I criticized the relaxed lifestyles of the Swedish as 'laziness' and despised them. It was only after discovering why they have such practices that I could

truly accept and appreciate them. Being curious also motivated me to find out the reasons behind the differences in other aspects such as the language and gestures they used. For example, I felt weird when everyone asked 'how are you?' and answered 'I'm fine, thanks. And you?' I thought it was fake and superficial at first because almost everyone was repeating the same thing. After I found out the rationale behind it, I eventually cast off my prejudice. I learnt to appreciate the virtue of this behavior and I tried to start this practice also. I felt lucky that I had the curiosity to find out why people have these habits at that time; otherwise, I would be blinded by my subjective lens forever.

While self-criticism can be very uncomfortable and intrusive, Lena did not shy away from this process. Highly motivated to become more intercultural, she scrutinized her own thoughts and behaviors. Gradually, as her understanding of intercultural competence evolved, she began to put her new understandings into practice.

Advice for Future Sojourners

At the end of the course, Lena and a classmate gave a presentation that was open to students who were going abroad the following semester. In their talk, they offered this advice:

Keep a positive attitude abroad. Acquire a new way of seeing things, i.e., learn new skills and discover new interests. Be adventurous! Ask "Why not?" Don't always say "no!" Be open-minded. Abandon your preconceptions. Appreciate the uniqueness of different cultures. Be curious. Observe, think, and ask! Reflect and evaluate your performance regularly and adjust your goals, if necessary.

Interestingly, most of their remarks centered on the characteristics of individuals who possess intercultural competence, providing further evidence of the positive impact of critical praxis.

Summary of Lena's Journey in the Intercultural Transitions Course

On entry into the *Intercultural Transitions* course, Lena was in Polarization (Defense/Reversal), an ethnocentric stage of development, as measured by the IDI. When she returned from her yearlong stay in Sweden, her narratives were punctuated with 'us' vs. 'them' discourse, with an overly critical view of her home culture and adoration of the host culture. As she gained exposure to intercultural communication/transition theories, 'unpacked' her experiences in class and online, learned about the journeys of her peers, and actively engaged in the process of guided, critical reflection, she became much more interculturally aware and balanced in her views. By the end of the semester, she had moved to the high end of Minimization, the transitional phase of intercultural development. Her rich oral and written narratives help us to understand the process of becoming intercultural, and underscore the benefits of blended intercultural praxis to help returnees make sense of international experience and take further steps towards intercultural competence.

REFLECTIONS

The process of crafting Lena's case affected me both as a researcher and practitioner. Working with her data, and that of her classmates in the *Intercultural Transitions* course, helped me to better appreciate the complexities involved in cross-cultural adjustment and re-entry, and further sensitized me to the idiosyncratic nature of sojourns. Some students may develop meaningful intercultural friendships during their stay abroad and experience tremendous growth in intercultural understanding, whereas others may find their hosts unwelcoming and spend nearly all of their free time with co-nationals (face-to-face or online). During the sojourn, they may have very limited contact with individuals who have a different linguistic and cultural background. Further, sojourners who have had negative intercultural experiences may return home with reinforced stereotypes and little interest in becoming 'more intercultural' conversely, returnees who had many positive experiences in the host environment may be more keen to invest in intercultural/ second language learning when they are back on home soil. The degree of reverse culture shock may also differ considerably among returnees, in part, due to their degree of immersion and the quality of their intercultural relationships in the host culture.

Through this study, I also became more aware of the potential impact of intercultural interactions on the evolving self-identities of student sojourners. Lena's case, for example, heightened my awareness of the sense of disequilibrium that returnees may experience, especially if they have really opened themselves up to "new ways of being" in the host environment and incorporated elements from the host culture into their sense of self. While some sojourners may find it exhilarating and empowering to embrace a broadened identity, others may find any change in their self-identification as threatening or disturbing, and it is essential for intercultural educators to be mindful of this.

It is through the analysis of the qualitative data, in particular, that I gained more awareness and understanding of factors that can lead to diverse sojourn and reentry experiences. The findings challenge the naïve assumption that student sojourners will have an in-depth immersion experience abroad, and magically transform into individuals with an advanced level of intercultural competence and second language fluency. It is also unrealistic to expect all student sojourners to acquire a more open, global identity simply by being present in the host environment. This means that returnees in an intercultural transitions course are apt to have varying degrees of intercultural sensitivity, and those who have a lot of international experience may not necessarily have a high level of intercultural sensitivity. The journey towards intercultural competence is highly individual, complex, and lifelong, and this needs to be taken into account when designing a learned-centered, intercultural communication/transitions course.

As I worked with Lena's data and those of her classmates, I also gained more understanding and appreciation of the amount of time, energy, and emotions required to 'unpack' international and re-entry experiences. As I read their stories, I felt privileged that they were willing to share so much of themselves with me, both orally and through their writing. The data was very rich and much of it was deeply personal. As I coded the material in NVivo, I recognized the risk-taking involved in laying bear one's innermost thoughts, weaknesses, and unfulfilled aspirations. At the same time, it became even more evident that individuals, like Lena, who are willing to fully engage in the process of critical reflection and meaning-making, can reap innumerable rewards. In her case, the IDI results, and written and oral data, offer ample evidence of personal growth and substantial steps towards interculturality. It is also likely that Lena may not fully realize the benefits of this reflective process until years later.

Lena's story, and those of her classmates, inspire me to continue with my efforts to link research with practice (e.g., develop intercultural communication/transition courses that draw on my investigations of the "whole person development" of our incoming and outgoing international exchange students). By tracking the learning of students in my *Intercultural Transitions* course, I have gained new insights that have helped me to refine subsequent offerings. This reflective process has also provided direction for the refinement of the interview and questionnaire protocols and email prompts that are employed in my large-scale investigations of our outgoing international exchange students. Research is informing my practice, and vice versa.

Finally, while *Intercultural Transitions* was conceived and implemented in an Asian setting, I hope this chapter will encourage intercultural educators in other contexts to employ reflective, technology-enhanced pedagogy to deepen and extend the intercultural learning of student sojourners and returnees. Research-driven interventions at all phases (pre-sojourn, sojourn, post-sojourn) have the potential to help both local and international undergraduates acquire higher levels of intercultural competence. Initiatives designed to optimize study abroad experience are well worth the investment as the rewards are many for both students and educators/researchers.

ACKNOWLEDGEMENTS

The intercultural curriculum initiative described in this paper has been supported by Teaching Development Grants (#4170338, #4170356) from the Chinese University of Hong Kong (CUHK) and competitive General Research Fund awards (#444709, #445312) from the University Research Grants Council of Hong Kong, which facilitated investigations of the learning of international exchange students. The author greatly appreciates the willingness of Lena and the other students in Intercultural Transitions to share their stories.

REFERENCES

Bathurst, L., & La Brack, B. (2012). Shifting the locus of international learning: Intervening prior to and after student experiences abroad. In M. Vande Berg, R. M. Paige, & K. H. Lou (Eds.), *Student learning abroad: What our students are learning, What they're not and what we can do about it* (pp. 261–283). Sterling, VA: Stylus.

Bazeley, P., & Jackson, K. (2013). *Qualitative data analysis with NVivo* (2nd ed.). Thousand Oaks, CA: Sage.

Bennett, J. M. (2004). Turning frogs into interculturalists: A student-centered developmental approach to teaching intercultural competence. In R. A. Goodman, M. E. Phillips, & N. A. Boyacigiller (Eds.), *Crossing cultures: Insights from master teachers* (pp. 312–342). London: Routledge.

Bennett, J. M. (2008). On becoming a global soul: A path to engagement during study abroad. In V. Savicki (Ed.), *Developing intercultural competence and transformation: Theory, research, and application in International Education* (pp. 13–31). Sterling, VA: Stylus.

Bennett, M. J. (1993). Towards ethnorelativism: A developmental model of intercultural sensitivity. In R. M. Paige (Ed.), *Education for the intercultural experience* (pp. 21–71). Yarmouth, ME: Intercultural Press.

Bennett, M. J. (2012). Paradigmatic assumptions and a developmental approach to intercultural learning. In M. Vande Berg, R. M. Paige, & K. H. Lou (Eds.), *Student learning abroad: What our students are learning, What they're not and what we can do about it* (pp. 90–114). Sterling, VA: Stylus.

Brockington, J. L., & Wiedenhoeft, M. D. (2009). The liberal arts and global citizenship: Fostering intercultural engagement through integrative experiences and structured reflection. In R. Lewin (Ed.), *The handbook of practice and research in study abroad: Higher education and the quest for global citizenship* (pp. 117–132). London, England: Routledge.

Gaw, K. F. (2000). Reverse culture shock in students returning from overseas. *International Journal of Intercultural Relations, 24*, 83–104.

Hammer, M. R. (2009a). The intercultural development inventory: An approach for assessing and building intercultural competence. In M.A. Moodian (Ed.), *Contemporary leadership and intercultural competence: Exploring the cross-cultural dynamics within organizations* (pp. 203–217). Thousand Oaks, CA: Sage.

Hammer, M. R. (2009b). *Intercultural Development Inventory v. 3 (IDI) education group profile report*. Retrieved May 12, 2013 from http://idiinventory.com/pdf/idi_sample.pdf

Hammer, M. R. (2011). Additional cross-cultural validity testing of the Intercultural Development Inventory. *International Journal of Intercultural Relations, 27*(3), 421–443.

Hammer, M. R. (2012). The intercultural development inventory: A new frontier in assessment and development of intercultural competence. In M. Vande Berg, R. M. Paige, & K. H. Lou (Eds.), *Student learning abroad, what our students are learning, what they're not, and what we can do about it* (pp. 115–136). Sterling, VA: Stylus.

Hammer, M. R. (2013). *A resource guide for effectively using the intercultural development inventory (IDI)*. Berlin, MD: IDI, LLC.

Jackson, J. (2006). Ethnographic preparation for short-term study and residence in the target culture. *The International Journal of Intercultural Relations, 30*(1), 77–98.

Jackson, J. (2008). *Language, identity, and study abroad: Sociocultural perspectives*. London, England: Equinox Publishing.

Jackson, J. (2010). *Intercultural journeys: From study to residence abroad, language and globalization series*. Basingstoke: Palgrave MacMillan.

Jackson, J. (2011, October). Assessing the impact of a semester abroad using the IDI and semi-structured interviews (Distinguished paper award). Paper presented at the 2nd Intercultural Development Inventory conference, Minneapolis, MN, USA.

Jackson, J. (2012). Education abroad. In J. Jackson (Ed.), *The handbook of language and intercultural communication* (pp. 449–463). London, England: Routledge.

Jackson, J. (2013a). Adjusting to differing cultures of learning: The experience of semester-long exchange students from Hong Kong. In L. Jin & M. Cortazzi (Eds.), *Researching intercultural learning* (pp. 235–252). Basingstoke, UK: Palgrave MacMillan.

Jackson, J. (2013b). ICT-enhanced intercultural transitions: Creating a community of engaged, reflective explorers. *World Conference on Educational Multimedia, Hypermedia and Telecommunications, 2013*(1), 1654–1663.

Kolb, D. A. (1984). *Experiential learning: Experience as the source of learning and development.* Englewood Cliffs, NJ: Prentice Hall.

Lou, K., & Bosley, G. W. (2012). Facilitating intercultural learning abroad: The intentional, targeted intervention model. In M. Vande Berg, R. M. Paige, & K. H. Lou (Eds.), *Student learning abroad: What our students are learning, what they're not, and what we can do about it* (pp. 335–359). Sterling, VA: Stylus.

Mendelson, V., & Citron, J. L. (2006). Bringing it home: Multifaceted support for returning education abroad students. *International Educator, 15*, 64–67.

Meyer-Lee, E. (2005). Bringing it home: Follow-up courses for study abroad returnees. *Internationalizing undergraduate education: Integrating study abroad into the curriculum* (pp. 114–116). Minneapolis, MN: University of Minnesota.

Mezirow, J. (2000). *Learning as transformation: Critical perspectives on a theory in progress.* San Francisco, CA: Jossey Bass.

Paige, R. M., & Vande Berg, M. (2012). Why students are and are not learning abroad. In M. Vande Berg, R. M. Paige, & K. H. Lou (Eds.), *Student learning abroad: What our students are learning, what they're not and what we can do about it* (pp. 29–59). Sterling, VA: Stylus.

Passarelli, A. M., & Kolb, D. A. (2012). Using experiential learning theory to promote student learning and development in programs of education abroad. In M. Vande Berg, R. M. Paige, & K. H. Lou (Eds.), *Student learning abroad: What our students are learning, what they're not and what we can do about it* (pp. 137–161). Sterling, VA: Stylus.

Szkudlarek, B. (2010). Reentry: A review of the literature. *International Journal of Intercultural Relations, 34*(1), 1–21.

United Nations Educational, Scientific and Cultural Organization (UNESCO). (2013). *Global flow of tertiary-level students.* Retrieved December 21, 2013 from http://www.unesco.org/new/en/

Vande Berg, M., Paige, R. M., & Lou, K. H. (2012). Student learning abroad: paradigms and assumptions. In M. Vande Berg, R. M. Paige, & K. H. Lou (Eds.), *Student learning abroad: What our students are learning, what they're not and what we can do about it* (pp. 3–28). Sterling, VA: Stylus.

Jane Jackson
Department of English
Chinese University of Hong Kong

NOTES ON CONTRIBUTORS

Mary Benbenek, PhD is a nurse practitioner with dual certification as a family nurse practitioner and a pediatric nurse practitioner. She has held various nursing positions in a variety of settings including intensive care, public health, and ambulatory primary care and ambulatory cardiology. She has practiced as a nurse practitioner for the past 20 years primarily in clinics serving the uninsured and underinsured. She is a clinical associate professor and coordinator of the Family Nurse Practitioner area of study at the University of Minnesota, School of Nursing. Research areas include health promotion, community participatory research, and immigrant health issues.

Jill E. Blondin, PhD serves as director of VCU Globe at Virginia Commonwealth University. She received her B.A. in art history from Indiana University, and her A.M. and PhD in art history from the University of Illinois at Urbana-Champaign. Before directing VCU Globe, Dr. Blondin helped to develop and to launch Global Awareness through Education (GATE), a globally-focused living-learning program, at the University of Texas at Tyler. Dr. Blondin has received numerous awards for her teaching and research, and has presented her work at AIEA, NAFSA, the NASPA International Symposium, the Workshop on Intercultural Competence (WISE) Conference, SUNY's Intercultural Horizons Conference, and the Assessment Institute at IUPUI.

Janet Bryant, PhD is currently an Adjunct Professor at Swinburne University, Melbourne, Australia. Her PhD is on Public Sector Reform in Victorian Local Government. She is a recipient of an ALTC citation for outstanding contributions to *'innovative curriculum on globalisation'*, including a study tour that exposes students to international business practice, different cultures and provides opportunity to enhance personal growth.

Izabela Buchowicz, PhD is an Assistant Professor of Economics in the Educational and Scientific Policy Unit of the Warsaw School of Economics, Poland. She has had long-term research and teaching experience. Her research interests are in the field of education policy and equalization of young people chances and chances of local population. She participated repeatedly in studies and research regarding the theory and practice of social policy. Carrying out her research interests, she participated in European Union and Poland projects (e.g. GOETE – *Governance of Educational Trajectories in Europe. Access, coping and relevance of education for young people in European knowledge societies in comparative perspective*; she participated in work on the problem of 5 level of qualification Framework for Qualification of European Education in Poland). Cooperates with the Pedagogy Department of the Warsaw University.

NOTES ON CONTRIBUTORS

Patricia Buckley, PhD is Associate Professor in Organisation Dynamics at Swinburne University. Her background includes working, teaching and researching in health, aged and community care sectors. She has held senior academic management positions in health and business and taught leadership and management in post graduate programs including entrepreneurship and innovation, business administration and human resource studies.

Ewa Chmielecka, PhD is a Professor at the Warsaw School of Economics, Head of the Unit of Educational Policy. Professor of the Educational Research Institute in Warsaw. Bologna Expert. Author of some 140 articles and books on the higher education systems and philosophy of science. The Polish representative in the EQF Advisory Group. Expert in national and international projects related to qualifications frameworks. Member of the Polish Academy of Sciences Committee "Ethics in Science". Member of the Polish Accreditation Commission. In 2009, she was awarded by the Students' Parliament of the Republic of Poland with the title "Authority of the Year".

Rose Cole is a third-year doctoral student within the Center for the Study of Higher Education at the University of Virginia's Curry School of Education. Before her doctoral program, she studied and worked at West Virginia University in Morgantown, WV as an academic program coordinator. She has degrees in English, history and public administration. She is currently engaged in research on human-rights based education initiatives in Charlottesville; teaching and learning in higher education; and the experiences of women in the academy. Her research interests include experiences of marginalization in higher education, retention of marginalized students in higher education, internationalization of higher education curriculum, and transformative pedagogy.

Elena Galinova, PhD, is a Senior Undergraduate Studies Advisor at the Pennsylvania State University. Her main research and professional interest areas are global citizenship education and global and intercultural advising. She coordinates a global citizenship advising program for undergraduates from all majors, encouraging them to get involved with global and intercultural issues and integrate them into their academic experience as majors, minors, general education courses, research, internship, and service projects. She also teaches a course on the foundations of global citizenship and global service learning and advises global service student organizations. She recently published an advising monograph on issues and strategies in working with international Chinese students. She holds two master's degrees (in Russian and English) from the University of Sofia, Bulgaria, and a dual doctorate in Educational Theory and Policy, and Comparative and International Education from the Pennsylvania State University.

Barbara Gibson, PhD has a unique combination of experience, encompassing business communication, social media, and intercultural communication. With more than 25 years' experience as a corporate communication professional, she is a past international Chair of the International Association of Business Communicators, and currently serves as President of SIETAR UK. She recently earned her PhD in intercultural communication at Birkbeck College, University of London, with research focused on the intercultural competencies needed by global CEOs. She has taught at both undergraduate and graduate levels since 2011, and joined Syracuse London in 2013. You can find her on Linked In (http://www.linkedin.com/in/barbaragibson),or on Twitter (http://twitter.com/barb_g).

Troy Gordon, PhD is Academic Director of the Syracuse University London Program, responsible for the curriculum, academic standards, and teaching and learning. He earned a BA from the University of Puget Sound, and an MA and PhD in English Language & Literature and Women's Studies from the University of Michigan, Ann Arbor. From 2001-2006 he lectured at UCLA in Writing Programs, and from 2007–2012 he served as Head of the Media & Communications Department and later as Associate Dean of London Hult International Business School in London. Dr. Gordon specializes in literature, media, gender studies, non-fiction writing, and the study of mass atrocities and conflict.

Sahtiya Hosoda Hammell is a third-year doctoral student in Social Foundations at the University of Virginia. Her undergraduate degree is in English from Princeton, where she focused on issues of normativity and post-colonialism. She has worked in education in Washington D.C, where she taught in DC Public Schools and at the University of the District of Columbia, wrote curriculum and directed out-of-school time programming. Sahtiya is the Curry Trustees' Fellow at the Curry Foundation, and currently serves as the Publications Co-Chair for the Comparative and International Education Society. Her current projects analyze the impact of global citizenship education and institutional efforts to promote diversity. Sahtiya's research interests include sociology of education, social justice pedagogy, and critical policy studies.

Meredith Hyde, PhD is the Director of Syracuse University London, a study abroad program which enrols over 500 American undergraduates a year. She earned her degrees at Yale and Oxford Universities, and was made a Fellow of the Royal Society of the Arts in 2007. Her research concentrates on metacognition and American undergraduates abroad and the ways in which students' autonomous learning skills can be developed. She has published and presented on a range of related topics at NAFSA, CIEE, Forum and BUTEX, and is a trustee of the Philosophy Foundation, an educational charity which works to bring the discipline into schools. She lives in London, and is the mother of twin boys.

Jane Jackson, PhD is a Professor in the English Department at the Chinese University of Hong Kong. She has had teaching and research experience in tertiary institutions in many countries/regions, including Canada, the United States, the Sultanate of Oman, Mainland China, the U.K., and Hong Kong. Her research interests include intercultural communication, language and identity, and education abroad. Recent books include *Introducing Language and Intercultural Communication* (Routledge, 2014), *The Routledge Handbook of Language and Intercultural Communication* (Routledge, 2012) (Editor), *Intercultural Journeys: From Study to Residence Abroad* (Palgrave MacMillan, 2010), and *Language, Identity, and Study Abroad: Sociocultural Perspectives* (Equinox, 2008).

Adam Jagiello-Rusilowski, PhD is an educator, researcher and social entrepreneur. He holds MA in English Literature and PhD in Educational Psychology from University of Gdansk. He studied Drama in Education at University of Northern Iowa (USA), Community Leadership at Columbia University (New York) and Social Economics at INSEAD Business School (Fontainableau, France). His PhD dissertation entitled "Involvement in Educational Drama and Self-efficacy of youth" was defended in 2007. Currently he works as Dean of Students and International Programs at Faculty of Social Studies, University of Gdansk. As a researcher he is interested in Lisbon Key Competences in Education in particular looking at activities promoting pro-social and entrepreneurial (innovation) attitudes in young Europeans and Arabs. He is involved in research projects on social and professional competences of higher education students and teaching methods which use artificial intelligence (especially language processing and learning analytics).

Ryan Jopp, PhD is a lecturer in management and tourism at Swinburne University, in Melbourne, Australia. He is also the Academic Director for Education Quality at the Faculty of Business and Law. His PhD research is on examining at climate change adaptation at regional tourism destinations. Ryan has taught a range of undergraduate and postgraduate units, across the fields of management, tourism and marketing.

Nue Lor is a Masters student in the Multicultural College Teaching and Learning program at the University of Minnesota. She graduated summa cum laude from the University of Minnesota with a Bachelors of Science in Family Social Science and minor in Applied Psychology in Educational and Community Settings. Nue completed an honors thesis on the impacts of social networks and capital on students' college accessibility and choice. Her research interests include college access, race and ethnicity in higher education, first generation and immigrant college students, and disability accommodations in higher education.

Kate Martin is the assistant director of the Center for Educational Innovation at the University of Minnesota. Martin's recent research centers on international student experiences during their first semester in the U.S. She co-created an innovative faculty development program for Internationalizing Teaching and Learning. Her M.A. is from the Monterey Institute of International Studies, and she is a certified administrator of the Intercultural Development Inventory.

NOTES ON CONTRIBUTORS

Josef A. Mestenhauser, PhD is Distinguished International Emeritus Professor in the Department of Organizational Leadership, Policy and Development at the University of Minnesota in its College of Education and Human Development. His more than fifty-year long career included being teacher, researcher, administrator, counselor and consultant. He published more than 120 books, monographs, articles and book chapters on international education, educational exchanges, international studies, transfer of knowledge, cross-cultural relations, leadership development, cultural change, educational reform and professionalism. He is three-time holder of senior Fulbright grants in the Philippines, Japan and Czechoslovakia. He was President of NAFSA:Association of International Educators, ISECSI (International Society for Educational, Cultural and Scientific Interchanges) and the Fulbright Association of Minnesota, and held offices in several professional associations. He holds doctorate from the Charles University, Faculty of Law, and PhD degree from the University of Minnesota in Political Science and International Relations. In addition, he held the post of Honorary Consul of the Czech Republic in Minnesota, Iowa, and North and South Dakota, from June 1, 1999 to June 2008.

Chrissie Monaghan, is a doctoral candidate in Comparative and International Education at the University of Virginia. In her dissertation, she utilizes historical methods to examine policies and programs in the post-Cold War era in protracted refugee situations. Christine is a fellow at the University of Virginia's Institute of Humanities and Global Cultures and the Virginia Foundation for the Humanities. She is currently conducting research on the reaches and limits of global citizenship education.

Mary Katherine O'Brien is an education program specialist at the University of Minnesota. She has worked in the field of international education since 2002 in the areas of education abroad, international student and scholar advising, and campus internationalization. O'Brien is a PhD candidate in Educational Policy & Administration with a focus in Comparative and International Development Education at UMTC. Her doctoral research focuses on the academic engagement of undergraduate international students in active learning contexts.

Diana Rajendran, PhD is a Senior Lecturer at Swinburne Business School, Swinburne University of Technology, in Melbourne, Australia. She has pursued her academic career overseas as well as in Australia. Her expertise and areas of teaching and research interest include Dynamics of Diversity, Intercultural Management, Migrant Studies, Quality of Work life, Emotional Intelligence and Management Education.

Marta Shaw, PhD is an Associate Professor of Public Affairs at the Jagiellonian University in Krakow, Poland and an Affiliate of the Jandris Center for Innovative Higher Education at the University of Minnesota. Her research agenda focuses on the impact of globalization on higher education in the areas of governance, research integrity, and intercultural education.

Catherine Solheim, PhD is a faculty member in the Department of Family Social Science at the University of Minnesota. She teaches graduate and undergraduate courses on financial management, family theory, and global family systems. She has co-led four learning abroad courses to Thailand to explore how culture and globalization impact families, health, and environment. Catherine's scholarship focuses on ways that culture and socioeconomic status impact the diverse ways families make financial resource decisions. She has conducted research on decision-making in Thai families, transnational Mexican-Minnesota families' resource and relationship decisions, and financial value, knowledge, and practices of two-generation Hmong immigrant families in Minnesota. Her current research focuses on mental health, relationship, and economic transitions of newly arriving refugee families and involves faculty colleagues, graduate students, and community partners.

Krista M. Soria, PhD works as an analyst with the Office of Institutional Research and is an adjunct faculty in the leadership minor program at the University of Minnesota, Twin Cities. Dr. Soria is interested in researching high-impact practices that promote undergraduates' development and success, the experiences of first-generation and working-class students in higher education, and programmatic efforts to enhance college students' leadership development, civic responsibility, and engagement in social change. Dr. Soria has worked for more than a decade in higher education, serving as an admission advisor, TRIO education advisor, academic advisor, and adjunct faculty for the University of Minnesota, Hamline University, the University of Alaska Anchorage, and St. Cloud State University.

Scott Spicer is associate librarian at the University of Minnesota Libraries (Twin Cities) He currently serves as Media Outreach and Learning Spaces Librarian and functions as head of the Library Media Services program, with primary responsibilities including outreach to instructors on the development and support for course integration of student produced media assignments and commercial educational media resources. Spicer has conducted research, published, and presented on a diverse range of media related topics in higher education, including the benefits and library support of student produced media, educational media resources, media literacy skill set development, and multimodal scholarship. Specifically, the emergence of video abstracts in science scholarly communication. Spicer received his MLIS from Dominican University and his MA in Curriculum and Instruction (Learning Technologies program) from the University of Minnesota (Twin Cities).

Carol Anne Spreen, PhD is an Associate Professor in the Curry School of Education, as well as a Visiting Professor at the University of Johannesburg. Dr. Spreen received her PhD in Comparative and International Education from Teachers College, Columbia University. She also holds an M.Phil. in Educational Policy Studies from Teachers College, an M.Ed. in Instructional Leadership from the University of Illinois, and a B.Ed. in International Education Development from the American University. Dr. Spreen's research centers on political and socio-cultural studies of educational change, particularly the influences of globalization on teaching and learning. Her current scholarship focuses on teacher's lives and work in rural South African schools, using participatory/action research to study the long-term impact poverty and inequality on educational access and outcomes.

Susan Staats, PhD is an Associate Professor in the College of Education and Human Development at the University of Minnesota. She is a mathematics educator and cultural anthropologist with field experience in indigenous communities of Guyana, South America. She teaches college algebra and interdisciplinary seminars for first year students. Her research interests include using sociolinguistic methods to understand collaborative mathematics learning and designing interdisciplinary learning activities for college algebra. Many of these interdisciplinary activities have involved international public health.

Lauren Ware Stark is a second-year doctoral student in the Social Foundations program at the University of Virginia's Curry School of Education. She earned a master's degree in French Studies at the University of Pennsylvania and spent five years teaching secondary English and French in public schools in Delaware and Texas. Lauren is currently the Events Coordinator for SEEDS (Students of Education Engaged in Diversity Scholarship) for Change at the University of Virginia, as well as a member of the editorial board for Cypher: Journal for the Social Foundations, Art and Culture. Her research interests include critical pedagogy; social justice and human rights-based education; ability grouping and tracking; teacher training, evaluation, and retention; critical race theory and whiteness studies; and teacher and student engagement in social movements.

Gayle A. Woodruff is the founding director for the University of Minnesota's system-wide efforts to internationalize the curriculum and campus. She co-created an innovative faculty development program for Internationalizing Teaching and Learning, and has been active in leadership for NAFSA: Association of International Educators' Teaching, Learning, and Scholarship Knowledge Community. Woodruff has published on international education and is a peer reviewer for the Journal of Studies in International Education. She has been awarded the University of Minnesota's John Tate Award for Excellence in Undergraduate Advising and NAFSA's Marita Houlihan Award for Distinguished Contributions to the Field of International Education. Her M.A. is in international development education from Minnesota.

NOTES ON CONTRIBUTORS

EDITORS

Rhiannon D. Williams, PhD is a Research Associate in the Department of Postsecondary Teaching and Learning at the University of Minnesota. Her research focuses on equitable access for marginalized populations into and within systems of higher education. Her research examines first-year experience programming and how intentional engagement with diversity in the classroom has the potential to support and further develop students understanding of themselves and each other as complex diverse individuals. Overall, her research grapples with the complexities, possibilities and limitations an equitable diversity discourse engenders in a higher education classroom. Recent publications include: Formative journeys of first-year college students: Tensions and intersections with intercultural theory *Higher Education Research and Development*); Engaging Diversity in Undergraduate Classrooms (*Josey-Bass, 2012*); Engaging Diversity in First-Year College Classrooms (*Innovative Higher Education, 2011*).

Amy Lee, PhD is a faculty member in and chair of the Department of Postsecondary Teaching and Learning (PsTL) in the CEHD. Her research focuses on the intersections of critical pedagogy, student and teacher development, and access/equity. She has authored and co-authored various articles and three books, Engaging Diversity in Undergraduate Classrooms (2012), Teaching Writing that Matters (2008), Composing Critical Pedagogies (2002). Amy has served in administrative positions at three public research universities, including director of an undergraduate English major, director of a writing program, and coordinator of community-action learning curricula and partnerships. She served for five years a mentor in the Center for Teaching and Learning's Early Career Teaching Program. She was a recipient of the University of Minnesota's Morse-Alumni Distinguished Teaching Award, a recipient of University of Massachusetts-Amherst 1999 University Distinguished Teaching Award and a recipient of the College Composition and Communication Association's James Berlin Award.